TEACHERS & SCHOOLING

Productive Pedagogies, Assessment and Performance

MAKING A DIFFERENCE

Debra Hayes, Martin Mills, Pam Christie and Bob Lingard

ALLEN&UNWIN

First published in 2006

Allen & Unwin
83 Alexander Street
Crows Nest NSW 2065
Australia
Phone: (61 2) 8425 0100
Fax: (61 2) 9906 2218
Email: info@allenandunwin.com
Web: www.allenandunwin.com

National Library of Australia
Cataloguing-in-Publication entry:

Teachers and schooling making a difference : productive
pedagogies, assessment and performance.

Bibliography.
Includes index.
ISBN 1 74114 571 6.

1. Effective teaching. 2. School improvement programs. 3.
Educational leadership. I. Hayes, Debra N. A. (Series :
Studies in education).

371.1

Set in 11/13 pt Caslon by Midland Typesetters, Maryborough
Printed by South Wind Production, Singapore

10 9 8 7 6 5 4 3 2 1

Table of contents

About the authors

Debra Hayes is Senior Lecturer in the Faculty of Education at the University of Technology, Sydney. **Martin Mills** and **Pam Christie** are Associate Professors in the School of Education at the University of Queensland. **Bob Lingard** is Professor in the School of Education at the University of Sheffield (formerly at the University of Queensland). They are the authors of *Leading Learning* (Open University Press, 2003).

Studies in Education
General Editor: Bob Lingard

Foreword

Over the past three decades, we have learned a good deal about seeing education as a political act. We have learned to think *relationally.* That is, understanding education requires that we situate it back into both the unequal relations of power in the larger society and into the relations of dominance and subordination—and the conflicts—that are generated by these relations. Thus, rather than simply asking whether students have mastered a particular subject matter and have done well on our all too common tests, we should ask a different set of questions: Whose knowledge is this? How did it become 'official'? What is the relationship between this knowledge, and who has cultural, social and economic capital in this society? Who benefits from these definitions of legitimate knowledge and who does not? What can we do as critical educators and activists to change existing educational and social inequalities and to create curricula and teaching that are more socially just (Apple 2000; Apple 2001; Apple & Beane 1999)?

These are complicated questions and they often require complicated answers. However, there is now a long tradition of asking and answering these kinds of critical challenges to the ways education is currently being carried on, a tradition that has grown considerably since the time when I first raised these issues in *Ideology and Curriculum* (Apple 1979; see also the new 3rd edition, Apple 2004). Over the past three decades the broad and diverse area of critical educational studies has made major gains in helping educators to understand the complex relationships between education and differential power. The intersecting dynamics of class, race, gender, sexuality, and how they are represented and struggled over in schools and the curricula, teaching and evaluative practices that go on in them, have been interrogated in powerful ways. Yet for all of the gains that have been made, too often these materials have been 'from the balcony'. They are often not sufficiently linked to the concrete realities of teachers' and students' lives and to the very personal pedagogic and political agendas of teachers, for example, who take the critical perspectives being produced and daily attempt to create a practice based on them (Apple 2001).

This situation is made much more complicated by the fact that in all too many nations what might best be called 'conservative modernisation' is now in the driver's seat in terms of educational policy and practice. Many of the rightist policies now taking centre stage in education, and nearly everything else, embody a tension between a neoliberal emphasis on 'market values' on the one hand and a neoconservative attachment to 'traditional values' on the other. For the former perspective, the state must be minimised, preferably by setting private enterprise loose; for the latter, the state needs to be strong in teaching *correct* knowledge, norms, and values. From both, this society is falling apart, in part because schools don't do either of these. They are too state-controlled and they don't mandate the teaching of what they are 'supposed' to teach. These positions are inherently contradictory, but as I have demonstrated elsewhere the neoliberal agenda has ways of dealing with such contradictions and has managed to creatively built an alliance that unites (sometimes rather tensely) its various movements (Apple 1996, 2000, 2001).

This new hegemonic alliance has a wide umbrella. It combines four major groups: (a) dominant neoliberal economic and political elites intent on 'modernising' the economy and the institutions connected to it; (b) economic and cultural neoconservatives who want a return to 'high standards', discipline and Social Darwinist competition; (c) some working class and middle class groups who mistrust the state and are concerned with security, the family, and traditional knowledge and values and who form an increasingly active segment of what might be called 'authoritarian populists'; and (d) a fraction of the new middle class who may not totally agree with these groups, but whose own professional interests and advancement depend on the expanded use of accountability, efficiency and management procedures that are their own cultural capital (Apple 2001; Apple et al. 2003).

The sphere of education is one in which the combined forces of neoliberalism and neoconservatism have been ascendant. The social democratic goal of expanding equality of opportunity (itself a rather limited reform) has lost much of its political potency and its ability to mobilise people. In my own nation, for example, the 'panic' over falling standards, dropouts, illiteracy, the fear of violence in schools and the concern over the destruction of traditional values have had a major effect and have led to attacks on teachers and teacher unions and to increasing support of marketisation and tighter control through centralised curricula and national testing. These fears are exacerbated, and used, by dominant groups within politics and the economy who have been able to shift the debate on education (and all things social) on to their own terrain—the terrain of traditionalism, standardisation, productivity, marketisation and economic needs. Because so many parents *are* justifiably concerned about the economic and cultural futures of their children—in an economy that is increasingly characterised by lower wages, capital flight and insecurity—neoliberal discourse connects with the experiences of many working class and middle-class people.

It should be clear to all of us that in education symbolic politics counts. Diametrically opposite policies often are wrapped in exactly the same vocabulary, something neoliberal and neoconservative educational 'reformers' have recognised and used all too well.

A fine example today is the struggle over the very meaning of democracy. We are witnessing a major transformation of our understandings of democracy (Foner 1998). Rather than democracy being seen as a fundamentally political and educative concept, its meaning is being transformed primarily into an economic one. Thus, under neoliberal policies in education and in society in general, democracy is increasingly being defined as simply consumer choice. The citizen is seen as a possessive individual, someone who is defined by her or his position in market relations. (Think, for example, of voucher plans in some areas of the United States where parents are in essence given cheques to send their children to any school, including private, for-profit ones.) When private is good and public is bad in education and so much else in this society, the world is basically seen as a supermarket and democracy is seen as making choices in that market. The withering of political and collective or community sensibilities here has had lasting effects, many of which, as I have shown, have been disastrous.

Among the key concepts now sliding around the map of meaning is *standards*. Indeed, the two movements, markets and standards/testing, go together since markets can't work unless the 'consumer' has sufficient knowledge about whether a 'product' is good or bad. Taken together, they can be truly damaging. I can think of no one who believes that having 'standards' is bad, who believes that educators shouldn't have high expectations for all of their students or who believes that what we should teach and whether we are successful in teaching it shouldn't be taken very seriously. Thus, standards are 'good'. But basically this is a meaningless position. What counts as standards, who should decide them, where they should come from, what their purposes should be in practice, how they are to be used, what counts as meeting them—these are the real issues.

Many people almost automatically think that having standards and testing them rigorously will lead to higher achievement, especially among our most disadvantaged children. By holding schools' and teachers' feet to the fire, so to speak, there will be steady improvement in achievement. Yet, like markets, such policies have been shown to just as often stratify even more powerfully by class and race, no matter what the rhetorical artifice used to justify them (Valenzuela 2005; Gillborn & Youdell 2000). In all too many cases the situation that has been created is the equivalent of an Olympic length swimming pool in which a large number of children already drown. The response is to lengthen the pool from 100 metres to 200 metres and give everyone an 'equal opportunity' to stand at the far end of the pool, jump in, and then swim the doubled length. But some children come from families who are affluent enough to have given their children swimming lessons or have sent them to expensive summer camps, while others couldn't even swim the earlier length because of not having such economic advantages. Yes, we guaranteed 'equality of opportunity', but basically all we really did was put in place another stratifying device that ratified prior advantages in cultural and economic capital. Given the historical role of Social Darwinist influences in education (Selden 1999), influences that were nearly always described in democratic language, we need to be cautious not to assume that the overt intent to use standards to improve schools will be what actually happens when they are instituted in institutions that are already starved for sufficient financial resources, have large numbers of teachers who are constantly treated as unworthy of serious respect, where the curricula and pedagogy are anything but responsive and where economic and social policies have literally destroyed the employment, health and housing of entire urban communities. Lengthening the pool in these instances may not have anywhere near the effect we desire, unless these policies are accompanied by serious economic and social policies that also change the life circumstances and chances of families and children in these communities. But, of course, this is exactly what current neoliberal and neoconservative policies are meant to have us forget.

Yet the movement for democratic schools, for critical curricula and teaching, and of publications such as the book you are about to read give us reason for hope. Even though this is a time when the right is gaining power, it is also a time when thousands of educators, community activists, critical scholars, students, and so many others in multiple communities and nations have shown that success can be won. In *Teachers and Schooling Making a Difference*, Debra Hayes, Martin Mills, Pam Christie and Bob Lingard have produced a volume that clearly demonstrates that it is possible to build an education that takes a vision of a truly serious education as seriously as it deserves. They carefully detail how in real schools and communities a rigorous, critical and thoughtful curriculum can be constructed. They portray how forms of teaching that are respectful and caring and which bring out the best thinking of students can be enacted. And they do not ignore the importance of dealing with whether or not the education that has been built actually works in the ways educators hope it will. That is, unlike many other critical educators, the authors know how important public accountability is during a time of rightist resurgence. They construct models of authentic assessment that are helpful rather than simply part of the increasingly dominant forms of public 'shaming'.

Teachers and Schooling Making a Difference does all this in a refreshingly clear way. It takes seriously the question that teachers ask, 'What do I do on Monday?', and answers it by situating it within larger relations of inequality; but it does provide answers. I want to stress that this is of considerable importance. I mentioned above that critical educators have become very good at 'bearing witness to the negativity' of current educational policies and practices—and rightly so. As Connell, Ashenden, Kessler and Dowsett showed in *Making the Difference* (1982), a book whose title the co-authors are playing off of, many existing policies and practices *create* differences. They play a role in reproducing the divisions that are central to the maintenance of inequalities. However, one of the reasons that so many people are turning to neo-liberal and neoconservative policies is because the right has been successful in providing answers to the question of

'What do I do on Monday?' Although there have been some successes such as those shown in the book *Democratic Schools* (Apple & Beane 1999), in general, educators who are committed to 'thick' democracy have been less successful in doing that. Life on the balcony may be a bit too comfortable. The authors of *Teachers and Schooling Making a Difference* refuse life on the balcony. They portray a democratic and critical education in action. It is an education that does not deny the importance of 'official' knowledge (Apple 2000) in the lives and futures of our children. However, it illuminates what can be done when such knowledge is both reconstructed and made available in respectful and critical ways so that students can understand and act on the world.

Reading books such as this is heartening. They remind me of the importance of linking our critical scholarship with an informed set of critical educational practices that make a difference in the lives of students, teachers and communities. In the end I remain an optimist without illusions. A truly critical and democratic education will take hard and continuing organised work; but after reading *Teachers and Schooling Making a Difference*, we know that it is possible.

Michael W. Apple
John Bascom Professor of
Curriculum and Instruction and
Educational Policy Studies
University of Wisconsin, Madison

References

Apple, M.W. 1990, *Ideology and Curriculum*, Routledge, New York.
Apple, M.W. 1996, *Cultural Politics and Education*, Teachers College Press, New York.
Apple, M.W. 2000, *Official Knowledge: Democratic Education in a Conservative Age*, 2nd edn, Routledge, New York.
Apple, M.W. 2001, *Educating the 'Right' Way: Markets, Standards, God, and Inequality*, RoutledgeFalmer, New York.

Apple, M.W. et al. 2003, *The State and the Politics of Knowledge*, RoutledgeFalmer, New York.

Apple, M.W. 2004, *Ideology and Curriculum*, 3rd edn., Routledge, New York.

Apple, M.W. and Beane, J.A. (eds) 1999, *Democratic Schools: Lessons From the Chalk Face*, Open University Press, Buckingham.

Connell, R.W., Ashenden, D.J., Kessler, S. and Dowsett, G.W. 1982, *Making the Difference: Schools, Families and Social Division*, Allen and Unwin, Boston.

Foner, E. 1998, *The Story of American Freedom*, Norton, New York.

Gillborn, D. and Youdell, D. 2000, *Rationing Education*, Open University Press, Buckingham.

Selden, S. 1999, *Inheriting Shame*, Teachers College Press, New York.

Valenzuela, A. (ed.) 2005, *Leaving Children Behind*, State University of New York Press, Albany, NY.

Preface

One of the largest classroom-based research projects undertaken in Australia was funded by Education Queensland for an amount of $A1.3 million. The study commenced in 1997 and concluded with the completion of its final report in 2001, the *Queensland School Reform Longitudinal Study* (QSRLS, 2001). This research is credited with the creation of the concept of *productive pedagogies*, which has become widely used nationally as a framework for describing classroom practice. We therefore refer to the study throughout this book as the Productive Pedagogies Research.

The members of the core research team who conducted this study were: Bob Lingard and James Ladwig (Co-directors); Martin Mills (Manager); Pam Christie, Debra Hayes and Allan Luke (Researchers); David Chant and Mark Bahr (Statistical Advisers); Merle Warry (Senior Research Assistant); Jo Ailwood and Ros Capeness (Field Researchers); and Jenny Gore (Consultant).

The lengthy and detailed process of coding student work samples and assessment tasks collected during the study was undertaken by two sets of teachers working in different cities. We are grateful to the Brisbane coders, Francine Barker, Carolynn Lingard, Glenda MacGregor and Noela Stark; and the Sydney coders, Susan French, Chris Greef, Anne Larkin,

Martin Lauricella, Celina McEwen, Jane Mowbray, Wolly Negroh and Nicola Worth.

While we recognise the contribution of the original researchers to many of the ideas contained in this book, the way these ideas have been developed and the opinions expressed are those of the four authors.

We often refer to our previous book, which focused on leadership and also drew on the Productive Pedagogies Research. Throughout, we refer to it as *Leading Learning* (Lingard, Hayes, Mills & Christie 2003).

Acknowledgments

This book has its origins in the *Queensland School Reform Longitudinal Study*, which was carried out by a team of researchers funded by the Queensland State Department of Education. As authors of this book, we wish to acknowledge the members of the original research team who contributed to many of the ideas we have developed here. We also thank the University of Wisconsin team at the Center on Organization and Restructuring of Schools headed by Professor Fred M. Newmann for agreeing to the use of some survey and other research instruments in the Queensland research. We thank Education Queensland for funding and supporting the research, and we express particular gratitude to Merle Warry for keeping the study on track and maintaining a sense of humour throughout.

We would like to acknowledge and thank the hundreds of school-based educators who welcomed us into their classrooms and schools and spoke to us at length about their work during the three years in which we were involved in the research. Their social support for their students should also be recognised.

Thanks are due to those who have provided feedback on draft chapters, including Judy Archer, Dawn Butler, Ann King, Maralyn Parker and our anonymous reviewers. Thanks are also due to Sue Anderson for editorial assistance, to Alex Gammie for the use of her ecology task, to Stanley Wong for permission to publish a work sample, and to Antoinette Rea for the Identity task.

Elizabeth Weiss provided invaluable guidance and support, which were important in getting the manuscript completed. We thank her most sincerely for her support throughout the process from commissioning to finalising of the manuscript.

We are grateful to our families, friends and colleagues for their sustained support and patience. In particular, we would individually like to thank Ali, Ann, Carolynn, Cristina, Dare, Dawn, Gill, Jane, Kirren, Lynne, Lucy, Marcia, Naomi, Nick, Paul, Ravinder, Ros, Tara, Vic and Wayne.

This book is the product of several years of collegial work and intellectual collaboration, from which all four authors benefited enormously. The order of authorship is not intended to reflect differential contributions to the conceptualisation and writing of the book, which we shared in equal measure. We thank each other for staying faithful to the task.

The cover art is a detail from Madonna Staunton's *Romantic Doubt* and was provided by Bellas Milani Gallery.

1 Introduction

When a local public school is lost to incompetence, indifference, or despair, it should be an occasion for mourning, for it is a loss of a particular site of possibility. When public education itself is threatened, as it seems to be threatened now— by cynicism and retreat, by the cold rapture of the market, by thin measure and the loss of civic imagination—when this happens, we need to assemble what the classroom can teach us, articulate what we come to know, speak it loudly, hold it fast to the heart. (Rose 1995: 4)

The research on which this book is based has confirmed what most teachers and many other people probably always knew: that apart from family background, it is good teachers who make the greatest difference to student outcomes from schooling. Individual teachers have more impact on student outcomes than do whole-school effects; and particular classroom practices are linked to high-quality student performance. Based on a large-scale research project and a broad range of the educational research literature, we describe in this book the classroom practices that make a difference. We detail and name such practices as *productive pedagogies* and *productive assessment*. Our claim is that these practices are important for *all* students, and that *all* these practices are especially important for those students from what are often described as disadvantaged backgrounds. The good news from our research is that quality teaching can improve outcomes for *all* students. The bad news is that it is not commonplace. And the reality is that quality teaching alone is not sufficient to bring about improvements in student outcomes. Indeed, there are limits to what teachers and schools can do, although they can make a difference.

We believe that in order to make a positive difference in the lives of young people, teachers need to share (with each other and with students and their communities) a common understanding of the types of student performances they are working towards. Such understandings are achieved in schools through rigorous engagement in a dialogue that displaces the more common fragmented monologues of teachers working in isolation in their classrooms. Our primary concern is to contribute to such dialogue by describing *what* makes a difference and suggesting *how* to make a difference in schools. The classroom practices we describe are our contribution to the former, and our description of alignment of these practices with performances is our case for the latter. Alignment is underpinned by context and a recognition that schools are located in places where people live. Schools that make a difference matter in these peoples' lives because they enrich and resource them, and they connect with their concerns and hopes. Alignment, then, is about teachers' pedagogies and assessment practices mediating the achievement of valued performances in the classroom.

This book reflects the process of alignment by detailing *productive pedagogies* in Chapter 2 and then showing how these may be linked to *productive assessment* and *productive performance* in Chapters 3 and 4 respectively. The key to alignment is not so much sequence as linkage—that there are explicit and coherent links between pedagogies, assessment practices and student performances, all of which should be intimately linked to the specific purposes and goals of schooling. We add the term 'productive' to signal in a clear and precise way those forms that make a difference and that, to our best knowledge, work in classrooms. *Productive pedagogies* and *productive assessment* practices make *a* difference to educational outcomes. Such practices in all classrooms will contribute to more socially just outcomes from schooling—*the* difference that is the focus of this book.

The pervasiveness of pedagogies

In countries where dental checkups are commonplace, lessons on brushing, flossing and whitening are now routine parts of such a visit. In other words, a trip to the dentist has become a clinical *and* pedagogical experience (often accompanied by a dose of product comparison). A similar pedagogical shift is experienced if we visit an art gallery or a science museum, shop for electrical goods or switch on the television or computer. Teaching and learning are permeating all aspects of life; pedagogical activity is spilling over from formal to informal spaces. This shift has multiple effects, not the least of which are new forms of marketisation and consumerism, but here we want to focus on its educative dimension. The spread of pedagogical discourse is evidence of the move towards what Bernstein (2001) has called the 'totally pedagogised society'. Pedagogy has moved out of the classroom; it has spread into other cultural and social spaces; and it is now an integral part of the practice of a wide range of workers other than teachers. Even family units have become sites of 'parenting skills', and the 'world of work translates pedagogically into Life Long Learning' (Bernstein 2001: 365). The imperative to keep improving reflects globalised labour markets and the insecurity of most employment today. As Rose (1999: 161) suggests:

> The new citizen is required to engage in a ceaseless work of training and retraining, skilling and reskilling, enhancement of credentials and preparation for a life of incessant job seeking: life is to become a continuous economic capitalization of the self.

Education and pedagogy are not constrained or contained by time and space in the way they once were. Individuals are now the subject of 'continuous pedagogic reformations', to use Bernstein's (2001: 365) evocative characterisation of this situation. However, schooling as an institution and set of practices remains an important site of pedagogy, despite the fact that learning (apart from a thinned-out conception linked to standardised testing) has disappeared from view in much of the educational policy landscape that has emerged in recent years.

This book is about teaching and learning in schools and classrooms. Based on the findings of a large-scale study—the Queensland School Reform Longitudinal Study (QSRLS 2001)—we describe the kinds of classroom practices and organisational processes that make a difference to the academic and social learning of students. We refer to this study throughout the book as the Productive Pedagogies Research (see preface). While we are concerned with improving the learning of all students, our particular focus is on improving the outcomes of students who traditionally underachieve and under-participate in education. We acknowledge that by declaring our intention in this way, we venture into highly problematic territory that has been thoroughly explored and raked over by the well-established arguments of critical, feminist, poststructural, postcolonial, race and other theorists over a long period of time. Their persistent articulation of minority standpoints, in the face of silencing discourses and other erasures, exposes the false assumption that a 'one-size-fits-all' approach works with the same level of effectiveness for all students (Reyes 1987; Delpit 1995; Rose 1995). Evidence continues to show the effects of social class, and of other factors such as race, gender, ethnicity and locality with which it is interwoven, on students' participation rates in schooling, their school performance, and their subsequent life opportunities (Anyon 1995; Lareau 2000; Van Galen 2004).

In presenting our research and discussion of teaching and learning in classrooms, we recognise that we risk being interpreted as positioning ourselves as outside arbiters and assessors of teachers' pedagogical practices. We specifically wish to distance ourselves from what Ball (2004) has identified as a discourse of derision of teachers that blames them for not doing their job properly. Rather, our intention is to take up the challenge to speak with teachers about their work—which centres on the day-to-day rhythms of teaching and learning in schools—while also speaking to a broader audience of principals, parents, policy makers, politicians and others about how to provide equitable and just schooling for all.

The relationship between research conducted in schools and the reform of teacher practices is a complex and ultimately political one. Suffice to say here that we reject a model that sees teachers as mere translators of research conducted elsewhere. In conducting the research on which this book is based, we sought to operate in ethical, open and collaborative ways in the research schools and with the teachers. In presenting our research and ideas, we are not seeking to provide a calculus of pedagogies and assessment practices that can simply be layered into schools or imposed on teachers. We do not wish to tame and regulate pedagogies at a time of 'multiplicity'—of multiple effects of globalisation and new technologies on identities, knowledges, practices, economies and nations (Dimitriades & McCarthy 2001). Rather, we report the research as a rigorously constructed but contestable map of pedagogical and assessment practices at a particular moment in Queensland government schools.

Schooling in Australia is ostensibly the constitutional responsibility of the state governments: there are some national developments but no national curriculum, for example, as in England; yet the state educational systems have much in common. While the research was conducted within one state educational system in Australia, and despite the contingent specificity of particular national and provincial schooling systems and indeed of individual schools, we argue that the research 'findings' have much broader applicability, given the common form of schooling across the globe (Meyer, Ramirez & Soysal 1992) and the emergent globalisation of educational policy developments (Lingard 2000). The issues facing schools and teachers in the Queensland research schools share some similarities with those being experienced by schools and teachers elsewhere.

Our intention is that the research reported throughout this book be used by teachers to engage in substantive professional dialogue of the sort that improves their classroom practices and takes account of their specific systems and school populations. Indeed, one of the 'findings' of the Productive Pedagogies Research, which we reported on in our earlier book *Leading Learning* (Lingard et al. 2003), was the importance of a school culture of professional dialogue and responsibility, supported by dispersed and pedagogically focused leadership, for enhancing the effects of schools on student learning (see Lee & Smith 2001). Thus our intention is that the research story of this book should be used, rearticulated and recontextualised by teachers and schools. It is also our intention to engage policy makers in debates about classroom practice, so that learning in its fullest meaning is given a central place in the educational policy landscape from which it is so often absent.

It is our belief, and hope, that we provide compelling arguments in this book as to why teachers and their practices should be at the centre of educational policy. In some educational systems this has been done—but in controlling and regulating ways, which have denied teachers the sort of space for professional dialogue that we are calling for here (Mahony & Hextall 2000; Ball 1994, 1997a, 1999, 2004; Apple 2001). Unfortunately, for the past decade or so policy has been done *to* teachers rather than *with* them. Perhaps the worst-case scenario is educational policy in contemporary England. As Ball (1994, 1999) has pointedly put it, teachers have been the objects rather than the subjects of recent educational policy changes, and multiple and competing discourses 'swarm and seethe' around the contemporary teacher. Mahony and Hextall (2000) have thoroughly demonstrated the deprofessionalising effects of such policy aimed at teachers in the UK context. Top-down imposed change works with a different logic of practice from that of classroom teaching, and pedagogical considerations are all too often absent. We suggest that more trust of teachers and more support for schools are needed in contemporary educational policy so as to constitute schools as reflective and inclusive communities of practice. Such trust would enhance professional dialogue about productive pedagogies and more likely align outcomes with those most often articulated in statements about the purposes of schooling. Those policy makers involved in the regulation of pedagogies desire the achievement of such outcomes but, paradoxically, the practices they encourage often work against the achievement of high-level intellectual outcomes for all.

As well as speaking to educational practitioners—teachers, school leaders, systemic personnel and policy makers—this research speaks to another community of readers, that of educational researchers and theorists. At a later point in this chapter we give an account of our research procedures, to open them to scrutiny, debate and further engagement. Throughout the text we address the work of a range of educational theorists to locate ourselves in, and advance, debates on the nature and purposes of schooling. Thus, a central aim of this book is to contribute to a professional discussion about classroom practices and their effects, while also contributing to broader debates about schooling, including consideration of the relationships between educational researchers, schools and policy makers. Underpinning our position is a valuing of schooling and an appreciation of the complexity of its purposes.

'Making a difference'

In picking up the discourse of 'making a difference', we acknowledge a significant tradition of research on schools, inequality and social justice, to which the work of Connell, Ashenden, Kessler and Dowsett (1982) in Australia made an exemplary contribution. In contrast to the optimism of early compensatory education programs, which assumed that educational interventions could redress the social inequalities stemming from students' home backgrounds, Connell et al. (1982) illustrated, through their empirical research and accessible analysis and argument, the complex ways in which social class, gender and family articulated with opportunities in schooling. This research appeared alongside the work of reproduction theorists—neo-Marxist and other—who provided compelling accounts of the ways in which schooling itself perpetuated inequalities, particularly those of social class. Subsequently, multiple voices from the margins—feminist, black, postcolonial, postmodern, gay and lesbian—have questioned whether mainstream schooling could ever valorise the nuances of difference without speaking over them. It is now clear that a plethora of institutional practices work to generate and reproduce inequalities in ways that are not easy to counter. Not least of these is the hegemonic or competitive academic curriculum at the core of schooling, and the ways in which it is taught and assessed.

Over two decades after Connell et al. published their research findings, more is known about schools and social inequality but possibilities for intervention remain as challenging as ever. While there is currently a more sophisticated understanding of schools and social inequality (Thrupp 1999), there is reduced state commitment to redressing it. Concern about schools and social justice has been shifted aside in current public debate by education policies that stress individualised responsibility for achievement, the importance of private contributions to school funding, and market approaches to school choice. In the current times of neoliberal globalisation, the gap between rich and poor within and between countries is widening; new patterns of dominance and marginalisation are developing around access to the network economy; identities are more fractured; and global violence and its visibility have sharpened with 11 September and the subsequent wars in Afghanistan and Iraq. Though current patterns of inequality are complex as new forms of disadvantage intermix with old, it is clear that schooling is imbricated in these patterns of inequality. In Australia, both old and new issues of difference are not adequately addressed through education. For example, Indigenous students are poorly served by schooling while asylum-seeker children are locked in detention with little priority given to their education. Arguably, here and perhaps elsewhere, the need for redistributive funding in schooling is greater than at any other time in the post-World War II period, while social justice frames are weaker. The same is true of public policies, which engage with difference in ethical and socially just ways.

This book is, then, in part a contribution to debates on schooling, inequality and social justice. A central concern of our research was to investigate classroom and school practices that might contribute to more equitable, improved outcomes for all students. The quality of teaching and learning experienced by students is a critically important social justice issue for schools today, and was a central underpinning value of the research on which this book is based. Of course, this is not to say that social justice issues can be effectively dealt with in the contemporary context through a focus on classroom practices alone. However, the quality of teaching and learning has to be one element of social justice approaches that aim to make a real difference. We also assert that, while schools are one important institutional basis of the sorting and selecting of individuals for different futures, a more equal distribution of the capacities and capabilities developed through education needs to be a goal of socially just schooling.

The recent school reform literature views the valuing of teachers, through strong support for their professional development in school and systemic policies, as the central element in effective school reform (Newmann & Associates 1996; Darling-Hammond 2000; Sachs 2003). Such reform seeks to spread the best classroom practices—pedagogies and assessment—across the whole school through certain leadership practices, culture and structures and support for teachers' professional development. Of course, such support must be accompanied by appropriate policy frames and funding at the systemic level. As with pedagogy, we stress that social justice issues cannot be effectively addressed in the contemporary context through teachers alone. Thus, while bringing classrooms into focus, we make the point that it is important not to decontextualise the work of teachers and schools. We distance our work from certain forms of school effectiveness research, which focus on school-level interventions without acknowledging broader social and economic influences, and which fail to recognise how these external features play out inside the school (see Chapter 5 and Thrupp 1999). We also recognise (though we do not develop this in our research) that spatial contexts influence schools in powerful ways. The spatial location of a school, both materially and metaphorically, has strong predictive influence on classroom experience, and this needs to be acknowledged in any study of teachers' practices. There is also a temporal component as policy contexts change, along with the patterns and nature of inequality. On the latter, research has shown how choice policies and educational markets, common in schooling systems around the globe today, tend to result in more homogeneous school populations, and 'school mix' in turn is known to have a strong effect on educational and social justice outcomes (Thrupp 1999).

Schooling today entails a complex interweaving of the modernist and postmodernist and the local and the global. Schools are modernist institutions *par excellence*, located in a postmodernist context. This is particularly so if we regard modernist institutions as those that contain the past in the present and seek to reconcile these (Augé 1995: 75). The physical and social architectures of schools speak most easily to standardised treatment of stable and predictable populations (see Macdonald 2003). In contrast, the postmodern floats free from the past, while the postcolonial that accompanies it constitutes multiple pasts and multiple yet always hybrid presents. Against this context, Dimitriades and McCarthy (2001: 21) have argued that mainstream educational thinkers and policy makers have tended 'to draw a bright line of distinction between the established school curriculum and the teeming world of multiplicity that flourishes in the everyday lives of youth beyond the school'. At the same time, the creation of the imagined community of the nation (Anderson 1983) and national citizens through schooling becomes more complex in the context of globalisation and the mix of national and postnational pressures that accompany such processes.

Information and computer technologies are tied in with these changes and contribute to the compression of time and space, as well as the creation of new identities and new cyber communities, especially for young people of school age. Students in schools today are positioned differently in relation to such technologies from the generation of their parents. There is also perhaps a greater generational cleavage between teachers and students today than ever before. This is nicely picked up on in Green and Bigum's (1993) assertion in relation to generations and new technologies: that there are aliens in the classroom and they are not the students. While new technologies hold real democratic potential in the free flow of ideas and information, they also potentially exacerbate inequalities; not all students have easy access to these technologies outside schools, and gendered and racialised identities play out differently in these contexts. Moreover, the scale and changing nature of learning throughout one's life suggests that schools are increasingly places where knowledge about learning and about how knowledges are constructed becomes as important as knowledge acquisition. These shifting conditions require even more from schools if they are to mediate the inequities that exist in society between those who are equipped to meet these challenges and those who are not.

Schools as modernist institutions are/were 'spaces of enclosure' (Lankshear, Peters & Knobel 1996)—in relation to written texts in book form, the architecture of classrooms and schools, and the written and constraining curriculum. Lankshear and his colleagues (1996) suggest that new technologies, with their effects of compressing both time and place, challenge these spaces of enclosure and thus challenge the authority of the teacher and school-based pedagogies of enclosure. One effect is that the construction of literacy is broadened in the direction of what have been called multi-literacies (New London Group 1997), which include computer literacy. Edwards and Usher (2000) have also written most persuasively about the effects of globalisation on pedagogy and the resultant challenges for modernist educational institutions of all sorts. All of these challenges complexify the work of teachers and the issue of pedagogies in schools. The response to such complexity ought to be to seek to open up a dialogue about the purposes of schooling today, given the changes briefly alluded to here, and to think through appropriate and effective curriculum and pedagogies in this context, including—as Cummins and Sayers (1995) suggest—consideration of how computer technologies should be incorporated in classroom practices. We intend this book to make a contribution to those dialogues as well as informing school and policy practices.

As Bernstein (2001) has noted, however, a focus on pedagogies can elide considerations of what knowledges are of most worth, and thus elide pressing considerations of the curriculum of contemporary schooling. Today, in the contexts of change alluded to already, disciplinary knowledges are being challenged and new knowledge forms are being produced. This has significance for school curriculum. Against such developments, Bernstein thus suggests that a sociology of the transmission of knowledges might be a more useful theoretical and research development than a sociology of pedagogy (2001: 367–68). We acknowledge here his earlier work, which argues that any consideration of pedagogy requires consideration of curriculum and assessment. Our approach then is to examine these three message systems of schooling through an analysis of numerous pieces of student work, assessment tasks and classroom observations in diverse school settings.

The conditions we have outlined raise important questions about what schools should teach—questions about the curriculum at the core of schooling. We suggest that there is need for informed public debate today about school curricula—a debate going well beyond considerations of what should be added to current curriculum offerings, which would simply further crowd an already crowded curriculum. An example of curriculum innovation related to our research on productive pedagogies is the New Basics project in Queensland (Department of Education 2001; Department of Education and the Arts 2004). The New Basics has developed an innovative curriculum framework around four new curriculum organisers: life pathways and social futures; multiliteracies and communications media; active citizenship; and environments and technologies. In its own words, the New Basics project is 'about dealing with new student identities, new economies and work places, new technologies, diverse communities and diverse cultures' (Department of Education 2001: 2). This project is significant in our view because it has sought to reconceptualise curriculum in a futures-oriented way and is thus one creative response to the curriculum questions facing educational systems around the globe. As a reconceptualist approach to curriculum, it recognises the globalised and changing contexts of schooling, as well as changes in the construction of knowledge. Systemic curriculum responses have tended to be much more incrementalist and add-on than this approach. Accompanying the New Basics is a significant form of assessment, Rich Tasks, which among other things seeks to maximise the collaborative use of new technologies. (See Macdonald [2003] for an analysis of one school's efforts in implementing the Rich Tasks.) An important intellectual resource for the New Basics and Rich Tasks was the Productive Pedagogies Research, which forms the basis of this book and which is considered in detail in the next section.

The research base

The Productive Pedagogies Research, one of the largest classroom-based studies ever undertaken in Australia, commenced in 1997. Within a broad context of globalising change, and the more specific local context of a move towards school-based management (Lingard, Hayes & Mills 2002), the Queensland government commissioned a group of university-based researchers to evaluate the contribution or otherwise of school-based management to student learning outcomes. The research team, which included the authors of this book, spoke back to this research purpose by proposing an alternative design, starting with classroom practices. The team made a case for looking at classroom practices to see which were most effective at producing positive student learning outcomes, both academic and social, and mapping back to consider what school structures and supports along with systemic policies were necessary to encourage these classroom practices. There was an interesting politics here which enabled the research team to 'remake' the research problem as constructed by the commissioning state depart-ment (see Lingard [2001] for a discussion of the politics surrounding the commissioning and reception of the research).

Over three years from 1998 to 2000 a team of researchers conducted formal observations in 975 classrooms using a coding instrument. These data were collected from 24 schools, eight per year, selected on the basis of reputation for school reform and a number of other features such as location, size and demographics. Each case-study school was visited twice in a single year, each visit lasting four to five days. During each visit, classes in English, Mathematics, Science and Social Science, in Years 6, 8 and 11, were observed. Based on recommendations in each school, we also observed teachers whose classroom practice was highly regarded by their colleagues. Classroom observations were accompanied by extensive interviews, surveys and analysis of whole-class sets of student work samples and their associated assessment tasks. We interviewed teachers about their pedagogies, assess-ment practices, and a broad range of issues related to their understanding of their schools and education in general. Extensive interviews were conducted with principals and other key personnel in each of the research schools during each visit. Data were analysed through a combination of quantitative and qualitative procedures. Throughout this book, we have attempted to preserve the anonymity of all teachers, principals and schools by the use of pseudonyms and the exclusion of identifying information. We reiterate the point we made in *Leading Learning* that there was an absence of student voice in the Productive Pedagogies Research. We would support further investigation into student perceptions of curriculum, assessment and pedagogy.

The Productive Pedagogies Research had direct intellectual links with the School Restructuring Study undertaken by the University of Wisconsin's Center on Organization and Restructuring of Schools (CORS) in the USA between 1991 and 1994. The CORS study was a comprehensive examination of interrelationships among what Fred Newmann and his colleagues came to refer to as four 'circles of support'. These circles were diagrammatically represented as nested layers in a concentric circle model, with student learning at the centre, then authentic instruction, school organisational capacity, and external support. Newmann and Associates (1996) argued that school restructuring for the enhancement of students' intellectual outcomes required a focus on pedagogy. This claim ran counter to the move at that time in many educational systems towards greater levels of school-based management, which was predicated on the assumption that structural change—in this case the relocation of more management tasks at the school site—would *ipso facto* enhance student learning outcomes. The CORS work perceptively and with a deep empirical base re-emphasised that it was teachers and their pedagogies that made the greatest difference of all the in-school factors in terms of student outcomes. Complementary school reculturing certainly contributes to this (Lee & Smith 2001), as does leadership focused on learning (see *Leading Learning*) together with good systemic policies. However, if the desire is for better student outcomes, support for teachers and their pedagogies ought to be at the centre of school culture and external funding and policy supports.

The Productive Pedagogies Research rearticulated the CORS study to emphasise social as well as academic outcomes from schooling (as described below) and to take account of the Australian, and specifically Queensland, context of school-based assessment and recognition of the professional contribution of teachers. The centrality of student learning and its mediation in schools through classrooms appealed to Education Queensland, which had commissioned the research. Queensland had come later to school-based management than many of the other state systems in Australia, and had learnt from their experiences, particularly in relation to the central importance of teachers to effective educational reform.

As well as its derivations from Newmann and the US school reform literature, the Productive Pedagogies Research built on strong traditions of research in Australia into school effectiveness (e.g. see Caldwell 1998; Hill & Rowe 1996, 1998; Rowe & Hill 1998), school development (Crowther et al. 2002) and social justice (e.g. see Connell et al. 1982; Rizvi & Kemmis 1987; Connell, White & Johnson 1991; Connell 1993; Gale & Densmore 2000; Thomson 2002). The Productive Pedagogies Research claims its place in Australian research from the basis of a government-commissioned research study, which utilised quantitative and qualitative methods and large data sets, as well as interview data. Our position is that statistical evidence has been central in the documentation of inequalities in schooling and that a new political arithmetic is required to map inequalities in these changing times (Brown et al. 1997). However, we further support a principled eclecticism in respect of methodological issues in research. There also needs to be a 'fit' between method chosen and research purpose.

Drawing on this research background, the Productive Pedagogies Research team sought to determine the kinds of classroom practices that would lead to students achieving the high-quality outcomes necessary to equip them to meet the demands of contemporary society, and to identify the kinds of school reforms that would promote such learning. The attempt to identify empirically which forms of classroom practice lead to improved outcomes for all students, especially those students who come from sociocultural backgrounds traditionally associated with weak school performance, is based on a deceptively simple question: *Which pedagogies will contribute to the enhancement of the academic and social performance of all students?* This question framed our study by making equity a particular and core concern, a point which differentiates and distinguishes its interests and approaches. It also refocuses attention away from school structures and management in suggesting that what happens in the classroom is directly connected to the achievement of student outcomes. This relationship may be obscured by the day-to-day concerns of schooling, which often emphasise management and organisational processes over learning and teaching, and by systemic reforms that emphasise structures rather than pedagogies. While recognising that the link between teaching and learning in the classroom is heavily mediated by factors within the classroom and beyond it (a point we return to in Chapter 5), we were nonetheless concerned to bring classroom practices into direct consideration.

The team of researchers who conducted the Productive Pedagogies Research came together in the summer of 1998 to develop a coding tool for describing teachers' classroom practices. The aim was to link these practices to indications of improvement in students' academic and social performances. An important influence on the development of this coding instrument was the work of Newmann and Associates at CORS. These US researchers had developed the notion of *authentic achievement*, which stressed the importance of intellectual quality in schooling, based on the premise that 'all students deserve an education that extends beyond transmission of isolated facts and skills to in-depth understanding and complex problem solving and that is useful to students and society beyond the classroom' (1996: 18). In the CORS study, authentic achievement referred to 'intellectual accomplishments that are worthwhile, significant, and meaningful, such as those undertaken by successful adults: scientists, musicians, business entrepreneurs, politicians, crafts people, attorneys, novelists, physicians, designers, and so on' (Newmann & Associates 1996: 23–4). The notion of authentic achievement was broken down into three main criteria, which in turn were translated into more specific standards for evaluating teaching. The main criteria for authentic achievement were: (1) student learning is focused on the *construction of knowledge* (producing, rather than simply reproducing, meaning and knowledge); (2) the cognitive work of the learning involves *disciplined inquiry* (the use of prior knowledge, developing in-depth understanding, and the expression of ideas and findings through elaborated communication); and (3) what is being done holds aesthetic, utilitarian or personal *value beyond school*. It is worth noting here that the CORS study of authentic achievement concluded that there was evidence that while authentic pedagogy did bring authentic academic performance for students, the overall levels of authentic pedagogy observed 'fell well below the highest levels on the proposed standards' (1996: 69).

In unpacking and recontextualising the notion of authentic achievement in an Australian context, the Productive Pedagogies Research team drew on its collective understanding of a range of educational research fields, with a particular focus on the literature that identified the pedagogical strategies and practices necessary for improving the academic and social outcomes of students from traditionally underachieving backgrounds. The literature included texts on school reform (Newmann & Associates 1996; Elmore, Peterson & McCarthey 1996; Darling-Hammond 1997), along with those in the fields of sociolinguistics and critical literacy (Cazden 1992; Freebody 1993; New London Group 1997); Indigenous education (Harris 1990; Groome 1994); constructivism (Daniels 2001); feminism (Davies 1993; Ellsworth 1989); sociology of education (Young 1971; Giroux 1989); and critical pedagogy (Shor 1980; Giroux 1983).

In designing its research instruments, the Productive Pedagogies Research team preserved the emphasis on intellectual outcomes developed by Newmann and

Associates, but added an emphasis on the social outcomes from schooling, such as responsible citizenship and the valuing of non-dominant cultural knowledges. Added to this was a range of classroom practices that were found by research to make a difference to student achievement, such as explicit pedagogy and the use of narrative. The result was the development of a classroom coding manual that included a larger range of classroom practices than those identified by Newmann and Associates (1996).

At the end of the first year of the study, and based on confirmatory factor analysis of classroom observation data in 302 classrooms, four underlying factors were constructed to form the four dimensions of productive pedagogies from the 20-element observation scale. These were initially called *intellectual quality, relevance, socially supportive classroom environment,* and *recognition of difference* (QSRLS 2001). After consultation with teachers and others during the course of the study, the term 'relevance' was changed to *connectedness* in order to reflect concern that relevance may lead to curricula that do not provide students with any cultural capital. After the conclusion of the study, the phrase *working with and valuing difference* was adopted in *Leading Learning* and here instead of the term 'recognition of difference'. This acknowledged teachers' concern that some individuals and groups claim to recognise difference—but for the purposes of discrimination and vilification; and that 'recognition' was not active enough in moving beyond a liberal multiculturalism of tolerance (also see Dimitriades & McCarthy 2001).

The 20 classroom practices that formed the basis of structured observations provided a lens through which researchers could consider existing teaching practices with a view to reconceptualising these in ways that would improve the academic and social outcomes of *all* students (see the Appendix for a more detailed discussion on the QSRLS research instruments). A major finding of the Productive Pedagogies Research was that, when holding all other factors constant, teachers' pedagogical and assessment practices *do* matter, and that they particularly matter for those students from disadvantaged backgrounds.

Productive pedagogies, assessment and performances

Throughout this book we utilise the concepts of *productive pedagogies, productive assessment* and *productive performances.* Here we provide a brief description of how these concepts were developed by the research team and utilised in the research.

In the CORS study, 'authentic pedagogy' was considered to encompass both instruction and assessment tasks. The Productive Pedagogies Research team favoured the term 'classroom practice' to encompass these, and replaced the term 'instruction' with 'pedagogies'. While the word 'instruction' seems to have reductionist connotations in the Australian context, we recognise its use in North America as a synonym for pedagogy. We use the word pedagogy in this book, and indeed used it centrally in the Productive Pedagogies Research, because we enjoy its constructivist heritage derived from Vygotsky (e.g. see 1994) and the view that pedagogy in all its forms is a central expression of humanity and what it is to be human. We also see it as a term and concept that can be appropriated by teachers as central to and expressive of their specific professional practice, while not supporting an elitist view of the profession. Further, we like this constructivist heritage because Vygotsky emphasised that pedagogy was intimately linked to both cognitive and social purposes.

Additionally, the plural form, 'pedagogies', was preferred over 'pedagogy' as a means of indicating that the framework was not to be interpreted as a 'one-size-fits-all' approach. Collectively, the classroom practices described by the coding instrument were called 'productive pedagogies'. As one line of research was to investigate how pedagogical and assessment practices influence student outcomes, whole-class sets of student work samples were collected from each of the teachers taking part in the study, along with the relevant assessment task. A coding manual was drawn up for analysing assessment tasks. This was based on the classroom observation manual and sought to determine the degree to which productive classroom practices were reflected in assessment tasks. In turn, a coding manual was drawn up to analyse productive performances. This was used to code whole-class sets of student work samples. The concepts of *productive pedagogies*, *productive assessment* and *productive performance* were thus developed out of the research in both conceptual and empirical terms.

The term 'productive' was adopted in preference to the US term of 'authentic', as an indication that there was not a 'true' or 'real' form of performance, pedagogy or assessment. Its adoption also acknowledges that teachers (like other professionals) are increasingly subjected to market forces (Gewirtz, Ball & Bowe 1995; Marginson 1997; Whitty 1997; Ball 2004) and called to account for the differential between 'inputs' and 'outcomes'. Such pressure can work to thin out pedagogies and limit the possibilities for achieving high-level intellectual outcomes. Our conceptualisation of what it means to be 'productive' is intended to challenge and resist such moves and related pressure to blame teachers for poor educational standards, and instead to 'set the terms' for what might count as productive. It is also to recognise that teachers do produce outcomes through their classroom practices.

As mentioned earlier, the 20 elements on the classroom observation instrument were based partly on the CORS model, and partly on the researchers' analysis of the various texts on classroom practices that make a difference to student learning, and in particular make a difference to students from disadvantaged and marginalised backgrounds. Social outcomes were added as a means of reflecting their importance in Australian schools, and the need for this addition was corroborated by a large group of Queensland principals early on in the research. The framework evolved further from the analysis of structured observations during the first year of the study and was confirmed in the following two years.

The elements of the Productive Pedagogies Research coding instruments are shown in Table 1.1. Those derived from Newmann, Secada and Wehlage (1995) are marked with

Table 1.1 Elements of the Productive Pedagogies Research coding instruments

Dimensions	Classroom practices		Productive performance (Academic° and Social† outcomes)
	Productive pedagogies	Productive assessment tasks	
Intellectual quality	• Problematic knowledge • Higher–order thinking* • Depth of knowledge* • Depth of students' understanding* • Substantive conversation* • Metalanguage	• Problematic knowledge: construction of knowledge* • Problematic knowledge: consideration of alternatives* • Higher–order thinking * • Depth of knowledge: disciplinary content* • Depth of knowledge: disciplinary processes* • Elaborated communication* • Metalanguage	• Problematic knowledge° • Higher–order thinking*° • Depth of understanding*° • Elaborated communication*°
Connectedness	• Connectedness to the world beyond the classroom* • Knowledge integration • Background knowledge • Problem–based curriculum	• Problem connected to the world beyond the classroom • Knowledge integration • Link to background knowledge • Problem–based curriculum • Audience beyond school*	• Connectedness to the world beyond school*†

Table 1.1 Elements of the Productive Pedagogies Research coding instruments (continued)

Dimensions	Classroom practices		Productive performance (Academic° and Social† outcomes)
	Productive pedagogies	*Productive assessment tasks*	
Supportive classroom environment	• Students' direction • Explicit quality performance criteria • Social support* • Academic engagement • Student self-regulation	• Students' direction • Explicit quality performance criteria	
Working with and valuing difference	• Cultural knowledges • Active citizenship • Narrative • Group identities in learning communities • Representation	• Cultural knowledges • Active citizenship • Narrative • Group identities in learning communities	• Cultural knowledges† • Responsible citizenship† • Transformative citizenship†

an asterisk (even where they have been renamed). A more detailed description of each coding scale and its constiuent elements is provided in later chapters.

The features of schooling that support productive performance

The study was also concerned to ascertain what features of *school organisational capacity* (Newmann & Associates 1996) and what external supports from the various systemic levels support productive performances through these types of classroom practices. The findings of that part of the research have been recorded in the report (QSRLS 2001) and elaborated on in *Leading Learning*. Newmann and Associates used the term *teacher professional learning community* (Louis, Kruse & Marks 1996) to describe the relationships among teachers in schools where these practices were evident. As previously noted, while the Productive Pedagogies Research was conducted during a period of enhanced school-based management in the Queensland state system of schooling, this research was not a study of the implementation of school-based management within a traditionally bureaucratic state system of schooling. Rather, the study explored the ways in which student performances could be enhanced through particular assessment and pedagogical practices, and identified the kinds of school and systemic supports and structures necessary to initiate and sustain such practices.

The findings of the study suggest that in order to improve student outcomes from schooling through improved classroom practices, there is a real need to value teachers, their knowledges and ongoing learning (see Darling-Hammond 2000) as central to a school's organisational capacity, as well as a central rationale for systemic infrastructural support for schools (see Fullan 2001). The final report of the study found independent yet positive effects of professional development for teachers of an internal school-focused kind and of an external type on the quality of class-room practices (QSRLS 2001). The provision of the money and time for such professional development in this study was a surrogate measure of valuing teachers and recognising their professionalism. In the research interviews when teachers were asked what they needed to enhance their practices, they inevitably answered 'more time' to think and to prepare.

Thus, given the centrality of teachers to effective school reform, there is a pressing need to place teacher professional practices—pedagogies and assessment practices linked to desired student outcomes—at the core of professional communities, both within and outside schools. Support for teacher professional learning communities in schools focusing on the links between student learning and teacher practice is one of the ways that has been explored to enhance whole-school effects on student outcomes. The key point here is that schools need to become real learning organisations structured around the ongoing relationship between teacher learning and student learning.

While teachers are the centrally important element of effective school reform, school leadership of a particular kind is also important—that is, the kind that disperses the practices of leadership across the school and creates a culture and structure linking ongoing teacher learning to the enhancement of student learning. Our conception here runs counter to that of heroic individual leaders as the way forward in school reform; it also recognises how dispersed leadership is almost the only way school leaders pragmatically can handle many of the increased demands made of them. Contemporary educational policy changes and restructuring have tended to pull school principals in the direction of being new managers rather than *educational* leaders (Ball 1994; Gewirtz 2002). At the same time, market pressure on individual schools in relation to enrolments has meant, in Apple's words (2001: 74): 'More time and energy is spent on maintaining or enhancing a public image of a "good school" and less time and energy is spent on pedagogic and curricular substance'. Learning needs to be reasserted in principal practices, and while the relationship between principal leadership practices and enhanced student outcomes is minimal and mediated, such practices can create the structure and culture that position effective classroom practices at the centre of their purview. Thomson's (2000) observation that principal practices should be saturated in pedagogies is most apposite here, as is Smyth's (1989) talk of educational leadership as pedagogy. We reiterate that it is good teachers and good pedagogies that make a difference, and school leadership ought to be about establishing the conditions that support such pedagogies.

Indeed, our research has encouraged us to conceptualise school leadership as a form of pedagogy—with its own learning goals, approaches to assessment and pedagogical activities. This stems from an understanding of schools as places of learning for students, teachers, head teachers and others. Teaching takes place in the classroom and in other sites within schools, thereby addressing the needs of different learners. For example, the issues and questions faced by teachers as they develop learning programs for students translate into those faced by heads of departments as they support the professional learning needs of teachers, and translate again into those faced by school executives as they build the capacity of their department heads to support the learning needs of teachers (Hayes 2004).

We believe that in order to sustain a focus on learning in schools, the challenges faced by practitioners at various levels of schooling should reflect common sets of concerns— concerns associated with enhancing the conditions of learning in schools. This alignment of concerns is facilitated and supported by a shared language, to talk about curriculum, assessment and pedagogy, as provided by the frameworks of *productive performance*, *productive assessment* and *productive pedagogies*, respectively; and, by time, for sustained professional dialogue among teachers, as provided by professional learning teams structured by protocols (see McDonald et al. 2003).

However, and as alluded to above, there is a danger in reasserting the centrality of pedagogies in school reform because of the parsimonious funding situation that education now faces. In Australia, the proportion of GDP expended currently on all education is just under 4.5 per cent, a figure that can be negatively contrasted with the 6.7 per cent expended in the 1970s. In some ways, Australia has returned to the unacceptable levels of investment in education of the 1960s, when both government and Catholic school systems were substantially underresourced and under pressure from increasing enrolment. This underresourcing is also located within an unhelpful—indeed divisive—debate about the funding of government and non-government schools. While these issues of funding manifest in a specific manner in the Australian educational policy context, stress on efficiency, accountability and parental choice is evident in policy in schooling systems around the world.

Consequently, this book has to be read against a backdrop of the need for more social and economic investment in education. Aside from funding and equity matters, educational policy has most often worked through curriculum and assessment. Teachers' professional autonomy has been practised in terms of pedagogy—that is, the way curriculum and assessment have been brought together in classroom practice. Some current approaches to assessment and testing potentially at least thin out pedagogies in ways that narrow the goals and purposes of schooling. This is what Mahony and Hextall (2000) have clearly demonstrated in the UK context, and what McNeill (2000) showed to be an effect of standardised testing in her US research. Effective school reform demands that the message systems of schooling—curriculum, pedagogy and assessment—be aligned and not work at cross-purposes. For instance, if we want a focus on higher-order thinking or on fostering strong citizenship attributes, our assessment practices need to be focused in that direction, as well as our pedagogies.

Structure of the book

Alignment of curriculum, assessment and pedagogy does not require the application of a sequence or a formula, although we have previously discussed the benefits of backward mapping as a way of disrupting the common tendency to disconnect classroom practices from the goals and purposes of schooling (Hayes 2003; Lingard & Mills 2003; Lingard et al. 2003). This disconnection often manifests itself in the form of an emphasis on classroom activities and strategies that have no clear links to assessment or the curriculum. In this book we emphasise the importance of transparent and coherent links between curriculum, assessment and pedagogy. In this way, the starting point of planning is less important than the process of shunting between these three systems to establish explicit links between them. The frameworks of classroom practice and performance that we describe in the following three chapters are thus translations of the curriculum through pedagogy and assessment to performance. In Chapter 5, we focus on the school-wide and systemic supports that are necessary to support teachers in creating productive classrooms. In each chapter we draw on the Productive Pedagogies Research and incorporate various combinations of field notes, maps of classroom pedagogies, collected work samples and assessment tasks, interview transcripts and findings. We also go beyond the research and draw on our broader experiences in schools working with school-based colleagues to make suggestions about how these ideas might be taken up.

Chapter 2 provides a description of the theoretical underpinnings of the *productive pedagogies* framework of classroom practice. Drawing on a range of literature, it argues that in order for students to demonstrate particular outcomes they need opportunities to practise related performances. And in order for students to have this opportunity, teachers need to engage in sustained professional dialogue about classroom practices. The *productive pedagogies* framework provides a descriptive language to support and enrich such dialogue.

The chapter provides accounts of actual classrooms to illustrate the elements of *productive pedagogies*. Interview data with teachers who participated in the Productive Pedagogies Research are also included.

Chapter 3 outlines *productive assessment* and describes how *productive performances* are demonstrated. The chapter provides a sketch of the current state of play regarding assessment. It notes how standardised testing regimens linked to accountability measures and league tables have worked against the encouragement of *productive assessment* practices. It also identifies the ways in which the association of assessment with testing has served as a means of distancing teachers from detailed considerations of the purposes of assessment. The chapter thus seeks to address this matter by arguing that assessment literacy among teachers is critical in order for assessment to support students' learning. It draws on both interview data collected through the Productive Pedagogies Research and on assessment tasks collected in that research, as well as other assessment tasks collected since the research, to illustrate the ways in which teachers regard assessment and to illustrate examples of productive assessment.

In Chapter 4 we contend that the purposes of schooling need to take into account the academic and intellectual development of students as lifelong learners. However, we also take a broader view of the purposes of schooling to argue that students need to be made aware of the ways in which they, as active participants in their world, can make a difference, for the better, to that world. Located within these purposes is a commitment to teaching for and about social justice. It is our contention that if these purposes are to be valued throughout the schooling process, then students need to be expected to demonstrate them when completing assessment tasks. While we acknowledge that many of these outcomes are often present in student activities that do not constitute the formal curriculum, for example in Amnesty International groups, environmental groups and the like (see Mills 1996; 1997b), it is only by incorporating them in the curriculum that they are given officially sanctioned status within schooling. Thus we outline *productive performance*, which encapsulates such outcomes, and in so doing we draw on actual student work to illustrate these performances.

Underpinning Chapter 5 is a recognition that teachers alone cannot make *the* difference to students' learning and that there has to be a consideration of the contexts for learning, including funding and policies. It argues that certain whole-school practices need to be set in place in order to produce more equitable student outcomes, and to support teachers as they work in classrooms to improve learning for all students. The chapter thus looks at how school organisation, teacher professional communities and school leadership can support and spread *productive assessment* and *pedagogies* across the whole school and at the same time recognises how different socioeconomic locations of schools affect their internal culture and operations, and thus their capacities for implementing such practices (Thrupp 1999). The chapter further recognises how the contemporary educational policy ensemble in many systems limits the possibilities for the sort of structural supports (funding and policy) being argued for (Apple 2000b; Ball 2004). It also considers the importance of locating the call for improved student performance, and concomitant classroom practices, alongside broader considerations of policy and funding support for schools. The central argument in the chapter is that the contexts in which teaching and learning occur matter, thereby stressing the need for a culture that recognises *and* values teachers through appropriate support structures.

Chapter 5 confirms the central argument of the book: that schools can make a difference and that quality of pedagogies and assessment practices, including their intellectually demanding character, are social justice issues. As Bourdieu (1973: 80) observed, 'By doing away with giving explicitly to everyone what it implicitly demands of everyone, the educational system demands of everyone alike that they have what it does not give'. The corollary of this is that all students, but particularly disadvantaged students, require intellectually demanding classroom practices. The research on which this book is based demonstrated the high levels of social support offered by teachers, but more than this is needed if schools are to make the difference in respect of socially just outcomes. Social support for student learning is a necessary but not sufficient condition in this respect. The chapter then analyses the school and systemic level changes that are required for schools to enhance their social justice effects, while simultaneously recognising the centrality of teachers, as well as broader social policy changes, to the achievement of this agenda.

In emphasising the importance of pedagogies as one central element of a socially just approach to schooling, we are not suggesting that teachers or pedagogies alone can achieve the sorts of schools or outcomes that we desire. Here we acknowledge the possibilities, as well as the limitations, of the critical pedagogies tradition within the sociology of education (Ellsworth 1989; Apple 2000b; Darder, Baltodano & Torres 2003). In providing a sociology *for* education, this book describes what critical pedagogies—what we have called *productive pedagogies*—look like in real classrooms while recognising that they can make *a* difference as one component part of a social justice project in education.

2 Productive pedagogies

Classroom practice is at the heart of schooling. As we have previously argued, what teachers do in their classrooms matters. When asked to describe what this is, teachers' accounts are usually personalised, contextualised and shaped by their professional experiences. This is not surprising, given the isolated nature of classroom practice, but it does limit what can be said in more general and collective terms about what goes on in classrooms, and consequently how these practices may be influenced. Hence, the heart of schooling most often remains hidden and cloaked in personal experiences layered by the particularities of time, location and relationships. As a consequence, most attempts to describe what happens in classrooms founder in the shallows of impression and superficial recollection. A key purpose of this chapter, then, is to elaborate the language of *productive pedagogies* that will serve as a framework for describing some of the richness, complexity and detail of classroom experiences from a research base.

The difficulties associated with influencing classroom practice should not be underestimated. Smylie and Perry (1998) note, in their review of a selection of major restructuring programs mainly to do with reorganisation, that, while restructuring promoted some change at the classroom level, the focus of change tended to be on making schools more efficient and in the process often introduced obstacles to broader educational improvement. These obstacles included internal struggles over resource distribution and reform goals, and the subsequent disillusionment experienced by some teachers. The reform environment was further weakened by growing workloads and the absence of strong leadership. With time, 'the most radical initial changes had eroded to resemble more traditional organizational forms and processes . . . While new organizational structures had been built, they failed to challenge or penetrate the *instructional core* of these schools' (emphasis added, p. 983).

We contend that the instructional or, as we prefer it, pedagogical core is a taken-for-granted part of schooling. Its formation is not announced but assumed; it is maintained by unspoken agreements; it requires very little to sustain it and make it functional; and it can remain out of sight or slip easily from view. Schools operate in these ways as their 'default mode'. Indeed, the collective experience of restructuring efforts suggest that even though school reforms may successfully challenge this pedagogical core, this is often only a fleeting disruption to the default mode of schooling.

This default mode is particularly deleterious and mysterious for students whose social, cultural and economic backgrounds are not strongly matched to the norms and practices of schooling (Delpit 1995; Bourdieu 1973, 1976). We believe that part of the challenge of improving the educational outcomes of these students is to expose the pedagogical core of schooling—to bring it out into plain view for all to see. Once exposed, it can become an object for discussion; it can then be described, justified and perhaps modified. But the nature of schooling is such that teachers understand each other in ways that generally go unspoken and unacknowledged. School colleagues teach the same students, work under the same conditions, are held accountable through the same processes and get on with the job of preparing and teaching in isolation from each other. Sizer's (1984) enduring narrative of 'Horace's compromise' continues to portray the isolation of teachers' professional experiences that run to parallel scripts, with the same characters, plots and settings. Dan Lortie's (1975) classic sociological study of US teachers also emphasised the endemic individualism of teachers and their practices. Lortie (1975: 240) noted:

> The ethos of the occupation is tilted against engagement in pedagogical inquiry. Reflexive conservatism implicitly denies the significance of technical knowledge, assuming that energies should be centred on realizing conventional goals in known ways. Individualism leads to a distrust of the concept of shared knowledge; it portrays teaching as the expression of individual personality. Presentism orientations retard making current sacrifices for later gains; inquiry rests on the opposite value.

Our purpose in this chapter is to elaborate the concept of *productive pedagogies* and to outline how it may be adopted as a means of challenging the pedagogical core of schooling by providing a common language to describe classroom practices and to develop shared understandings between teachers of their professional practice. We believe that the conversational framework provided by *productive pedagogies* is only one, albeit important, aspect of this challenge. Hence, this chapter must be read alongside the other chapters in this book, as pedagogy should not be separated from considerations of student performance and assessment. Nor should such reflection about and reform of pedagogy be thought through in isolation from whole-school reforms and system-level supports—the focus of the final chapter. Such reforms challenge the reflexive conservatism, individualism and presentism of teacher practice. What we support here is a concept of the teacher as activist professional engaging in all aspects of schooling and reform efforts (Acker 1999; Sachs 2003). In contrast, much contemporary educational policy reform has implicit in it a passive view of teacher professionals. The *productive pedagogies* framework should also be treated as an example that can inform, supplement or be replaced by school-based traditions of pedagogy that reflect the concerns of local communities—their cultures, traditions and desires for schooling. Having said that, we would also emphasise the research base to this model of pedagogies. Our experiences in schools remind us that if the pedagogical core of schooling goes unchallenged, there remains the persistence of the default mode of schooling.

Findings of the Productive Pedagogies Research and overview of the dimensions

As discussed in Chapter 1, the four dimensions of *productive pedagogies*—namely, *intellectual quality, connectedness, supportive classroom environment* and *working with and valuing difference*—were derived from an extensive mapping of teachers' practices, involving both statistical analyses and theoretical interrogation of the classroom observational data. The dimensions may also be considered as organisers of classroom practice. As such, they provide a framework for planning, discussing and analysing teachers' work. In this section we provide a rationale for each dimension before discussing its elements. This rationale is based on the research literature and on our conceptualisation of the nature and purposes of schooling outlined in Chapter 4. It is not based on the assumption that these practices are already present, universally valued or easily achieved in classrooms. Indeed, the Productive Pedagogies Research suggested that such practices were quite rare, a point consistent with the findings of Newmann and Associates (1996) on authentic pedagogy and achievement. We reiterate the point made in Chapter 1 that we recognise that critical pedagogies alone cannot make all the difference to students' educational outcomes and social justice concerns (Apple 2000b), but assert that the absence of what we have called *productive pedagogies* exacerbates unequal outcomes from schooling (Lingard, Mills & Hayes 2000).

The Productive Pedagogies Research found high levels of supportiveness in classrooms across the sample, but low levels of the other three dimensions. Even so, the findings suggest that each of these dimensions makes an important contribution to the development of students with the skills, understandings, dispositions and knowledge base that would enable them to be active and informed citizens and to access further education.

The *productive pedagogies* framework is based on the premise that all students need to be provided with *intellectually challenging* classrooms, and that this is especially the case for students from marginalised backgrounds (Coleman et al. 1966). If students from such backgrounds do not experience classrooms where they are intellectually challenged, we argue that this is a matter of social injustice. When pedagogic disadvantage is combined with deficit thinking—that is, thinking that simply blames students and/or their families for students' lack of academic success, and fails to consider the contribution of schooling—then schooling fortifies and multiplies the broader inequities in society. For example, where there is not a strong match between the social and cultural norms of home and school, it is sometimes assumed that students are not capable of doing work of high intellectual quality, and they are thus not given such work to do. This situation benefits those who are at ease with the implicit cultural values and demands of schools, and reinforces the marginalisation of others. In contrast, the findings of the Queensland School Reform Longitudinal Study (QSRSL) confirm those of other research, which demonstrates that when students from marginalised backgrounds are presented with intellectually demanding work, their outcomes are likely to improve (Newmann & Associates 1996; Boaler 1997). This is where our work draws on the insight of the French sociologist Bourdieu, in his work on how social reproduction occurs through cultural reproduction in which schooling is closely involved. Bourdieu (1973, 1976, 1986; Bourdieu & Passeron 1977), in much of his writing, demonstrates how the reproduction of inequality through schooling occurs when the cultural values implicit in schooling remain tacit. Thus we utilise Bourdieu to construct a positive thesis about what schooling might be able to achieve through pedagogical reform. As we state throughout this book, the quality of pedagogy is a social justice issue; intellectually undemanding pedagogy and inexplicit cultural demands benefit the already advantaged and confirm the disadvantage of the already disadvantaged.

Nonetheless, providing students from marginalised backgrounds with work of high intellectual quality is seldom sufficient for improving their outcomes. Attempting to make the curriculum relevant through pedagogies that *connect* classroom learnings with the 'real world' may well provide a bridge that motivates all students to engage with the learning process, a motivation that is often missing when the curriculum is divorced from the lives of students. Many students who struggle with the mores and social practices of schooling—that is, have trouble 'doing school'—need to see that schooling has some meaning for them. It tends to be middle-class students who best handle decontextualised school knowledge. This means that classroom practices should recognise and value students' background experiences while connecting with their worlds beyond the classroom. Students with the cultural capital to 'do school well' may be able to do work of high intellectual quality in the absence of connectedness, but a schooling system that serves the *whole* community should seek to ensure that *all* students are able to demonstrate connectedness between the classroom and the world beyond it.

A range of earlier research (Bernstein 1971a, 1971b; Anyon 1981; Connell et al. 1982) has demonstrated that in schools serving disadvantaged communities, the pedagogy is sometimes socially supportive but not 'intellectually demanding'. Our research suggests that good social outcomes are more likely to be achieved by classroom practices that are intellectually demanding, connected to the students' worlds beyond schools and socially supportive than by socially supportive classrooms alone. This is not to downplay the importance of social support for all students—rather to suggest that social outcomes may be more effectively achieved when social support is combined with connectedness and works with and values differences.

Connecting the classroom with the world beyond the school does not, however, ensure that students are exposed to various forms of cultural capital. Indeed, a curriculum that deals only with students' worlds may simply involve studying popular music, sporting stars and movie idols. While a curriculum that does study these topics potentially has much to offer students, they also need to be provided with a variety of powerful knowledges that open up opportunities for them in the broader societal context. A skilful teacher will of course demonstrate how such things as a Shakespearean play can be connected to students' lives. A connected classroom, however, like an intellectually demanding classroom, is not sufficient for ensuring that students' outcomes are improved.

In a variety of research studies (e.g. Rose 1995; Lingard et al. 2002; Yates, McLeod & Arrow 2003) students speak of the importance of having positive relationships with their teachers. This is clearly critical for all students. However, *social support* goes beyond good relationships. It is also about creating classrooms where students are not scared to fail (or to 'have a go', to use the Australian vernacular) and are prepared to take risks with their learning (see Rose 1995). Students from marginalised backgrounds will often not engage with classroom expectations through fear of failure. Thus teachers need to create classroom environments that take into account ways in which student learning can be supported, by providing an environment where students are not criticised for their efforts and where students are provided with the structures to help them achieve. Mike Rose's (1995) research in the USA also recognises the need for classrooms to be supportive intellectual environments. Indeed, Rose (1995: 414) talks about the need for safety and respect in all classrooms.

A critical and important aspect of *productive pedagogies* is the dimension of *working with and valuing difference*. For many students from traditionally underachieving backgrounds, recognition and valuing of their cultural difference is necessary to achieve good outcomes. However, we acknowledge that the valuing of difference, as suggested by this dimension, is not an uncontested notion. For instance, the debate about whether Muslim girls should be forced to remove their headscarfs, or hijabs, while attending public schools is manifesting itself in various forms in the West. In France, the case for its removal taps into deeply held beliefs enshrined in the country's centuries-old laws aimed at preserving its secular identity; whereas in the USA the case for wearing the hijab is based on the constitutional protection of a citizen's right to religious freedom (see also McConaghy & Burnett [2002] for a critique of the *working with and valuing difference* dimension in the *productive pedagogies* model). We do not suggest that the application of the dimension of *working with and valuing difference* provides a solution to this debate in schools, but we contend that the ongoing questioning by teachers about whose differences are valued is a critically important consideration for effective classroom practice. Schooling for the contemporary world involves providing students from all backgrounds with opportunities to engage in positive ways with non-dominant cultures as part of its social outcomes. For instance, all students need to know that the world can be seen from multiple perspectives and that what is often constructed as 'truth' is the product of power relations (Berlak & Berlak 1981). A good critical education would therefore provide students with opportunities to understand the ways in which various 'regimes of truth' (Foucault 1997) have been constructed. Such an education would also encourage students to understand the intimate relationships between power and knowledge.

In presenting the *productive pedagogies* framework we emphasise that in order to make a difference for students, our findings suggest that these classroom practices must also be supported by leadership focused on learning; supportive and professionally enabling relationships among staff, and between staff and students; strong community relations; and appropriate structures that support a focus on learning (see Chapter 5). In the schools that participated in the Productive Pedagogies Research, these factors were present in varying degrees. It is worth noting that one of the schools in which all factors were strongly present was Casuarina State School. It was set apart from the rest of the case-study schools by demonstrating high levels of the *intellectual quality* dimension in combination with high levels of the *supportive classroom environment* dimension. Importantly for this discussion, Casuarina was also set apart by being located in an area of poverty. It had one of the lowest measures on the Index of Relative Socioeconomic Disadvantage (IRSED) of all schools in the study. The variables on this measure include family income, educational attainment, occupation, unemployment, dwelling ownership and occupancy, single-parent families, marital status, and fluency in English. Even so, the school demonstrated pedagogic advantage when compared with the other schools in the study.

We have always stated that we do not expect all elements of *productive pedagogies* to be present in a single class, and that a more reasonable expectation is to build each element in a unit of work. However, during our fieldwork we occasionally encountered an exceptional class in which all elements coded high. The classes were rare but memorable moments. The following field notes describe one such class.

> The Year 6 teacher I was meant to observe was absent today, so the principal filled in at the last moment. He brought a guitar, tape player and photograph into the class. He sat all the students in a circle and began to play the song *From little things, big things grow*. Soon the students were all singing along and he held their attention for the rest of the lesson. This song connected with their background knowledge because it's a popular song by a popular Australian songwriter, Paul Kelly. When they'd finished, copies of the lyrics were passed around and they listened to it on the tape player. This time the teacher stopped after each verse and explained the story of how in 1975 the then Prime Minister, Gough Whitlam, handed back the land of the Indigenous Gurindji people in Western Australia to their representative, Vincent Lingiari. The photo depicted the moment the tall white man let red earth fall through his fingers into the outstretched hand of the Aboriginal elder. This was not just a history lesson, it was a story of survival. Throughout, the teacher interrupted the flow

of the narrative to provide cultural knowledge and explain the terms and language required to grasp the significance of this symbolic act in the history of colonisation and dispossession of land. The focus shifted to the present day, and a conversation followed in which the students made sense of their own experiences within this historical context. This part of the lesson was deeply connected to the world beyond the classroom and underpinned by a strong sense of group identity and social support born out of shared experiences. As an act of protest, the class decided to compose some letters to the current prime minister in support of Indigenous peoples' ongoing struggle for justice and land rights. This social history lesson transformed into an English lesson as the students practised the style of formal letter writing, the art of persuasion and the construction of an argument. They read aloud to each other their drafts and made corrections and suggestions. By the end of the lesson, the letters were almost ready to be sent, there was some discussion about whether they should be typed, but in the end they decided to post their handwritten letters.

In the following section we more fully explore the ways in which this lesson reflected the dimensions of *productive pedagogies* by being intellectually challenging, connected with the world beyond the classroom, and conducted within a socially supportive environment while working with and valuing difference.

Intellectual quality

Productive pedagogies take the description of *higher-order thinking* and *substantive conversation* directly from the work of Newmann and Associates (1996). Two of the other elements in this dimension, *deep knowledge* and *deep understanding*, represent a disaggregation of Newmann and Associates' single variable *depth of knowledge and understanding*. To these elements were added *problematic knowledge* and *metalanguage*, with the former highlighting the constructed nature of knowledge and the latter recognising different language uses and the specificities of technical vocabularies.

When observing for the *intellectual quality* items, researchers asked the following questions:

- *Higher-order thinking*—Are higher-order thinking and critical analysis occurring?
- *Deep knowledge*—Does the lesson cover operational fields in any depth?
- *Deep understanding*—Do the work and response of students provide evidence of depth of understanding of concepts or ideas?
- *Knowledge problematic*—Are students critiquing and second-guessing texts, ideas and knowledge?
- *Substantive conversation*—Does classroom talk break out of the initiation/response/evaluation pattern and lead to sustained dialogue between students, and between teachers and students?
- *Metalanguage*—Are aspects of language, grammar and technical vocabulary being foregrounded?

The items that make up the dimension of *intellectual quality* within the *productive pedagogies* framework are detailed below.

Higher-order thinking required students to manipulate information and ideas in ways that transformed their meanings and implications. This transformation occurred when students combined facts and ideas in order to synthesise, generalise, explain, hypothesise or arrive at some conclusion or interpretation, as would be the case if students were asked to define the difference between a 'terrorist' and a 'freedom fighter'. Manipulating information and ideas through these processes allowed students to solve problems and discover new (for them) meanings and understandings. When students engaged in the construction of knowledge, an element of uncertainty was introduced into the instructional process and made instructional outcomes unpredictable; in such cases, the teacher was often not certain what was going to be produced by students. In helping students become producers of knowledge, the teacher's main instructional task was to create activities or environments that provided students with opportunities to engage in higher-order thinking.

Deep knowledge concerned the central ideas and concepts of a topic or discipline, and such knowledge was judged to be crucial to a topic or discipline. Knowledge was deep when relatively complex relations were established to central concepts, such as colonisation, evolution, photosynthesis and probability. For students, knowledge was deep when they developed relatively complex understandings of these central concepts. Instead of being able to recite only fragmented pieces of information, students developed relatively systematic, integrated or holistic understandings of concepts. *Deep understanding* was demonstrated by the students' success in producing new knowledge by discovering relationships, solving problems, constructing explanations, and drawing conclusions. Evidence of shallow understanding by students existed when they did not or could not use knowledge to make clear distinctions, or arguments, to solve problems and develop more complex understandings of other related phenomena.

Presenting *knowledge as problematic* involved an understanding of knowledge, not as a fixed body of information but rather as constructed, and hence subject to political, social and cultural influences and implications (Berlak & Berlak 1981). Multiple, contrasting and potentially conflicting forms of knowledge are represented, whereas treating knowledge as given involved the subject content within the class being represented as facts, a body of truth to be acquired by students. In such cases the transmission of the information varied, but was based on the concept of knowledge as static and able to be handled as property, perhaps in the form of tables, charts, handouts, texts and comprehension activities.

Knowledge as problematic is illustrated in the following description of a class from our field notes:

> As an introductory lesson to a topic about the environment, a Year 8 Social Science teacher drew a long horizontal line across the blackboard and wrote 'very concerned' at one end and 'not concerned' at the other end. She asked students to place a mark on the line representing their degree of concern about the environment. This required that the students make a

'low-key' public statement about their position and then justify it in writing by answering the question: 'Why I chose my position'. The teacher made a number of statements that could be interpreted as supporting multiple positions, thus reinforcing that there was no one correct position. It was clear from the way that this task was managed that the teacher anticipated divergent and potentially conflicting views to surface during the activity. She skillfully and continually kept opening the discussion up by reinforcing the complexity of the issues and the need to consider multiple viewpoints and experiences.

In classes where *substantive conversation* is present, there are considerable teacher–student and student–student exchanges; the interaction is reciprocal; and it promotes coherent shared understanding. This item sought to assess the extent of talking to learn and to understand in the classroom. In classes where there was little or no substantive conversation, teacher–student interaction typically consisted of a lecture with recitation, where the teacher deviated very little from delivering information and routine questions; students typically gave very short answers. Discussion here followed the typical IRE (initiate/response/evaluate) pattern: with low-level recall/fact-based questions, short utterances or single-word responses, and further simple questions and/or teacher evaluation statements (e.g. 'Yes, good'). This was an extremely routine, teacher-centred pattern that amounted to a 'fill in the blank' or 'guess what's in the teacher's head' format. The IRE pattern referred to here is well known and documented in sociolinguistic studies of classroom discourse (e.g. see Cazden 1988; Mehan 1979).

Metalanguage refers to teaching where there were high levels of talk about talk and writing, about how written and spoken texts work, about specific technical vocabulary and words (vocabulary), about how sentences work or do not work (syntax/grammar), about meaning structures and text structures (semantics/genre), and about issues of how discourses and ideologies work in speech and writing. Teachers who stressed metalanguage tended to do a good deal of *pulling back* from activities, assignments, readings and lessons, and foregrounded particular words, sentences, text features, discourses and so on. Such classrooms were replete with fairly sophisticated talk about language.

Metalanguage is illustrated in the following description of a class from our field notes:

> A Year 11 English class was being introduced to the concept of 'discourse'. The teacher asked the students to examine how medical, legal and mechanical languages operate within particular contexts to construct speakers, listeners and subjects. The students gave some concrete examples of these and explored how power operates in each situation by considering the questions: Who gets to speak?; and Who must listen?. By reversing the speaker and the listener, students were able to consider alternative discourses and to examine how power relations can be disrupted. There was consistent use of metalanguage throughout as the teacher and students examined how discourses constitute texts, knowledge and power.

The elements within the dimension of *intellectual quality* draw their significance from a number of different sources. The early self-fulfilling prophecy studies (Rosenthal & Jacobson 1968; Rist 1970) and studies of streaming and tracking (Oakes, Gamoran & Page 1992) show that one of the main reasons some students do not achieve high academic performance is that schools do not always require students to perform work of high intellectual quality. In contrast, Newmann and Associates (1996) found that when students from all backgrounds are expected to perform work of high intellectual quality, overall student academic performance increases and equity gaps diminish. The need for intellectual quality in schooling has been argued by philosophers and educational theorists for centuries (Presseisen 2000). At the *Fourth International Teaching for Intelligence Conference*, Sizer (1998) pressed this claim in terms of the need for informed scepticism, Greene (1998) in terms of the importance of rich dialogue in learning, and Sternberg (1998) in terms of tacit knowing and the need for the learner to become sensitive to what is not openly expressed.

Despite the strength of the arguments for the need for intellectual quality in schooling, our findings indicated that students are often expected to simply take notes, fill in worksheets, complete textbook activities, or perform acts of rote learning. However, the research confirmed that all students benefit from being provided with activities that require them to be actively engaged in the construction of knowledge. This means students need to be engaged in higher-order thinking, where they have to hypothesise, generalise, synthesise, evaluate and so on; they need to learn important concepts and processes in depth, rather than be engaged in superficial learning, and be provided with opportunities to demonstrate a deep understanding of such concepts and processes; they need to be provided with opportunities to use discussion as a means of learning; they need to see that knowledge is a social construction, that is it is made by people and as such can be changed; and they need to be exposed to critical literacy perspectives which enable them to see how language is used to construct particular kinds of realities.

In our interviews with teachers, they often explained how they attempted to integrate particular concerns into their teaching. One secondary Science teacher who had demonstrated high levels of *productive pedagogies* explained how her understanding of constructivist theories helped her look for a depth of understanding in her classrooms:

> I've found that I can tell students anything and they won't believe me if they've already got their own idea, so if I tell them that they have to explain it to somebody younger than them, then they then revert to their own ideas. So if they can tell me what they would tell a Martian or what they would tell their five-year-old niece, then I can see whether . . . they have taken note of what I have said. (Teacher, Melaleuca Secondary College)

While the Productive Pedagogies Research team observed some teachers engaging students from diverse social and cultural backgrounds in work of high intellectual quality, these practices were not widespread. When we spoke to teachers about their classroom practices, many expressed the view that course requirements (curriculum to be covered) constrained their ability to teach in-depth knowledge, and inhibited their repertoires of practice. That is, these teachers offered structural reasons for the lack of intellectually demanding pedagogies in their classroom practices. While we observed other teachers working under the same constraints who did not express these views, we highlight the following comment as a common teacher refrain expressed across the study:

> I think I'm constrained by the content that I have to cover, and so I do a lot of stand up, didactic teaching. There's a great deal of content to get through because we're bound by the Board of Secondary Senior Schools syllabus and all those papers, all those assessment instruments are externally peer monitored so that, you know, you are bound (a) to follow the syllabus and (b) to cover the content of questions which will be monitored. [This constrains the way I teach] because when I'm presenting something which I think is conceptually diffi-cult for a student, I don't see another way of presenting it other than didactically. (Teacher, Wattle State High School)

While didactic teaching of in-depth knowledge may be adequate in circumstances where students are motivated and well suited to the cultural and social practices of schooling, this approach is unlikely to re-engage already marginalised students in work of intellectual quality. Teachers' percep-tions of their roles, such as those contained in the above quote, reflect their personal and professional experiences. In schools where there is limited time for professional dialogue, these perceptions are not easily changed. Thus, a real chal-lenge for improving students' academic performance is in improving teachers' professional knowledge and collegial support structures.

Teachers who demonstrated many of the elements of *productive pedagogies* in their classroom practices tended to think of themselves as facilitators of learning. They focused more on the development of students' skills and concepts and less on the transmission of knowledge. Such teachers also felt a real sense of responsibility for student learning. In contrast, low-scoring teachers more often saw themselves as explainers of information and placed emphasis on information transmission, most often blaming contextual factors totally for poor student performance. How teachers positioned themselves in relation to knowledge appeared to strongly influence their pedagogic practices and perception of their role in the classroom. Those with strong disciplinary knowledge and solid understanding of how knowledge is constructed were better able to mediate their students' critical engagement with knowledge in the classroom. The way in which knowledge was treated in classrooms was often reflected in the form of verbal communication between teachers and students. Teachers who coded low on the elements of *productive pedagogies* tended to tightly script classroom talk and relied heavily on superficial IRE (initiate/response/evaluate) exchanges. In contrast, those who coded high engaged students in substantive conversations about deep knowledge; they encouraged critical reasoning, such as making distinctions, applying ideas, forming generalisations and raising questions. Interestingly, good schools in the study also had cultures saturated with substantive professional conversations.

Another aspect of classroom talk within the *intellectual quality* dimension is *metalanguage*. It has been strongly argued that students from disadvantaged backgrounds need to be provided with explicit instruction about language use. Such explicitness entails a focus on vocabulary and word morphology, sentence-level grammar, and reading and writing demands of subject-specific text types (Freebody, Ludwig & Gunn 1995) in order to develop a 'metalanguage'—based on what Halliday (1994) refers to as systemic functional grammar—for talking about written and spoken texts (Cope & Kalantzis 1995; see also Hasan & Williams 1997). Within the context of schooling, metalanguage facilitates students' access to powerful codes. Its link with equity programs points to its particular relevance for students from disadvantaged backgrounds who traditionally underachieve at school. However, there is evidence to suggest that such productive classroom practice is not widespread (e.g. see Freebody, Ludwig & Gunn 1995; Baker & Freebody 1989). Somewhat similar to Bourdieu, Baker (1997) attributes this to a progressivist pedagogical orientation that in fact conceals the criteria and practices of school literacy. Such implicitness disadvantages students who do not possess the appropriate cultural capital. The criticisms of such classrooms often lie in the claim that they are too preoccupied with discussions about beliefs, values and 'affect'. However, we would not want to take an either/or position on this: both discussions about beliefs and values alongside explicit discussions about language are needed.

When observing these elements in classrooms, the researchers made judgments on a 1–5 scale. The structure of the coding for *higher-order thinking* is shown in Figure 2.1. This structure was replicated in the coding instrument for all the elements.

Figure 2.1 Higher-order thinking coding scale

TO WHAT EXTENT DO STUDENTS USE HIGHER-ORDER OPERATIONS?

Lower-order thinking occurs when students are asked to receive or recite factual information or to employ rules and algorithms through repetitive routines. Students are given pre-specified knowledge ranging from simple facts and information to more complex concepts. Such knowledge is conveyed to students through a reading, worksheet, lecture or other direct instructional medium. The instructional process is to simply transmit knowledge or to practise procedural routines. Students are in a similar role when they are reciting previously acquired knowledge: i.e. responding to test-type questions that require recall of pre-specified knowledge. More complex activities still may involve reproducing knowledge when students need only to follow pre-specified steps and routines or employ algorithms in a rote fashion.

Higher-order thinking requires students to manipulate information and ideas in ways that transform their meaning and implications. This transformation occurs when students combine facts and ideas in order to synthesise, generalise, explain, hypothesise or arrive at some conclusion or interpretation. Manipulating information and ideas through these processes allows students to solve problems and discover new (for them) meanings and understandings. When students engage in the construction of knowledge, an element of uncertainty is introduced into the instructional process and makes instructional outcomes not always predictable: i.e. the teacher is not certain what will be produced by students. In helping students become producers of knowledge, the teacher's main instructional task is to create activities or environments that allow them opportunities to engage in higher-order thinking.

HIGHER-ORDER THINKING

Lower-order   Higher-order
thinking   1 . . . 2 . . . 3 . . . 4 . . . 5   thinking

1 = Students are engaged only in lower-order thinking: i.e. they receive, or recite, or participate in routine practice, and in no activities during the lesson do students go beyond simple reproduction.

2 = Students are primarily engaged in lower-order thinking, but at some point they perform higher-order thinking as a minor diversion within the lesson.

3 = Students are primarily engaged in routine lower-order thinking for a good share of the lesson. There is at least one significant question or activity in which some students perform some higher-order thinking.

4 = Students are engaged in at least one major activity during the lesson in which they perform higher-order thinking; this activity occupies a substantial portion of the lesson, and many students are engaged in this portion of the lesson.

5 = Almost all students, almost all of the time, are engaged in higher-order thinking.

One of the lessons we observed that coded high on the *higher-order thinking* element, along with many of the other elements on the *intellectual quality* dimension, occurred in a multi-age early-childhood class (Years 1–3). The teacher who taught this lesson was highly regarded in the school by students, teachers and parents alike. The lesson described here was not a 'one-off' but is representative of the kinds of pedagogies that were observed in her classroom on numerous occasions. From our field notes, we describe a philosophy lesson that led into a discussion on the nature of justice:

The students, girls and boys, from 6 to 8 years old, form a circle on the floor with the teacher who announces to the class that it is time for philosophy. No one asks what is meant by 'philosophy'. There appears to be a clear understanding of what this lesson will entail. The students sit quietly and listen as the teacher reads them the story of *The Little Red Hen*. They smile and silently mouth the hen's and other farmyard animals' repetitive phrases such as:

Little Red Hen: 'Cow, will you help me plant my seeds?'
Cow: 'Not I, not I. It is too hot to do such work.'

They are obviously intent on this story of a hen seeking assistance from a variety of farmyard animals to help her with planting, harvesting, grinding and baking. There are outbursts of laughter as the teacher mimics the various animals' excuses as to why they are currently unable to help her. Their satisfied nods and quiet comments indicate that they are siding with the red hen who, after all her hard work, refuses to share the bread with the other animals when, at the completion of the baking, they are suddenly no longer busy but more than happy to share in the task of eating the bread. A brainstorming session follows the story where students indicate questions they would like answered. On butcher's paper the teacher writes down the series of questions posed by the students, such as: 'Why is the hen baking bread?', 'Why won't the other animals help her?'. The students then discuss some of these questions. Rolling a bright yellow ball between them (indicating that the person with the ball has the right to speak uninterrupted), they suggest that possibly the animals had helped the hen before and she had not delivered on her promises; they give examples of how this has happened to them before where they have been promised something that they never receive in return for help they have given someone. One student suggests that even if this were the case it is important to give people a second chance and the animals should have helped the hen. Another student puts up his hand and the ball is rolled to him. He says that he 'sort of agrees' with the girl, but then disagrees and says it is up to the hen to make amends by sharing the bread and then perhaps the other animals will help her in the future. Interestingly, the reading position that these students have taken in relation to this story has changed: no longer are the other farmyard animals the 'villains' in this piece but the little red hen. The teacher then takes the story down another path, and somewhat restores the dignity of the red hen. She changes some of the reasons why some of the animals were unable to help her with the baking of the bread; for example, what if the cow was unable to help her because she was tired from being in the fields eating grass all day to make milk to help bake the bread? Would that change the hen's response? The discussion then moves to questions such as 'Should all of the animals be treated the same?' and 'Does fairness mean treating people the same?'. Enthusiastically the students give examples how they were treated unfairly because they were either treated the same as or differently from someone else. Other students either agree or disagree with the statements being made: some just say 'I agree' or 'I disagree', for example, while others give long, sometimes circular, arguments as to why they disagree or agree.

Higher-order thinking was clearly present in this lesson. The students manipulated the various ideas within the story to give it a variety of meanings. They were learning to hypothesise about various scenarios and about the various consequences of each. They were demonstrating an ability to explain their views as well as being able to justify them. Although the process was firmly regulated, the students took the class discussion in a direction that did not appear necessarily predictable. This was very much an activity in which the teacher's main role had been to create opportunities for higher-order thinking to occur. There were also a number of other items from the *intellectual quality* dimension present in this observed class. These children were dealing in depth with philosophical concepts related to complex questions on the nature of justice (e.g. see Rawls 1971; Young 1990, 1997; Fraser 1995, 1997; Benhabib 2002). They were practising substantive conversations as they hypothesised and interacted with each other's points of view, or added to and expanded on points raised by other students. The extent to which the students understood that these were complex questions that had multiple answers was evident in the classroom dialogue. Students recognised the validity of each other's responses without necessarily agreeing with them.

Connectedness

The Productive Pedagogies Research sought to determine the extent to which classrooms in the study were connected to the world beyond them. We prefer the term 'connectedness' to 'relevance' (which was used initially), as the latter can imply, for some, a lack of intellectual demand. This dimension includes the item *connectedness to the world* from Newmann and Associates (1996). To this concept *knowledge integration, background knowledge* and *problem-based curriculum* were added. Hence, the elements in this dimension seek to describe the extent to which knowledge is built on students' existing knowledge; connections are made between different bodies of knowledge (rather than compartmentalising the curriculum); connections are made with the world beyond the classroom; and students' knowledge and skills are developed in the context of solving real-life issues or problems.

When observing for the *connectedness* elements, researchers asked the following questions:

- *Knowledge integration*—Does the lesson range across diverse fields?
- *Background knowledge*—Is there an attempt to connect with students' background knowledge?

- *Connectedness to the world*—Do the lesson and the assigned work have any resemblance to or connection with real-life contexts?
- *Problem-based curriculum*—Is there a focus on identifying and solving intellectual and/or real-world problems?

The elements that make up the dimension of *connectedness* within the *productive pedagogies* framework are detailed below.

Knowledge integration was identifiable when either: (a) explicit attempts were made to connect two or more sets of subject area knowledge; or (b) no subject area boundaries were readily seen. Themes or problems that either required knowledge from multiple areas or that had no clear subject areas basis in the first place were indicators of curricula which integrated school subject knowledge.

Knowledge integration is illustrated in the following description of a class from our field notes:

> At this high school growing enrolments necessitated increasing the number of sporting houses by two for various inter-house sporting events. To accommodate this change, two extra lanes had to be marked on the running track in time for the school athletics carnival. This prompted a group of Year 8 teachers from different curriculum to work together on an integrated unit with the same group of students. An HPE teacher worked with the students to design the new track and athletics field so that it would accommodate the extra competitors. Extra areas had to be allocated for the new house groups, for more marshalling space and for specialised events such as discus and long jump. A Mathematics teacher worked with her class to determine the actual lengths of the new tracks and the position of the starting blocks for events over various distances. An English teacher worked with his class to draw up programs, advertising material, results lists and signage. A Computer Studies teacher worked with her class to construct a website for the carnival; there were continual updates made to this website.

Integration in this example occurred around a common topic with subject boundaries remaining intact. This appears to be the most common form of integrating knowledge across subject boundaries in the schools participating in the Productive Pedagogies Research.

In classes where there were high levels of *background knowledge*, lessons provided students with opportunities to make connections between their linguistic, cultural and everyday experiences, and the topics, skills and competencies at hand. *Background knowledge* was deemed to include community knowledge, local knowledge, personal experience, media and popular culture sources. Little or no connection was noted in those lessons that introduced new content, skills and competencies without any direct or explicit opportunities to explore what prior knowledge students had of the topic, and without any attempt to provide relevant or key background knowledge that might enhance students' comprehension and understanding of the 'new'.

The element *connectedness to the world* sought to measure the extent to which the class had value and meaning beyond the pedagogical context. A lesson scored highest on this element the more there was a connection to the larger social context within which students live. Two areas in which student work could have exhibited some degree of *connectedness* were: (a) a real-world public problem—i.e. students confronted an actual contemporary issue or problem, such as applying statistical analysis in preparing a report to the city council on the homeless; (b) students' personal experiences—i.e. the lesson focused directly or built on students' actual experiences or situations.

In the item *problem-based curriculum*, problems were defined as having no specified correct solution, thereby requiring knowledge construction on the part of the students and sustained attention beyond a single lesson. A problem-based curriculum was identified by lessons in which students were presented with a specific practical, real or hypothetical problem (set of problems) to solve or were already engaged in the solving of such problems.

In discussing the elements within the dimension of *connectedness*, we want to emphasise that linking classrooms to the world beyond them is not a substitute for intellectually demanding work but an important and complementary dimension of such work. This understanding is confirmed by the findings of the Productive Pedagogies Research and prior findings within a range of research fields. For example, sociological arguments suggest that knowledge integration is related to specific cultural codes themselves associated with specific sociological groups (Grumet 1988; Bernstein 1996; McConaghy 1998). The question of how knowledge integration relates to specific social groups remains an open theoretical debate, but its inclusion in the dimension of *intellectual quality* recognises that the ability to integrate knowledge may act as a gatekeeper to success within the curriculum.

In a very different field during the 1980s and early 90s, there was an extensive corpus of experimental and applied research in cognitive psychology that argued that learning occurs optimally when there is 'goodness of fit' (Anderson 1994) between students' background knowledge and the new knowledge structures of curriculum and instruction. Similarly, support for the inclusion of connectedness to the world has come from progressive educators tracing back to the work of Dewey (1916). Within the rating criteria of *connectedness*, higher ratings were allocated to lessons that had actual and present utility, as opposed to hypothetical or future utility.

'Problem-based learning' is a specific approach to connecting the classroom to the world beyond it that was advocated by a number of cognitive psychologists. Ashman and Conway (1993, 1997), for example, argue that cognition and skills are developed by a direct focus of classroom teaching and curriculum on the identification, analysis and resolution of intellectual, practical and disciplinary problems. A final example comes from ethnographic and sociolinguistic research. In the 1980s, research in these fields began to document models of cultural and linguistic 'mismatch' in knowledge, texts and practices between home/community and school. It was argued that this was a principal cause of minority educational failure (Heath 1983; Delgado-Gaitan 1995; Cazden 1992).

This last set of findings was illustrated by one of the secondary English/History teachers we observed. She described how she needed to be aware that students might not share the same linguistic and cultural experiences:

> I think a lot of times . . . successful lessons have come out of making the information relevant to them, [even] fairly difficult concepts if I can make it relevant to their own lives then that helps . . . You have to be aware of that all the time, especially as a teacher if you're lively and have a good vocabulary but you don't listen to the students then that is a danger and sometimes you are completely unaware that something you said has gone completely over their heads because they have not understood the meaning of a word and one that you may have taken for granted. Sometimes it is because it is not in their experience. I was surprised when I did *Gulliver's Travels* last year and most of the kids in this group had not even heard of Gulliver . . . You always have to be conscious of that and try to make it as relevant as possible.
> (Snappy Gum State High School)

It is important to distinguish between forms of connectedness that expose students to powerful cultural codes and those that limit their exposure. For instance, it is quite imaginable that a curriculum dominated with studies of popular culture would limit students' exposure to other cultural forms. Such a focus is unlikely to be of long-term benefit for students unless it is done in ways that ensure that the curriculum also promotes students' intellectual engagement with the subject matter, rather than just catering to their current interests. Furthermore, there is a danger that in providing relevance by simply working with students' interests, stereotypical representations of, for instance, gender will be treated as unproblematic. This is where making connections between students' cultures and aspects of the dominant culture become important. The making of such connections clearly requires substantial intellectual engagement on the part of the students.

A number of teachers we interviewed made efforts to link the experiences of their students to aspects of the dominant culture. One senior English teacher described how she used a film for this purpose:

> Last year [we did] Shakespeare and we used Baz Luhrmann's new film . . . They didn't like Shakespeare, [but] they couldn't help themselves, and they liked the movie . . . one of the kids, who was probably one of the most against going to it, [said] 'that wasn't a bad movie. It was just like a boy/girl movie wasn't it?'. [If I were to just tell them] you are going to do Shakespeare, they'd say, 'You can't understand what they are talking about'. (Mulga State High School)

The knowledge integration coding scale is given in Figure 2.2.

Figure 2.2 Knowledge integration coding scale

TO WHAT DEGREE IS SCHOOL KNOWLEDGE INTEGRATED ACROSS SUBJECT BOUNDARIES?

School knowledge is typically segregated or divided in such a way that specific sets of knowledge and skills are (relatively) unique and discrete to each specified school subject area. Segregated knowledge is identified by clear boundaries between subject areas. Connections between knowledge in different segregated subject areas are less and less clear the stronger the dividing knowledge boundary. In the extreme, such boundaries prevent any interrelating of different subject areas.

Integrated school knowledge is identifiable when either: (a) explicit attempts are made to connect two or more sets of subject area knowledge; or (b) no subject area boundaries are readily seen. Themes or problems that either require knowledge from multiple areas or that have no clear subject areas basis in the first place are indicators of curricula which integrate school subject knowledge.

SCHOOL KNOWLEDGE INTEGRATED

Knowledge   Knowledge
segregated   1 . . . 2 . . . 3 . . . 4 . . . 5   integrated

1 = All knowledge strictly restricted to that explicitly defined within a single school subject area. No intrusion of other contents permitted.

2 = Knowledge mostly restricted to that of a specific subject area, with minor intrusions limited to connections with one other (separate) discipline.

3 = Knowledge from multiple subject areas connected or related, but still treated as separate and distinct subjects.

4 = Near-complete integration of multiple subject areas; however, some minor inclusion of knowledge that is still treated as unique to a subject area.

5 = Complete integration of subject area knowledge to the degree that subject area boundaries are not recognisable.

The following example illustrates a lesson that would code high on the dimension of *connectedness*. Students in a Year 6 class were developing a report on bullying, complete with sets of recommendations to go into a school bullying policy, to be submitted to the principal. The students in this class had identified a problem in the school regarding bullying. The class teacher then asked the students to investigate the problem. Was it a serious concern for many students? Which ones? Where were the problem areas in the school? Was the school doing enough about the problem? What should it do? And so on. The students gave maps of the school to younger students and asked them to colour in red the areas where they didn't feel safe; green where they did; and yellow where they were a little unsure. The Year 6 students then collated these data into sets of graphs that were to be included in the final report. The students were involved in constructing surveys to be given to older students. They then had to put their various findings in report form, including sets of recommendations to be submitted to the principal. There was significant intellectual activity in the pedagogical practices associated with this task, in that students were investigating a topic in depth, were canvassing various viewpoints, and were translating and synthesising these into various recommendations. However, there was also significant connectedness in relation to the elements of the *productive pedagogies* framework.

The students in this class were working with an integrated curriculum. The subjects being integrated here were: Human Relationships Education in relation to issues of bullying; Mathematics in relation to the collation and representation of data; Social Science in relation to considering the ways in which the data were affected by such things as gender and ethnicity; and English in relation to report writing and interviewing activities. *Background knowledge* was also important, because students had to be familiar with their surroundings and with other students to investigate this topic. Furthermore, it was their background knowledge that initiated the project and thus what gave the students motivation to engage with the topic and to complete the project. The students were eager to engage with this investigation because it was transparently connected with their day-to-day experiences.

Perhaps most significantly, the whole project was set around a series of problems that the students wanted solved. This was very much a problem-based curriculum. This meant for many students that they were learning how to solve problems within a highly relevant and engaging context. For instance, many of the Mathematics skills that these students were learning would normally have been part of the standard curriculum. However, in this context the students were learning that these skills had meaning beyond the classroom, and that this meaning partly derived from the degree to which their report was sufficiently credible and convincing to present to the principal.

Supportive classroom environment

Supportive classroom environment is the dimension of *productive pedagogies* that is most often identified by teachers and students as an important aspect of good classrooms. The opportunity to learn in a socially supportive environment is critical to all students, but we would stress that this support must also be intellectually demanding. As one school principal said in his interview, if care was all there was, schools would not be educative in the ways they ought to be. What this may look like for individuals or different groups of students may of course vary. However, the elements that make up the *supportive classroom environment* dimension include student direction of activities, social support, academic engagement, explicit criteria and self-regulation. Thus a classroom that was demonstrating these elements of *productive pedagogies* would be giving students some say in what they are doing in the classroom; being explicit about what is expected from students so that those students who struggle with knowing how to 'do' school have their learning scaffolded in ways that enable them to achieve; and encouraging students to take risks without fear of 'put-downs' from the teacher or other students (see Rose 1995). According to this framework, socially supportive classrooms would also be characterised by students being 'on-task' without the teacher having to refer to their behaviours. Our research seemed to suggest that good teachers focused on making their lessons interesting and demanding, and that this focus ameliorated the need to focus on managing students' disruptive behaviour.

When observing for the *supportive classroom environment* items, researchers asked the following questions:

- *Engagement*—Are students engaged and on-task?
- *Student self-regulation*—Is the direction of student behaviour implicit and self-regulatory or explicit?
- *Student direction of activities*—Do students have any say in the pace, direction or outcomes of the lesson?

- *Social support*—Is the classroom a socially supportive and positive environment?
- *Explicit criteria*—Are the criteria for judging student performances made explicit?

The elements that make up the dimension of *supportive classroom environment* within the *productive pedagogies* framework are detailed below.

Academic engagement was identified by on-task behaviours that signalled a serious psychological investment in class work; these included attentiveness, doing the assigned work, and showing enthusiasm for this work by taking the initiative to raise questions, contribute to group tasks and help peers. Disengagement was identified by off-task behaviours that signalled boredom or a lack of effort by students; these included sleeping, day-dreaming, talking to peers about non-class matters, making noise or otherwise disrupting the class. It was assumed that these behaviours indicated that students were not taking seriously the substantive work of the class.

Student self-regulation was evident in a classroom where teachers did not have to make frequent statements aimed at managing students' behaviour (e.g. 'You're not being good today, put your pens away') or to regulate students' bodily movements and dispositions (e.g. 'Sit down', 'Stop talking', 'Eyes this way').

Student direction of activities occurred when students influenced the specific activities and/or tasks they would do in the class and/or how these were to be realised. Such tasks were likely to be student-centred, as in group work or individual research and/or investigative projects, whereby the students assumed responsibility for the activities with which they engaged and/or how they completed them. Where students did not influence the class activities, the teacher, or some other educational/institutional authority, explicitly determined what activities students did, and hence how they met the specified objectives required within the period. Despite much talk over many years about the need for a negotiated curriculum, we found little evidence of student direction of activities in the Productive Pedagogies Research. While the *supportive classroom environment* dimension was almost universally present to high degrees in the research classrooms, if the element of student direction of activities had been extracted from the dimension, the mapped scores would have been even higher. There was little student direction of activities, which probably reflects the crowded curriculum and imperatives to complete a unit of work in a particular time.

Social support was present in classes when the teacher conveyed high expectations for all students; these expectations included that it is necessary to take intellectual risks and to try hard to master challenging academic work, that all members of the class can learn important knowledge and skills, and that a climate of mutual respect among all members of the class contributes to achievement by all. Mutual respect meant that students with less skill or proficiency in a subject were treated in ways that continued to encourage them and make their presence valued. In a similar fashion, Rose (1995: 413) in his research talked about the importance of classrooms in which students felt safe 'from insult and diminishment'. If disagreement or conflict developed in the classroom, the teacher helped students resolve it in a constructive way for all concerned. Social support could be undermined by teacher or student behaviour, comments and actions that tended to discourage effort, participation and taking risks to learn or express one's views. For example, teacher or student comments that belittle a student's answer, and efforts by some students to prevent others from taking seriously an assignment, served to undermine support for achievement. Support could also be absent in a class when no overt acts like the above occurred, but the overall atmosphere of the class was negative due to previous behaviour.

The presence of *explicit criteria* was identified by frequent, detailed and specific statements about the nature of high-quality student achievement. This involved overall statements regarding tasks or assignments, about a specific lesson or program of work, or about performance at different stages in a lesson. Such explicitness, as we have argued elsewhere in this book, is important if schools are to operate in socially just ways.

Two of the elements of this dimension, *academic engagement* and *student self-regulation*, are descriptors of productive classrooms and thus indirectly reflect actual teacher practices. However, they did provide classroom observers with a picture of the kinds of classrooms that engage students, thus relieving teachers of the need to continually bring students back on to task. While these items gave a good indication of the classroom atmosphere, they need to be read in conjunction with elements within the *intellectual quality* dimension in order to distinguish 'busy work' from academic engagement. The structure of the coding instrument for the *academic engagement* scale is shown in Figure 2.3.

Figure 2.3 Academic engagement coding scale

TO WHAT EXTENT ARE STUDENTS ENGAGED IN THE LESSON?

Disengagement is identified by off-task behaviours that signal boredom or a lack of effort by students: these include sleeping, day-dreaming, talking to peers about non-class matters, making noise or otherwise disrupting the class. It is assumed these behaviours indicate that students are not taking seriously the substantive work of the class.

Engagement is identified by on-task behaviours that signal a serious psychological investment in class work: these include attentiveness, doing the assigned work, and showing enthusiasm for this work by taking the initiative to raise questions, contribute to group tasks and help peers.

ACADEMIC ENGAGEMENT

Disengagement 1 . . . 2 . . . 3 . . . 4 . . . 5   Engagement

1 = Disruptive disengagement; students are frequently off-task, as evidenced by gross inattention or serious disruptions by many; this is the central characteristic during much of the class.

2 = Passive engagement; most students, most of the time, either appear lethargic or are only occasionally active in carrying out assigned activities, and some students are clearly off-task.

3 = Sporadic or episodic engagement; most students either appear indifferent or are only occasionally active in carrying out assigned activities, but very few students are clearly off-task.

4 = Engagement is widespread; most students, most of the time are on-task pursuing the substance of the lesson; most students seem to be taking the work seriously and trying hard.

5 = Serious engagement but not universal; almost all students are deeply involved, almost all of the time, in pursuing the substance of the lesson.

While most educators would defend a socially supportive classroom as a valued educational goal, it is important to acknowledge that the degree of social support for achievement is typically not achieved evenly across student populations. This has been especially strongly documented in analyses of classroom practice linked to educational inequalities and the educational production of social inequalities. Early findings of the British sociology of school knowledge (Young 1971) indicated an uneven social distribution of socially supportive classroom environments. These findings have been corroborated by more recent US studies of the relationship between classroom management and curriculum (McNeil 1986). These studies paint a similar picture to Australian studies of the educational production of inequality (Connell et al. 1982; Teese & Polesel 2003). Simply put, the prevalence of low social support, especially for traditionally disadvantaged students, has been documented repeatedly.

Interestingly, while *social support* was the most prevalent dimension in the Productive Pedagogies Research, the element of student direction of activities was seldom found. In many of the interviews we conducted with teachers, and in subsequent workshops, teachers indicated that they thought it was important for students to have a say in their own learning. However, this commitment was seldom translated into practice. There was a perception that involving students too much would slow down classroom processes and limit the amount of content that could be covered. When this dimension was present, it was usually within constraints that had been set by the teacher, as in the example below:

> We are looking at Greece in the 400s and 500s with them and focusing on Greek culture, and they could choose any aspect of Greek culture. I gave them a great list out of the work program of areas they could select from and within those areas I made suggestions, and so they have really gone with their own preference. And it was surprising that a couple of the girls offered to look at, well not surprising now, to look at religion and gods and goddesses in mythology, and I thought, okay well I'll be interested to hear. (Mulga State High School)

In Australia, there is some recognition of the curriculum being 'overcrowded', and this may account for teachers' reluctance to relinquish control of the class by valuing students' interests alongside syllabus outcomes. However, there is research evidence to suggest that student direction of activities is a crucial factor in encouraging students' engagement with the learning process. As indicated by Boaler (2002: 81):

> The independence and responsibility encouraged in the students at Phoenix Park seemed to have a direct effect on their approach to mathematics. In a general sense, the students seemed less oppressed and constrained than many students of mathematics, and they seemed to take a more creative approach to mathematics than was typical for school students.

Explicitness is also relevant when students are more involved in planning activities. For instance, in the earlier example of a bullying project, the students, in consultation with the teacher, came up with the idea of submitting a report to the principal. The teacher then had to ensure that the students were presented with explicit criteria as to what constituted a high-quality report. We have previously emphasised the need for explicitness, particularly for students who lack the particular kinds of capital for 'doing school'. For these students, explicit criteria help to make clear what is expected of them in order to succeed, otherwise they can feel alienated by learning programs that appear shrouded in mystery and accessed by secret passwords. In Boaler's (2002) influential *Experiencing School Mathematics*, she writes of the need for students to learn how to learn. She indicates how these students react unfavourably to 'progressive' Mathematics programs because they would rather be working from textbooks than doing problem solving. This emphasises the importance of encouraging students to take up new ways of learning within supportive environments.

The notion of social support is thus also based on the need for students to take risks with their learning in an environment where they are not 'put down' for their attempts. Thus, this is about creating an environment that is warm and comfortable for students, but also one where students are encouraged to participate in the classroom in such a way that they hypothesise, challenge and discuss possible ideas with each other in a safe environment. This occurred in most classrooms that we visited—which is not to deny that there were some instances of sexism and racism present in some classrooms.

Working with and valuing difference

We believe that the *working with and valuing difference* dimension of *productive pedagogies* is crucial in terms of improving the academic and social outcomes of marginalised students, at the same time as improving the social outcomes of all other students. This dimension is also important for the sort of future society that we desire and the position of equality and difference and active citizenship within that society. The elements that are included in the valuing of difference dimension are: *cultural knowledges, inclusivity, narrative, group*

identities in a learning community and *active citizenship.*
Pedagogical practices that reflect this dimension would
involve providing students with knowledge about non-
dominant ways of being in terms of gender, ethnicity/race,
sexualities and so on and explicitly valuing diversity; ensuring that all students are included in classroom activities
through active participation; employing a range of teaching
styles (e.g. including the use of narrative in order to explain
abstract concepts); ensuring that students' various identities
are acknowledged and valued within the classroom in ways
that build a community based on difference; and presenting
students with opportunities to take an active role in making
a difference to their classroom, school or broader community.

When observing for the *working with and valuing difference*
elements, researchers asked the following questions:

- *Cultural knowledges*—Are diverse cultural knowledges
  brought into play?
- *Inclusivity*—Are deliberate attempts made to increase
  the participation of students of different backgrounds?
- *Narrative*—Is the style of teaching principally narrative, or is it expository?
- *Group identities in a learning community*—Does the
  teaching build a sense of community and identity?
- *Citizenship*—Are attempts made to foster active citizenship?

In answering these questions the research team utilised the
following understandings of each item.

Cultural knowledges were treated as being valued when there
was explicit valuing in the classroom of the non-dominant
culture's beliefs, languages, practices and ways of knowing.
Valuing all cultural knowledges required more than one culture being present, and given status, within the curriculum.
Cultural groups are distinguished by social characteristics
such as gender, ethnicity, race, religion, economic status, sexuality or youth. Thus, their valuing meant legitimising these
cultures for all students, through the inclusion, recognition
and transmission of this cultural knowledge. Curriculum

knowledge that is constructed and framed within a common set of cultural definitions, symbols, values, views and qualities—thus attributing some higher status to it—stands in contrast to this.

The *inclusivity* scale was designed to measure the degree to which non-dominant groups were represented in classroom practices by participation. For the purposes of this scale, non-dominant groups were identified in relation to broad societal-level dimensions of social inclusion/exclusion.

Narrative was identified as a sequence of events chained together and was marked by an emphasis in teaching and in student responses on structures and forms. These may include the use of personal stories, biographies, historical accounts, and literary and cultural texts.

Group identities in a learning community took into account a contemporary social theory that emphasises the need for schools to create learning communities in which difference and group identities are positively recognised and developed within a collaborative and supportive classroom community. This requires going beyond a simple politics of tolerance. A classroom that demonstrated this ideal was one where differences and group identities were both positively developed and recognised at the same time as a sense of community was created. For example, in a given classroom, non-Anglo identities could have been given positive recognition in classroom practices and representations; non-Anglo students and teachers would be given opportunities to pursue aspects of the development of their identities and cultures; all class participants would value this as a positive and legitimate aspect of their classroom community; and racism would be challenged within the classroom, school and wider community.

The *active citizenship* item acknowledged that in a democratic society all individuals and groups have the right to engage in the creation and re-creation of that democratic society; have the right to participate in all of the democratic practices and institutions within that society; have the responsibility to ensure that no groups or individuals are excluded from these practices and institutions; and have the responsibility to ensure that a broad definition of the political includes all relationships and structures throughout the social arrangement (see Freire 2001). Active citizenship was treated as present in any classroom in any subject domain when the teacher elaborated on the meaning of such citizenship and facilitated its practice both within and outside the classroom. For instance, active citizenship is a key component of one of Education Queensland's 'Rich Tasks', which are part of the New Basics project, where Years 7–9 students are required to construct a project that improves the wellbeing of the community (Queensland Department of Education, 2001).

There are numerous studies suggesting that the elements contained in the dimension of *working with and valuing difference* contribute to the academic performances of students from marginalised backgrounds. For example, the classic White and Lippitt (1960) study indicated that democratic classrooms, which were inclusive and respectful of difference, produced academic outcomes of equal quality to those produced by more authoritarian and laissez-faire classrooms, which paid little attention to matters of inclusivity or of respecting difference (see also Christie 1985; Harris & Malin 1994; Hymes 1996).

An example of the ways in which focusing on *working with and valuing difference* can support the academic and social outcomes of students can be seen in relation to gender (e.g. see Keddie 2004). For instance, in some schools, anti-learning cultures among boys are supported by homophobic and misogynist sentiments. Boys in such cultures will often suggest that they do not want to work hard and don't like school, especially subjects such as the humanities or English (in case they might be perceived as 'gay' or 'a girl') (Mills 2001; Epstein & Sears 1999; Lingard et al. 2002). Many acts of misbehaviour in classrooms and playgrounds and sexual harassment by boys of girls and other boys involve boys seeking to demonstrate their heterosexuality and 'manliness' (Mills 2001; Mahony 1998; Epstein & Sears 1999). In those classrooms where difference is valued, boys and girls are enabled to act outside what is often considered as 'normal' gendered behaviours in ways that have positive effects for them and others in their classrooms. There is research that suggests that some non-mainstream learners, particularly Indigenous children, may learn best through narrative structures, because of the strong oral traditions and narrative practices extant in their communities (e.g. Christie 1985; Harris & Malin 1994; Hymes 1996). The element *narrative* was present in many classrooms. Many teachers were comfortable locating difficult concepts in narrative. *The Little Red Hen* lesson discussed previously is a good example of this. The use of narrative in this case enabled very young students to grasp aspects of the difficult concept of justice. Most of the classrooms that we visited were also inclusive, in that they involved all students, and we rarely saw students excluded on the basis of gender, ethnicity or race. However, in many cases this was a product of assimilation, or of treating everybody the same. When observing classrooms, researchers sought to identify the extent to which *inclusivity* was accompanied by a *recognition of group identities in a learning community* (see Figure 2.4).

Figure 2.4 Group identities in a learning community coding scale

TO WHAT DEGREE IS THE CLASS A SUPPORTIVE ENVIRONMENT FOR THE PRODUCTION AND POSITIVE RECOGNITION OF DIFFERENCE AND GROUP IDENTITIES?

Contemporary social theory emphasises the need for schools to create learning communities in which difference and group identities are positively recognised and developed within a collaborative and supportive classroom community. This requires going beyond a simple politics of tolerance. A classroom that manifests this ideal is one where differences and group identities are both positively developed and recognised at the same time as a sense of community is created. For example, in a given classroom, Aboriginal identities are given positive recognition in classroom practices and representations; Aboriginal students and teachers are given opportunities to pursue aspects of the development of Aboriginal identities and cultures; all class participants value this as a positive and legitimate aspect of their classroom community; and racism is challenged within the classroom, school and wider community.

GROUP IDENTITIES IN A LEARNING COMMUNITY

No evidence of community or production of difference, focus on individuals	1 . . . 2 . . . 3 . . . 4 . . . 5	Development and positive recognition of difference, within community

1 = There is no evidence of community within the classroom; no positive recognition of difference and group identities; and no support for the development of difference and group identities. Students are all treated as individuals.

2 = Limited evidence of community exists within the classroom; no positive recognition of difference and group identities; and no support for the development of difference and group identities.

3 = Some evidence of community exists within the classroom; some recognition of difference and group identities; and no support for the development of difference and group identities.

4 = There is a strong sense of community within the classroom; positive recognition of difference and group identities; and limited support for the development of difference and group identities.

5 = There is a strong sense of community within the classroom; positive recognition of group identities; and a supportive environment for the production of difference and group identities.

While the occurrence of *working with and valuing difference* was low in the case-study schools, we have seen examples of its introduction into the classroom with good effect. For instance, in an English class with a significant number of bilingual students whose first language was Mandarin, students were encouraged to work in first-language groups for some of the lesson. When we observed this class, they were studying Emily Bronte's *Wuthering Heights*, and even those students who had English as a first language found the text difficult. Working in small first-language groups enabled those students who had a good grasp of the text to unpack it for those who were struggling with this piece of nineteenth-century English literature. This recognition of these students' 'difference' occurred in ways that did not detract from the community created in this class.

In those cases in the study where we did see non-dominant cultural knowledges, it was usually in the form of youth culture as a specific focus of the curriculum. In the first instance, we saw one Grade 8 English class that was being conducted on a unit called *Planet Teenager*, where students were making comparisons between the music they listened to and the music that their parents had listened to when they were teenagers (see Chapter 3 for the assessment task associated with this lesson). In the second instance, non-dominant cultural knowledge was present in social science units such as Aboriginal Studies. It was something that was virtually non-existent in Maths and Science classrooms. This is of course not inevitable. There is significant research that has demonstrated some of the ways in which Maths and Science classrooms can be sensitive to non-dominant cultural knowledges (e.g. see Harding 1993).

One instance that we have written about already (*Leading Learning*, Chapter 2), where we observed active citizenship, involved students working on an environmental plan to regenerate the vegetation around the creek that was running through their school (see also Mills 1996, 1997b; Freire 2001). This item of the *working with and valuing of difference* dimension is advocated in numerous syllabus documents, can be found in *The Adelaide Declaration on National Goals for Schooling in the Twenty-First Century* (MCEETYA, 1999a), and is a core component of the New Basics project in Queensland. While these refer to the kinds of outcomes we want students to be able to demonstrate, students that are to demonstrate these outcomes have to be given opportunities to practise them in the classroom.

Attempting to value difference can be fraught with difficulty. One teacher in a western Queensland high school situated in a town well known for its racial tensions explained how her attempt to engage in a 'Reconciliation' activity had not worked as planned. The town had a history of 'race-related riots'. In Australia, this term is often used to diminish the political nature of uprisings by Indigenous communities protesting against endemic forms of racism. After one such incident, a government inquiry was conducted and recommended the establishment of a school for Indigenous students in a nearby town. This led to a major exodus of Aboriginal students from the established school to the Indigenous school. The art teacher explained how the mural outside the art room had been constructed as part of a Reconciliation process:

> We had very few interactive activities [between the two schools]. So we decided we'd try this reconciliation mural . . . it was for any students of Aboriginal descent in the school who wanted to work on it plus a spattering of my Art students across the whole year level. So it wasn't one particular class. So we spent time developing images that we wanted to use and that we wanted to show a progression from traditional times to middle times to more symbolic representations of contemporary times. The same thing was supposedly happening at [the other school] . . . So it actually fell on its face. It was a forty-five degree day in the middle of summer and all our kids were just . . . I had briefed them about, you know, when the bus arrives, we'll go over, meet each other. How we'll go about it, how we'll make each other feel comfortable. The bus didn't come. No they just didn't come . . . I've organised lots of these things before and I've been the one in the control seat. I've had expectations and they've always worked and I just assumed they would this time and I really didn't do enough homework.

The kids from here were disappointed so then we had to kind of debrief . . . but that was okay. It was still a learning experience . . . and I was quite open about admitting that perhaps I'd been a bit naïve in putting them in that situation. So that was our reconciliation mural.

The teacher then went on to talk about the importance of the mural for the Aboriginal students at the school:

. . . they don't often get an opportunity within the school to, really overtly, expose their cultural heritage . . . in that they're really putting it in your face and it's there for a long time . . . that's a really demonstrative activity and it's something that lasts. It's not just a performance on stage or a recital or something.

This event demonstrates a number of things in relation to elements within the *working with and valuing difference* dimension. First, it is indicative of some of the mishaps that can occur in attempting to engage in cross-cultural work. Indeed, a number of teachers since the study have told us they are nervous about this dimension in case they 'get it wrong'. However, what is needed are more professional development opportunities to raise the threshold of teachers' knowledges around a variety of questions, including Indigenous issues and others relating to difference (Martino, Lingard & Mills 2004). Teachers in the research talked about how they were often perplexed by such questions and had not received policy or professional development support in relation to them. Such issues should also be a focus of professional dialogue within schools.

Second, and importantly, this teacher recognised that she played a major part in the lack of success, in her view, of the event. It is often the case that teachers, and others, deploy deficit models of students and Indigenous communities to explain their own failures. This was not the case with this teacher, who was highly regarded by her school community and who demonstrated high levels of *productive pedagogies* in her art classes. Instead, she considered ways in which her aims of furthering awareness of Reconciliation issues were hindered by her own lack of knowledge, despite having made attempts to learn about Aboriginal cultures.

Third, while in her view the event failed, clearly there was a valuing of difference in the final product. As she says, this did have an impact on the school, in that a final product was created that has had a lasting presence in the school for both those working and studying at the school and those visiting the school. Furthermore, it is a product that meets all the criteria of the *productive performance* outlined in Chapter 4.

Engagement with Productive Pedagogies Research

As the concept of *productive pedagogies* has acquired a high degree of purchase in various state systems and schools throughout Australia, through school, teacher and system interest as well as through professional development work and conference presentations, a number of recurring sets of questions arise. Many of these questions stem from the way in which a research tool has evolved into a professional tool for professional dialogue. Here we look at some of these questions and comment on the ways in which this framework has evolved.

It is important to recall that the *productive pedagogies* framework of classroom practice was designed as a coding instrument for undertaking structured classroom obser-vations within a research project. That is, it was a research tool, and the four-dimensional framework was derived from statistical interrogations of 302 classroom observation data at the end of the first year of the study and then confirmed through a total of 975 classroom observations. In research terms, this original purpose is both a strength and a limit-ation. The strength of coding a large number of classrooms with a structured observation instrument is that it is pos-sible to say something about how these classrooms compare with each other, albeit within the terms of the coding instru-ment. Additionally, the Productive Pedagogies Research did provide a useful snapshot of teachers' classroom practice at a particular policy moment in the history of education. However, the narrow range of observations permitted by the structure of the instrument is a major limitation: the unexpected, particular and uncoded occurrences that take place in the classroom are not captured adequately by such a process.

Although the *productive pedagogies* framework was developed as a research tool and coding instrument, we do not recommend that it be widely used for this purpose in schools. While peer observation may provide a powerful learning experience for both observer and observed, such practice requires high levels of trust; it should be framed by explicit agreements about how the observations will be conducted, recorded and discussed; and it should be embedded in a mechanism of sustained professional dialogue between teachers. As these conditions are generally not common in schools and are often limited to a small group of teachers, we suggest that it is preferable to utilise video recordings of lessons or model lessons when undertaking coding activities, and that participants in these activities should agree to certain principles of professional dialogue, such as those described by protocols (e.g. see McDonald et al. 2003).

We are often asked whether or not all 20 elements of *productive pedagogies* are necessary for improved student outcomes. The research data are inconclusive on this. However, we argue that items from all four dimensions should be present to ensure that the academic and social outcomes of all students are maximised. It is perhaps more reasonable to consider a unit of work, rather than a single lesson, when considering the distribution of *productive pedagogies*. In this way, the framework can operate as a planning tool and the elements can suggest a range of teaching strategies.

There has also been the suggestion that this framework is too demanding of students and teachers. This would perhaps be true if the expectation were that all 20 elements of the four dimensions had to be present in the classroom all the time. We do argue for the need to have high expectations, and indeed those teachers who have high expectations of their students are those most likely to demonstrate high levels of *productive pedagogies* (Rosenthal & Jacobson 1968; Lingard et al. 2003; see also Boaler 2002). We also acknowledge that some necessary and valuable classroom activities would not code high, such as practising handwriting scripts or quiet reading. It is important to remember that *productive pedagogies* describe a range of classroom practices, rather than the many and varied ways in which young people learn.

There are also times when teachers think that the *productive pedagogies* framework of classroom practice should include other items. For instance, there have been suggestions that creativity is missing, and scaffolding of learning has also been mentioned, along with sequencing and pacing. We welcome these suggestions, as we have always worked from the assumption that the *productive pedagogies* framework occupies only some of the bandwidth on the spectrum of classroom practices. A key use of the framework is to stimulate professional dialogue. We encourage teachers to adapt it to their locally developed understandings of students' learning needs. In so doing, we encourage them to review what the research literature might say about the topic.

There have also been suggestions that the framework is too large and that an effective way of implementing it is to focus on one dimension at a time. However, we would be concerned by this uptake, because the framework is a holistic one. The focus in such instances is usually on *intellectual quality*. We cannot emphasise enough the importance of intellectual quality for all students, but we would argue that it is not sufficient. The other three dimensions are also necessary—especially for those students who struggle with schooling. That all the dimensions can work nicely together is well captured in a comment made by a teacher at Waratah State Primary School, the one who taught the lesson on *The Little Red Hen*, who regularly demonstrated high levels of *productive pedagogies* in her classroom:

The philosophy is so inclusive as we are always drawing on their own experiences and so every child knows that they can come in with an example from their own life and we will talk about it. We talk about the rules of philosophy and one of the rules is philosophy is a safe place to speak. You can say what you want to say as long as it doesn't hurt other people. There are no right or wrongs and so just because someone has given a good answer to the question that doesn't mean it is the answer, that is just their opinion. It is very inclusive and you are going to see it tomorrow. Already the year ones are participating right from the word go; they can say something and no one will laugh as it is their own opinion. The fact is that straight away they can come in with an experience from home, like we have been doing fairy tales of late and we did the three little pigs, and one of the questions after the story was why was the wolf so mean. We started to get into the area of meanness and of course they all had examples they could give.

Within the philosophy program at this school there is an emphasis on students engaging in higher-order thinking, where in this case young children are expected to speculate and hypothesise on the reasons for the characters' decisions and in the process provide supporting evidence. However, the teacher also picks up on the importance of other aspects of *productive pedagogies*. Dealing with a philosophy in which there are 'no right or wrongs' can occur only in a supportive environment, where students have a 'safe place to speak'; philosophy engages the students because the teacher connects the topics and issues to their experiences and worlds, there is clearly the narrative element of the valuing of difference dimension, and 'You can say what you want to say as long as it doesn't hurt other people' entails a valuing of different cultural knowledges and learning to see the standpoint of others. This was not a relativist position: comments that were clearly objectionable and vilified particular groups of people not in the classroom were also forbidden.

The *productive pedagogies* framework has been reshaped and incorporated in the New South Wales Quality Teaching Model (Professional Support and Curriculum Directorate 2003). Given what we know about quality teaching and learning from prior research, there is little doubt that the items within the New South Wales model reflect the kinds of classroom practices that, when present in high measure, will lead to improved learning outcomes for students. However, the explicit omission of the dimension *working with and valuing difference* is puzzling, as it appears out of step with the long history and preservation in New South Wales of redistributive funding regimens, and as it removes the focus on the philosophy of inclusion and representation underpinning this dimension. The fact that these approaches to quality teaching and learning were not found in high levels in the Queensland study suggests that they need to be supported and highlighted more, not less. While recognising the complexity of these matters, we note that the schools in the Productive Pedagogies Research seemed to be better at incorporating aspects of this dimension in their whole-school culture or in some subject teaching such as Aboriginal Studies, rather than across all subject domains.

Conclusion

In the current political and policy context, the placing of teachers and their knowledges at the core of schooling practice and policy is in a sense a dangerous strategy (Apple 2000a; Smyth 2001). Pedagogy is that which teachers have accrued to their professional identities and held, to differing extents in different educational systems, outside the state's purview. The state in many Western countries has been concerned to articulate and mandate curriculum and assessment in particular ways in the current policy moment, while not explicitly mandating a particular pedagogy. Nonetheless, accepting Bernstein's account that curriculum, pedagogy and assessment constitute the three message systems of schooling and that changes to one of the message systems affects the workings of the others, the new reductionist approaches to curriculum and assessment (linked to accountability) such as the English and Welsh National Curriculum have real effects on pedagogy. These effects are in the direction of 'thinning out' the pedagogy rather than broadening it in the direction of what we have called *productive pedagogies* (Hartley 2003). However, calling for an alignment between the three message systems potentially opens up pedagogy to its regulation by the performative and evaluative state, and potentially increases the state's surveillance of teachers. This appears to be the case in English schools. Nonetheless, it is our considered view, on the basis of the Productive Pedagogies Research and other related research, that pedagogy needs to become the focus of substantive professional conversations within schools—edifying conversations, to use Ball's (1997b) terms. For us, the concept of *productive pedagogies* provides a vocabulary for teachers to discuss their pedagogies and reflect on them. It most certainly does not provide a calculus that can simply be layered over existing classroom practices. The framework of pedagogies being argued for here instead acknowledges the need always for the mediation of the concept of *productive pedagogies* by teachers' considered professional readings of their subject matter and their students. Opportunities for teacher reflection about pedagogies need to be built into the culture of schools. It is to these whole-school and educational system matters that we turn in Chapter 5. In Chapter 3 we look at assessment as a means of encouraging students' learning and argue that the achievement of good outcomes requires good assessment practices. In this we agree with Barnes et al. (2000: 624) '. . . that the performances privileged by assessment should be precisely those performances that constitute the goal of the curriculum. Where this is the case, it is entirely appropriate that there be a close link between assessment and instruction'.

3 Productive assessment

Assessment is perhaps the most maligned aspect of teaching and learning processes in schools. This is often a consequence of its association with the ranking and sorting of students, with external examinations, with league tables, with standardised tests, with various reporting systems, with judging teacher performance, and with the restriction and containment of teacher practices. Such uneasiness about assessment plays out in different ways in educational systems around the globe due to the dominance and differing effects of these and other assessment practices. In England, for example, standardised testing is linked to a mistrustful regulation of teacher work (Mahony & Hextall 2000; Ball 2004). An extensive top-down testing regimen, combined with high-stakes public examinations, results in less space for teachers' professional judgments and some considerable demoralisation of the profession, even at the primary level (Ball 1999, 2004; Jeffrey & Woods 1998; Lingard & Ozga 2004; Ozga & Simola 2004). Throughout much of the USA, teaching is reduced to improving test results and the complementary creation of what McNeil (2000) has insightfully called defensive teaching. She begins her scarifying critique of this testing situation in the USA with the observation (2000: 3) that:

Standardization reduces the quality and quantity of what is taught and learned in schools. The immediate negative effect of standardization is the overwhelming finding of a study of schools where the imposition of standardized controls reduced the scope and quality of course content, diminished the role of teachers, and distanced students from active learning.

In contrast, the Queensland school system has not had external public examinations for over 30 years, utilising instead in the senior school a very professionalising mixture of school-based assessment and system moderation via teacher panels and a core skills test for moderation purposes. All of these things seek overtly to operate in socially just ways through an emphasis on teacher-established standards across schools. We would note here as well that the core skills test focuses on desired higher-order skills from across the panoply of curricular offerings in the last two years of secondary schooling. This higher-order demand appears to fuel pedagogy focused on higher-order thinking at the senior levels of schooling.

The Productive Pedagogies Research found very positive effects of this long period of senior teacher ownership of assessment practices and the requirement for alignment of pedagogy and assessment with curriculum (syllabus) goals. Senior teachers in the study often demonstrated high levels of assessment literacy. Interestingly, however, these good practices and their effects were not anywhere near as evident in the practices of assessment in the lower secondary schools. Differences in assessment regimens also operate in differing ways in the primary or elementary years, with assessment at the secondary level becoming potentially more disfiguring of the educative process as selection and sorting pressures come to bear more harshly and with high-stakes effects.

Queensland's moderation system through teacher panels is unique in Australia and persists in stark contrast to, say, New South Wales's system of external examinations. We also note the worldwide pressures for more testing of student achievement across systems, as part of political desires for outcomes accountability and input–output measures in a time of fiscal constraint. Such pressures also exist globally in terms of multiple country comparisons of educational indicators. Think here of the OECD's indicators, which now play an important policy role within member nations (Henry et al. 2001). However, assessment can be read differently. Despite such pressures and policy constraints, assessment can, and indeed should, also be a pedagogical tool. It is this aspect of assessment that we pursue in this chapter—assessment as educative and socially just.

Having said that, we need to acknowledge and recognise distinctions between different forms of assessment and testing and their different purposes. Sometimes the issue becomes the desire at system level for assessment/testing to serve multiple purposes, for example accountability and monitoring over time and prognostic and diagnostic assistance for teachers. Teachers almost always support assessment for the latter purposes, while feeling somewhat de-professionalised by system-imposed testing for accountability and a range of other political purposes (Mahony & Hextall 2000; Ball 2004). Our focus here is on assessment that forms part of teachers' classroom practices, while recognising the need for a politics around the nature and effects of systemic testing.

Assessment at the classroom and systemic level mostly relates to individual performance, yet we note as well the significance of the social purposes of schooling, which are variously defined in terms of the contemporary world, and their contribution to the collective social good. Assessment of these purposes should be valued alongside individualised performance measures. Alignment supports this valuing: by ensuring that assessment practices shape pedagogy in ways that support students' learning; and by providing measures of the success of schooling in achieving the broad range of academic and social outcomes.

Assessment in education—the state of play

As already noted, there have been many challenges posed to current education systems by the changing nature of modern society as a result of globalisation, risk and uncertainty. The collapse of metanarratives (Lyotard 1984) usually associated with postmodernity has also seen the collapse of a clear value consensus and horizon of expectation (Laidi 1998), with increased demand for numerical evidence and portfolio-demonstrated performance as one outcome (Yeatman 1994; Ball 2004).

Changes in education have at times been driven through assessment. Black (2001: 65) has noted that '. . . as reformers dream about changing education for the better they almost always see a need to include assessment and testing in their plans and frequently see them as the main instruments of their reform'. For example, Black and Wiliam (1998) have shown ample evidence that strengthening formative assessment, which provides regular feedback, raises the standards of pupil performance, while Barnes et al. (2000: 623) have shown that, in the case of mandated high-stakes assessment, changing assessment can leverage curriculum reform, though not always for the better. They state that '. . . the important debate on the role of assessment as either catalyst or engine for reform is not assisted by the exclusive identification of assessment with testing' (2000: 625). Contemporary education systems increasingly draw control back towards the centre and monitor performance at the local level through the imposition of standards testing and even audits of teacher performance. These tendencies towards reporting and accountability—more pervasive in some educational systems than in others—work against more progressive and educative assessment practices and the desires of such reformers.

We consider that these varying effects of assessment reflect struggles over the purposes of schooling as much as the nature of assessment practices themselves. Schools are implicated in and affected by the major sweeps of history; debates about the purposes of schooling at any time reflect competing political readings of desirable forms of schooling and its message systems of curriculum, pedagogy and assessment (Bernstein 1973; Apple 2000b). Acknowledging the political character of schooling, our approach to assessment does *not* assume that it is a neutral mechanism or simply an educational measurement tool. We understand assessment as a discourse of schooling that produces multiple effects— some anticipated, others not; some clearly visible and others hidden. We acknowledge that power operates through assessment and is one of its effects. Like other discourses of schooling, assessment positions students in particular ways in relation to knowledge—its construction, manipulation, utilisation and transmission. This positioning reflects how power operates more broadly in society, in particular its stratifying effects. As Delpit (1995: 25) explains:

> The upper and middle classes send their children to school with all the accoutrements of the culture of power; children from other kinds of families operate within perfectly wonderful and viable cultures but not cultures that carry the codes of power.

We argue that many high-stakes testing regimens do not offer opportunities for *all* students to engage in high-quality intellectual activities. Indeed, in many instances assessment tasks, and associated teaching practices, operate as instruments of power and gatekeepers to the codes of power. We make this observation while recognising the meritocratic promise of schooling to sort and select fairly within a culture of achievement, rather than one of ascription. Although it seems almost inevitable in a stratified society that schooling will continue to sort and select, a more equitable distribution of social capacities is necessary to a society informed and affected by robust citizenship. Put simply, schools need to create active citizens of all students and contribute to some notion of collective wellbeing (see Brown & Lauder 2000). This needs to be kept in mind when set against the individualising and dividing practices of most assessment in schools.

The form of assessment in schools that is our focus in this chapter involves a wide range of practices. These are shaped by *when* the assessment takes place and *how* the information gained is used. It can be oriented towards testing content, the achievement of outcomes and the performance of skills; and it can take specific forms such as exhibitions, standardised tests, online projects and Rich Tasks, to name just a few. These practices respond to a variety of pressures: systems accountability through comparisons between schools; employers' requests for 'plain language' comparisons between students, and measurement of employability skills; and parents' expectations to be able to track their children's progress through time and by comparison with their peers. These enduring demands are now occurring when, Eisner (1998: 132) claims, 'if ever there was a time in which the calls were clearer or more strident for new, more authentic approaches to educational assessment, I cannot remember when they occurred'. Within this context, we focus here on the purposeful connection of assessment to curriculum and pedagogy—the alignment issue, and its realisation through students' achievement of academic and social performances. In our view, this connection is mediated by a shared vision for learning among teachers that reflects local concerns, makes explicit the broad purposes of schooling and, in turn, the purposes of classroom practices. In the absence of such a vision, learning may be equated with the acquisition of content knowledge or success on a test.

Productive assessment

There is a wealth of literature on formative assessment, authentic assessment and performance assessment from which the *productive assessment* framework outlined in this chapter draws its inspiration (e.g. see Lambert & Lines 2000; McNeil 2000; Torrance 1995; Broadfoot 1996; Murphy & Broadfoot 1995; Newmann & Associates 1996; Cumming & Maxwell 1999). *Productive assessment* is a specific title we have allocated to an approach to assessment that aligns with our concept of *productive pedagogies*, outlined in Chapter 2, and with *productive performances*, considered in some detail in Chapter 4. *Productive assessment* thus links pedagogy to student performance through assessment. In this chapter we describe the types of assessment practices that are linked to *productive pedagogies*, which support the achievement of these *productive performances*.

There is also a strong social justice element to the construction of our framework of *productive assessment*. There has been much said about the need to consider the question of whose knowledge is represented in assessment (e.g. see Chilisa 2000; Thompson & Gitlin 1995; Gipps & Murphy 1994). *Productive assessment* is concerned with the levels of achievement of *all* students, but particularly those from traditionally marginalised backgrounds and those who are currently underachieving. However, at the same time, as Chilisa (2000) has indicated, discrimination and social justice may not be apparent in the achievement levels of students but in the ways in which students come to perceive themselves as a result of the particular knowledges valorised within an assessment piece. This occurs in such instances where, as Thompson and Gitlin (1995) argue, knowledge is linked into the standpoint of the dominant culture in an unconsidered way. Global flows of people associated with local conflicts rub up against existing tensions between, for example, Indigenous and established colonial populations in ways that challenge tenuous and unsatisfactory settlements between existing interests in society. Competing accounts of the world need to be considered in the school curriculum in order to make problematic the processes of knowledge production that result in such settlements (Dimitriades & McCarthy 2001).

Productive assessment tasks

For students to demonstrate *productive performance*, there needs to be a move away from traditional forms of testing and measurement. This move entails assessment processes and practices that enable students to demonstrate a richness of outcomes, rather than a limited set of knowledges. We regard the narrow assessment instruments—typified by short-answer tasks, rote essay responses and multiple choice tests—used in many school situations to be inadequate indicators of these outcomes (McNeil 2000). Unfortunately, these narrow kinds of assessment dominated most of the tasks collected from schools that participated in the Productive Pedagogies Research (QSRLS 2001). In many ways such assessment does not measure the kinds of outcomes that it purports to be doing. For instance, it is difficult to know whether student responses on an exam actually reflect their acquisition of knowledge of a topic or whether such knowledge is fleetingly lodged in the student's short-term memory. Furthermore, as Torrance (1997: 321) has argued: '[T]hese measures pay no regard to the many other personal, practical, and social outcomes of schooling that most governments (and individuals) would claim are important'. The notion of *productive performance*, addressed in Chapter 4, takes into account these other outcomes alongside academic ones. As such, it requires assessment tasks that allow students the scope to demonstrate these outcomes, and requires forms of pedagogy that develop in students the requisite skills and knowledges. In order for students to do well on *productive performance* measures, the assessment tasks must provide opportunities for students to demonstrate these performances and the pedagogical practices must provide students with the requisite skills and knowledges to complete these tasks. The *productive assessment* framework describes the characteristics of tasks that allow students to demonstrate such outcomes.

The *productive assessment* framework consisted of 18 elements. Like the pedagogies framework outlined in Chapter 2, the assessment framework we outline here has four dimensions—*intellectual quality*, *connectedness*, *supportive classroom environment*, and *working with and valuing difference*. The distribution of the 18 elements into these four dimensions is detailed in Table 1.1 and discussed below.

Productive assessment tasks incorporate seven elements drawn from Newmann and Associates' (1996) model of authentic assessment tasks. However, the Productive Pedagogies Research team slightly modified the names of these elements, while retaining their substantive nature, in order to make more explicit the links between the pedagogy assessment and performance scales. For example: 'organisation of information' has been renamed *higher-order thinking*; and 'consideration of alternatives' has been renamed *problematic knowledge (consideration of alternatives)*.

Intellectual quality

We support the view that all students should be given tasks that require them to demonstrate high-quality academic outcomes (see also Newmann & Associates 1996; Boaler 2002). This is a form of social justice premised on the assumptions that all students have a right to learn, a right to the equitable distribution of educational resources and a right to experience quality teaching. The items that make up the dimension of *intellectual quality* within the *productive assessment* framework are detailed below.

The *higher-order thinking* item requires students to manipulate information and ideas in ways that transform their meanings and implications. This transformation occurs when students combine facts and ideas in order to synthesise, generalise, explain, hypothesise or arrive at some conclusion or interpretation. Manipulating information and ideas through these processes allows students to solve problems and discover new (for them) meanings and understandings. When students engage in the construction of knowledge, an element of uncertainty is introduced into the instructional process and makes instructional outcomes not always predictable: that is, the teacher is not certain what students will produce. In helping students become producers of knowledge, the teacher's main instructional task is to create activities or environments that allow them opportunities to engage in higher-order thinking.

The *problematic knowledge (consideration of alternative knowledges)* item refers to the ways in which the assessment task asks students to consider alternative solutions, strategies, perspectives or points of view as they address a concept, problem or issue. Tasks that score highly on this scale involve students considering alternatives, either through explicit presentation of the alternatives or through an activity that could not be successfully completed without the examination of alternatives implicit in the work.

The *problematic knowledge (construction of knowledge)* item recognises the importance of expecting students to demonstrate an understanding of how knowledge is constructed. Such an expectation is based on an understanding of knowledge as contested, rather than as a fixed body of information; and as subject to political, social and cultural influences and implications. A task that requires students to demonstrate this understanding might compare and contrast potentially conflicting forms of knowledge. It might also seek explanations as to why some forms of knowledge are more valued and considered to be of higher status than others. For example, as students increasingly seek information from the Internet, they are required to interpret, use and apply this knowledge. This relies on their understanding of how knowledge is constructed, and on their ability to differentiate between various paradigms and interests.

The *depth of knowledge (disciplinary content)* item is an indication of the need to set assessment tasks that promote students' understanding of and thinking about ideas, theories and perspectives considered critical or essential in an academic or professional discipline or in interdisciplinary fields recognised in authoritative scholarship. For example, in Science this would include increasingly sophisticated understandings of living things and the relationships between them. Examples in Social Science would include deepening understandings of democracy, social class or theories of revolution. Reference to isolated factual claims, definitions or algorithms are not indicators of significant disciplinary content unless the task requires students to apply powerful disciplinary ideas that organise and interpret information.

The *depth of knowledge (disciplinary processes)* item requires students to be 'doers' of the discipline. An assessment task where this is present would expect students to use methods of inquiry, research or communication characteristic of an academic or professional discipline. Some powerful processes of inquiry may not be linked uniquely to any specific discipline (e.g. interpreting graphs), but they would be valued if the task called for their use in ways similar to important uses in the discipline. Examples of methods of disciplinary inquiry would include looking for mathematical patterns or interpreting primary sources.

The *elaborate communication* item in an assessment task expects that students will respond to the assessment item with a coherent communication of ideas, concepts, arguments and/or explanations. In the Productive Pedagogies Research, due to logistical reasons, the focus was on elaborate written communication; however, *productive assessment* recognises that elaborate communication can occur through a variety of media. What is important is that this form of communication is expected to be rich in detail, qualifications and argument.

The coders evaluating the assessment tasks were asked to consider the following questions in relation to each of the items in the *intellectual quality* dimension of *productive assessment*:

- *Higher-order thinking*—To what extent does the assessment task expect students to engage in higher-order thinking?
- *Problematic knowledge (consideration of alternative knowledges)*—To what extent does success in this task require consideration of alternative solutions, strategies, perspectives or points of view?
- *Problematic knowledge (construction of knowledge)*—To what degree are students expected to demonstrate knowledge as constructed?
- *Depth of knowledge (disciplinary content)*—To what extent does the assessment task require students to

demonstrate an understanding of ideas, theories or perspectives central to an academic or professional discipline?

- *Depth of knowledge (disciplinary processes)*—To what extent does the task lead students to use methods of inquiry, research, communication and discourse characteristic of an academic or professional discipline?
- *Elaborate communication*—To what extent is elaborate communication expected?

In asking each of these questions, the researchers made judgments on a 1–5 scale. The structure of the coding scale for *depth of knowledge (disciplinary content)* is shown in Figure 3.1. This structure was replicated in the coding instrument for all the elements.

Figure 3.1 Depth of knowledge (disciplinary content) coding scale

TO WHAT EXTENT DOES THE ASSESSMENT TASK REQUIRE STUDENTS TO DEMONSTRATE AN UNDERSTANDING OF IDEAS, THEORIES OR PERSPECTIVES CENTRAL TO AN ACADEMIC OR PROFESSIONAL DISCIPLINE?

This scale identifies the extent to which an assessment task promotes students' understanding of and thinking about ideas, theories and perspectives considered critical or essential in an academic or professional discipline, or in interdisciplinary fields recognised in authoritative scholarship. Examples in Mathematics could include proportion, equality or geometric space. Examples in Social Science could include democracy, social class or theories of revolution. Reference to isolated factual claims, definitions or algorithms will not be considered indicators of significant disciplinary content unless the task requires students to apply powerful disciplinary ideas which organise and interpret information.

DISCIPLINARY CONTENT

Limited disciplinary content	1 . . . 2 . . . 3 . . . 4 . . . 5	High disciplinary content

1 = Success in this task can be achieved without any understanding of concepts, ideas or theories central to any specific discipline.

2 = Success in this task can be achieved with a superficial understanding of concepts, ideas or theories central to any specific discipline.

3 = Success in this task can be achieved with a moderate understanding of concepts, ideas or theories central to any specific discipline.

4 = Success in this task requires a substantial understanding of concepts, ideas or theories central to any specific discipline.

5 = Success in this task requires a substantial understanding, and a comparison, of concepts, ideas or theories central to one or more specific disciplines.

In this chapter we draw on a number of assessment tasks to illustrate various elements of *productive assessment*. Most of the tasks were collected as part of the Productive Pedagogies Research. These tasks illustrate the findings of the study and, according to our agreements with research participants, the teachers and schools are not identified. In addition, where noted, other tasks have been developed by school-based colleagues to illustrate elements of *productive assessment*. These tasks are used with permission of the authors listed in the acknowledgments.

One such task demonstrates high expectations regarding disciplinary content (see Figure 3.2). It is a Year 8 Science task in which students were asked to design an ecosystem for a new zoo. The school in which this task was developed is located on the western plains of the Great Dividing Range in New South Wales, which is known for its wheat and cotton industry. The central disciplinary content being investigated

Figure 3.2 Year 8 Science ecosystem design

Year 8 Science Assessment Task
Topic—Ecology

THE PROBLEM:
A new zoo is opening in the area. The zoo is seeking to create new enclosures for its animals, in order to make them more realistic. The decision has been made to place a variety of different animals and plants in each enclosure. The management hopes that the new displays will give visitors a better idea of how animals live in the wild. You have been employed to design an 'ecosystem' for the zoo to house a variety of different plant and animal species.

THE DESIGN BRIEF:
Your ecosystem must contain both plant and animal species (between 10 and 20 species in total). Animals must be selected from AT LEAST THREE of the following groups:
- Mammals
- Birds
- Reptiles
- Fish
- Insects

You need to specify the type of geographical area in which the species live (for example, Australian desert, Alpine region, Ocean shore, Mangrove Swamp, Sandy Desert, Tropical rainforest). The area you choose should be reflected in the design itself.

The ecosystem must contain food chains and food webs that will sustain those organisms present. Some animals will need to be fed regularly, to prevent them from eating each other. You will need to make decisions about feeding, and indicate which animals need feeding.

THE PROCESS:
You will need to submit progress reports to your supervisor, indicating the direction and achievements of you project. These will be required at regular intervals throughout your work.

Task	Requirements	Date due
Progress report #1 (8 marks)	• A plan for your enclosure, including: type of ecosystem, features, possible organisms • A proposal for the zoo manager, describing why your enclosure will be a worthwhile investment	Week ____ , Term 3
Progress report #2 (12 marks)	• A list of likely organisms, classified into producers, consumers etc. (give reasons) • A description of any special requirements needed by the organisms to ensure their survival	Week ____ , Term 3
Final submission (20 marks)	• Labelled map or model of the enclosure • Your predicted food web(s) for the ecosystem • Adaptations—description & labelled diagram • Discussion of the impact a bushfire, drought OR flood might have on your enclosure • Bibliography (Author, Title, Year of Publication)	Week ____ , Term 3

in this task relates to food chains. The students are required to prepare a design brief for an enclosure to be incorporated into a new zoo in their town. This task can be applied to the design brief in ways that reflect each student's interests and depth of understanding of food chains. However, success in the task does require a substantial understanding of food chains, and the inclusion of progress reports provides opportunities for the students to obtain feedback during the design process. Also, the marking criteria are designed to encourage students to produce complex food chains that include all the organisms in the proposed enclosure. The design element of this task requires students to demonstrate more than the ability to interpret and describe food chains: it requires that they demonstrate a deep understanding of how food chain concepts are central elements of the functioning of ecosystems. The teacher provides a cautionary note by reminding the students that: 'Some animals will need to be fed regularly, to prevent them from eating each other'. In addition, they must take into account the unpredictable but all too familiar nature of their local environment by considering the impact of fire, drought or flood on their ecosystem. It is the embedding of this disciplinary content within a task that extends over a period of time and that requires an understanding of the local environment that makes this task particularly challenging and connected to the students' experiences.

Connectedness

While the items within the *intellectual quality* dimension are critical to evoking student performances of the kind represented by the *productive performance* outcomes identified in Chapter 2, engagement with a task is more likely to occur for traditionally underachieving students when the task has meaning for them. This means being explicit with students about the types of performances they are expected to achieve while providing opportunities for them to practise these performances. This may involve students presenting to an audience beyond the teacher, and usually beyond the rest of the class, which may entail Exhibitions of the type developed by the Coalition of Essential Schools (Cushman 1990). We have seen, for instance: students writing storybooks for younger children, which they have then taken to read to students in younger grades; students constructing local environmental impact statements which have been sent to various members of the community; and students preparing a collaborative submission in response to a call for designs of a work of public art. In these instances, students were concerned with the demands, and indicators of success, of real-life audiences.

The items that make up the dimension of *connectedness* within the *productive assessment* framework are detailed below.

Integrated school knowledge is identifiable in an assessment task when either: (a) students are expected to make explicit attempts to connect two or more sets of subject area knowledge; or (b) subject area boundaries are not readily seen. Themes or problems that either require knowledge from multiple areas, or that have no clear subject areas basis in the first place, are indicators of curricula that integrate school subject knowledge.

Connectedness (link to background knowledge) is present in an assessment task when students are provided with opportunities to make connections between their linguistic, cultural, world knowledge and experience and the topics, skills and competencies at hand. Background knowledge may include community knowledge, local knowledge, personal experience, media and popular culture sources.

The *connectedness (problem linked to world beyond classroom)* scale measures the extent to which an assessment task has value and meaning beyond the instructional context. In a task with little or no value beyond the classroom, activities are deemed important for success in school (now or later) but for no other aspects of life. Thus, to score highly, the task should ask students to address a concept, problem or issue that is similar to one that they have encountered, or are likely to encounter, in life beyond the classroom.

The *connectedness (audience beyond school)* scale measures the degree to which an assessment task expects students to communicate their knowledge, present a product or performance, or take some action for an audience beyond the teacher, classroom and school building. This refers to the nature of the students' final product, not to the process of working on the task. To score highly on this scale, student responses to assessment items should be taken seriously by the intended audience.

Problem-based tasks are defined as those having no specified correct solution, requiring knowledge construction on the part of the students, and requiring sustained attention beyond a single lesson. A problem-based assessment item is one which presents students with a specific practical, real or hypothetical problem (set of problems) to solve.

The questions associated with evaluating *connectedness* in *productive assessment* tasks are listed below:

- *Integrated school knowledge*—To what degree is school knowledge integrated across subject boundaries?
- *Connectedness: link to background knowledge*—To what degree does the assessment task draw on students' background knowledges?
- *Connectedness: problem linked to world beyond classroom*—To what extent is the assessment task connected to competencies or concerns beyond the classroom?
- *Connectedness: audience beyond school*—To what extent does the assessment task expect students to address an audience beyond the classroom?
- *Problem-based tasks*—To what extent is the assessment task based on solving a specific problem(s)?

The structure of the coding scale for the element *link to background knowledge* is shown in Figure 3.3.

Figure 3.3 Link to background knowledge coding scale

TO WHAT DEGREE DOES THE ASSESSMENT TASK DRAW ON STUDENTS' BACKGROUND KNOWLEDGES?

Low *connection* assessment tasks introduce new content, skills and competencies without any direct or explicit opportunities to explore what prior knowledge students have of the topic, and without any attempts to draw on relevant or key background knowledges that might enhance students' comprehension and understanding of the 'new'.

High *connection* assessment tasks provide students with opportunities to make connections between their linguistic, cultural, world knowledge and experience and the topics, skills and competencies at hand. Background knowledge may include community knowledge, local knowledge, personal experience, media and popular culture sources.

Note: Background knowledge does not mean content that would have been studied for a test as part of that unit.

LINK TO BACKGROUND KNOWLEDGE

No		High
background		background
knowledge	1 . . . 2 . . . 3 . . . 4 . . . 5	knowledge

1 = No connection is made in the assessment task to students' background knowledge.

2 = Students' background knowledge and experience are mentioned within the task, but are not connected to the requirements of the task.

3 = Some connections to students' background knowledges and experiences are mentioned and minimal amounts are necessary for completion of the task.

4 = Some connections to students' background knowledges and experiences are mentioned and moderate amounts are necessary for completion of the task.

5 = Students' background knowledge and experiences are a significant aspect of the assessment task.

The following task (see Figure 3.4), Planet Teenager, scored highly on the *link to background knowledge* item. It was a Year 8 English task, so most of the students undertaking it were twelve to thirteen years old. The students were required to do an in-depth study of what it means to be a teenager in Australia today. This drew on students' knowledges of contemporary culture, and asked students using this knowledge to investigate various aspects of the culture.

We have used this assessment task in numerous workshops with teachers to create conversations with them about assessment. It has been a useful task in that it has always created interesting discussions about what makes a high-quality assessment piece. It is always lauded for its connectedness: here is a piece that clearly links into students' worlds. Teachers have in many instances used it as a starting point for creating their own assessment tasks. They like the focus on music, on predicting the future, on identifying key issues of the moment and so on. And, as was the case in our observations of students working on this task, they acknowledge that it will engage the students. However, the one concern that comes up over and over again is that it is possible to do some of these activities without engaging in any degree of intellectual quality, and that the choice within the task could mean that some students do the easier work rather than the more in-depth activities. These teachers also often suggest that the idea about writing for the metropolitan daily newspaper—the *Courier-Mail*—is a little artificial. An idea that has often arisen as a means of improving the task and of taking into account the 'audience beyond the school' item has been a public museum-style exhibition for parents, and others, where students do one or more of these items in real depth about what it means to be a teenager today contrasted with a teenager perhaps 20 to 30 years ago. There have also been suggestions that in order for students to demonstrate *productive performance* on this task they will need to be supported in their learning. Much of this support for learning will come through the pedagogical interactions in the classroom during the course of the unit. However, there

Figure 3.4 Year 8 English, 'Planet Teenager'

PLANET TEENAGER

State High School
YEAR 8 ENGLISH
TASK - MAGAZINE LIFT-OUT

"Talkin' about my Generation"

As the end of the millenium approaches, the <u>Courier Mail</u> is running a series of weekend specials profiling various generations and highlighting issues of relevance to each.

YOUR TASK – As the <u>Courier Mail</u>'s Youth Affairs reporter, you have been asked to prepare a special on teenagers. Your lift-out must reflect what's important to young people and should be original and creative in ideas and presentation. It must include at least FOUR of the following. . .

OUR TIME IN 2000

As a key feature of your lift-out you must write a REFLECTIVE PIECE of between 200 and 300 words in which you discuss the general beliefs and attitudes of your generation and culture. You must also discuss your own ideas about the world you live in, your thoughts on the future and being an adult and what your ideal world would be like. This will be used as an introduction to your lift-out and is a compulsory component of the task.

THE PLANET OF SOUND

This segment looks at music as a symbol that's important to teenagers. It should include a short CD Review of a popular artist, the current top 10 songs and a 10 point profile on an artist or band. This profile should include information on style of music, degree of influence of artist/s, interesting facts about them etc are ways in which the assessment task can support the students' learning.

Supportive classroom environment

Productive assessment requires all students to accomplish tasks at high levels. The findings of the Productive Pedagogies Research suggest that supportive classroom pedagogies are significantly correlated with student academic performance. Such pedagogies provide multiple opportunities for students to practise, demonstrate and receive feedback on their performance, relative to explicit criteria on tasks over which they feel a sense of ownership.

The elements that make up the dimension of *supportive classroom environment* within *productive assessment* are detailed below.

When *student direction of assessment tasks* is present, students are able to influence the tasks they will do in order to complete the assessment requirements of a particular unit. Such tasks are likely to be student-centred and involve group work or individual research and/or investigative projects, whereby the students assume responsibility for the activities with which they engage and/or how they complete them.

The need for students who struggle with schooling to be provided with *explicit criteria* has been well documented (e.g. see Bourdieu & Passeron 1977; Freebody 1993; Cope & Kalantzis 1995; Freebody, Ludwig & Gunn 1995). An assessment item that adequately scaffolds learning identifies through detailed and specific statements what it is students are to do in order to achieve. The main focus of this item is on explicit statements about what constitutes high-quality student performances. Criteria, requirements or benchmarks that simply lay out expectations of what constitutes completed work do not make explicit, in themselves, what constitutes high-quality performance.

The questions that need to be asked to ensure that supportiveness is present in an assessment task are:

- *Student direction of assessment tasks*—To what degree do students determine the assessment task?
- *Explicit quality performance criteria*—To what degree are criteria for what counts as a high-quality student performance made explicit?

The structure of the coding scale for the element *explicit quality performance criteria* is shown in Figure 3.5.

Figure 3.5 Explicit quality performance criteria coding scale

TO WHAT DEGREE ARE CRITERIA FOR WHAT COUNTS AS A HIGH-QUALITY STUDENT PERFORMANCE MADE EXPLICIT?

Explicit criteria in an assessment task are identified by detailed and specific statements about what it is students are to do in order to achieve.

Note: The main focus of this scale is on the explicit statements of what constitutes high-quality student performances. Criteria, requirements or benchmarks that simply make explicit expectation of what constitutes completed work do not make explicit, in themselves, what constitutes high-quality performance.

EXPLICIT QUALITY PERFORMANCE CRITERIA

No explicit criteria	1 . . . 2 . . . 3 . . . 4 . . . 5	Explicit criteria

1 = The assessment task makes no mention of the criteria that are being used to determine levels of student performance in this task.

2 = The assessment task makes no mention of the criteria that are being used to determine levels of student performance in this task. It does contain procedural parameters or advanced organisers to assist students' completion of the task.

3 = The assessment task outlines only the criteria that are being assessed in this task; it does not contain procedural parameters, advanced organisers or explicit criteria relating to what constitutes a high-quality performance by students in this task.

4 = The assessment task contains procedural parameters, advanced organisers and the criteria that are being assessed in this task but it does not contain explicit criteria relating to what constitutes a high-quality performance by students in this task.

5 = The assessment task contains procedural parameters, advanced organisers and the criteria that are being assessed in this task and also contains explicit criteria relating to what constitutes a high-quality performance by students in this task.

The element of *explicit quality performance criteria* was evident in the marking criteria (see Figure 3.6) for the Year 8 zoo design task described earlier. While the description of the task alone would suffice to enable students to complete it (see Figure 3.2), it does not detail the quality of performance or degree of application required. An additional grid formed the second part of this assessment task and made explicit the criteria by which quality performance would be judged.

Grids such as that in Figure 3.6 are more commonplace now, especially in Queensland, where regional panels of teachers establish agreed standards. While these standards are an attempt by teachers to be more explicit about the quality of student performance required, they tend to relate to scholarly attributes that may be demonstrated through the task rather than to the specific requirements of the task. This is in part due to the fact that the development of these grids is a time-consuming task, and so teachers tend to adapt previously or externally developed grids to new tasks. This is generally a straightforward modification, as the scholarly attributes the grids describe have transdisciplinary relevance as well as relevance across the years as students develop and practise these attributes. However, these grids may work for

Figure 3.6 Year 8 Ecology marking criteria

SYLLABUS OUTCOMES:

Prescribed Focus Area
4.3　Identifies areas of everyday life that have been affected by scientific developments

Knowledge and Understanding
4.10　Identifies the factors affecting survival of organisms in an ecosystem
a)　Describes some adaptations of living things to factors in their environment
b)　Describes how producers, consumers and decomposers in Australian ecosystems are related, using food chains and food webs
c)　Describes the roles of photosynthesis and respiration in ecosystems
d)　Discusses some effects of bushfires, drought and flood on Australian ecosystems

Skills
4.13　Clarifies the purpose of an investigation and, with guidance, produces a plan to investigate a problem
4.19　Draws conclusions based on the information available
4.21　Uses creativity and imagination to suggest plausible solutions to familiar problems

Values and Attitudes
4.23　Demonstrates confidence and a willingness to make decisions and to take responsible actions

MARKING CRITERIA　　　Name: _____　Total Mark: /40

Outcome	Task	Indicators—How will you show you have achieved the outcome?				Your mark
		1 mark	2 marks	3 marks	4 marks	
4.3	Progress report # 1.	Basic plan for enclosure. Very little detail included.	Plan includes one of: type of eco-system, possible features, organisms.	Plan includes two of: type of eco-system, possible features, organisms.	Detailed plan, including all aspects. Detail provided by diagrams &/or descriptions.	
4.13	(8 marks)	Plan is not related to the problem. Purpose of investigation is unclear. No consider-ation of issues.	Plan is generally related to the problem. Relevant information is included.	Plan demonstrates clear understanding of the problem & possible solutions.	+Plan considers many aspects of the problem, and draws conclusions about how to solve it.	
4.10 c)	Progress report #2.	Organisms listed, but not correctly classified as producers or consumers.	Organisms correctly classified as producers or consumers.	+Reasons given for classification, mentioning making or eating food.	+Mention of photo-synthesis and respiration as means of producing and converting energy.	
4.10	(12 marks)	Requirements for organisms listed in general terms (e.g. food, water).	Requirements for organisms (or groups of organisms) listed specifically.	Requirements for organisms (or groups of organisms) described specifically.	Requirements specifically described, including affect on survival for each organism.	
4.23		Teacher assistance sought in decision-making throughout the task. Skills are not applied.	Some independent decision making occurs. Skills are used, but not directly related to project.	Information & skills from lessons are used to confidently make decisions about direction of project.	+confidence and responsibility demonstrated throughout development of task.	
4.21	Final submission.	Little creativity used. Map/model is basic &/or follows teacher scaffold directly.	Some creativity used. Map/model is practical and own initiative is displayed.	Substantial initiative &/or creativity shown in either design or presentation of map/model.	Map/model demonstrates high level of creativity and practicality in both design and presentation.	
4.19	(20 marks)	Conclusions are drawn without reference to relevant concepts. conclusions.	Understanding of some concepts is shown, but not related to final submission &	Understanding of concepts is generally related to final submission & conclusions.	Use of a variety of relevant concepts and applications to reach conclusions about appropriate solutions.	

continued

4.10 d)	Final submission (cont.)	Possible impacts of the disaster are presented as a list.	Possible impacts of the disaster are described in general terms.	Impacts on organisms and the ecosystem are considered. Discussion text type is used.	+Evaluation of impacts &/or hypotheses about the future of the ecosystem are included.	
4.10 a)		General list of adaptations of three organisms.	General description OR labelled diagram indicating how organisms are adapted to the chosen environment.	General description AND labelled diagram indicating how organisms are adapted to the chosen environment.	Detailed description and labelled diagram clearly relates adaptations to the chosen environment.	
4.10 b)		1 or more correct food chains, each consisting of 3 or more organisms.	Simple food web(s) include only some of the organisms in the ecosystem.	Complex food web(s) include all organisms in the ecosystem.	+Potential 'feeding' needs are considered & indicated on the food web(s).	

some students and not for others because they lack explicitness and assume an understanding of the codes or rules of power (see Delpit 1995). In this task students needed to access the scholarly attributes of analysis, definition and application. As Teese explains, when there is a close match between 'the conceptual demands laid up in the curriculum and the family cultural resources available to the average student' (Teese 2000: 5), these types of descriptions may enhance the clarity of a task for some students and shroud it in complexity for others. A critical mediating element that determines how these grids operate is the classroom practice of teachers and the degree to which they explicitly teach the performances they wish to assess in their students.

We collected numerous examples of carefully assessed tasks that gave students multiple opportunities to practise and develop a wide range of skills and scholarly attributes. This is well illustrated through a teacher's feedback to a bilingual student of Legal Studies in the second-last year of high school in Brisbane's outer suburbs. The topic was criminal law in society, and the task required an essay to be written. A set of criteria for this task related to written expression and language competence: logical and sequential expression; lucid and fluent expression; and mechanical aspects, such as spelling, grammar, punctuation and genre convention. The teacher made numerous margin notes related to these criteria throughout the essay and concluded with the long comment in Figure 3.7.

Figure 3.7 Year 11 Legal Studies

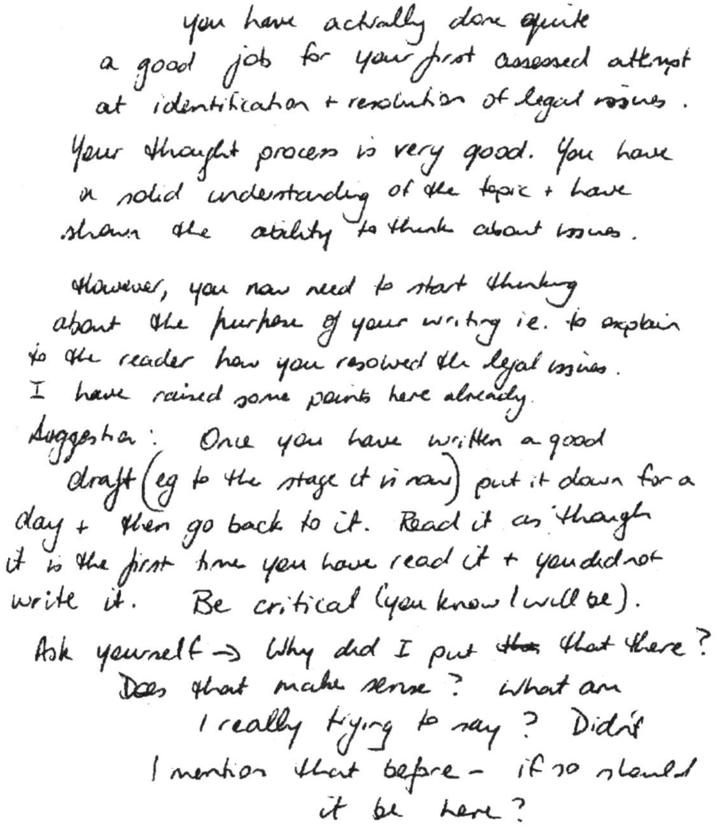

you have actually done quite
a good job for your first assessed attempt
at identification + resolution of legal issues.
Your thought process is very good. You have
a solid understanding of the topic + have
shown the ability to think about issues.

However, you now need to start thinking
about the purpose of your writing ie. to explain
to the reader how you resolved the legal issues.
I have raised some points here already.
Suggestion: Once you have written a good
draft (eg to the stage it is now) put it down for a
day + then go back to it. Read it as though
it is the first time you have read it + you did not
write it. Be critical (you know I will be).

Ask yourself → Why did I put that there?
Does that make sense? What am
I really trying to say? Didn't
I mention that before – if so should
it be here?

Through her detailed feedback and encouragement, this teacher was making explicit how language codes work for a bilingual student. This type of close alignment between assessment and teaching practices is an essential feature of *productive assessment*. It is underpinned by an acceptance of learning as the core business of schools and teaching as a central activity. In our interview with this teacher, we asked her to describe how she assessed students, both formally and informally. In her response, she emphasised the need to monitor student progress in an ongoing way using both academic and social indicators:

> Oh, body language is huge. So it's a matter of always being alert the entire time throughout the unit to just little subtle things like is a particular child becoming a bit more sarcastic or I suppose indirectly asking for help, you've always got to be alert to those signals. And taking the opportunity, if you can just take a child aside and say 'Oh look, I've noticed that you seem a little bit negative, is something wrong? Do you need some help with that?' So there is that level of assessment and also questioning in class . . . making sure that they understand their work, that type of thing . . . I try to monitor it all the [time].

Paying attention to body language and mood shifts is seldom associated with assessment, but it illustrates how this teacher understood the relationship between her teaching and her assessment practices.

Working with and valuing difference

We believe that assessment tasks that incorporate elements in the *working with and valuing difference* dimension support the development of social and academic performances in all students, especially those from marginalised groups. As we illustrate below, assessment tasks that work with and value difference (as distinct from simply recognising difference) are highly likely to engage students in critical thinking about the nature of differences and how they are produced. This requires higher-order thinking skills in order to describe, analyse, evaluate and synthesise differences. A key difference between tasks that work with and value difference and those that don't is that the former tend to make knowledge problematic, whereas the latter tend to assume that their modes of knowledge production need no explanation—a trait of dominant forms of knowledge.

The items that make up the dimension of *working with and valuing difference* within *productive assessment* are detailed below.

Cultural knowledges are valued in an assessment task when there is explicit valuing of non-dominant beliefs, languages, practices and ways of knowing. Valuing a range of cultural knowledges requires more than one culture being present, and given status, within the curriculum. Cultural groups are distinguished by social characteristics such as gender, ethnicity, race, religion, economic status or youth. Thus, their valuing means legitimising these cultures for all students, through the inclusion, recognition and transmission of this cultural knowledge. This element seeks to develop an understanding of how cultures come to be valued differently. It involves students developing an understanding of how some beliefs, languages, practices and ways of knowing have come to be given priority over others and why this has occurred.

Group identities are present in an assessment item where differences and group identities are both positively developed and recognised. For example, young people's multiple identities may be given positive recognition, and they may be given the opportunity to pursue various interests associated with these identities. This could take the form of examining youth culture through music, marketing and the media.

Active citizenship is present in any assessment item in any subject domain when the students are expected to elaborate on the meaning of such citizenship and the completion of the assessment item facilitates its practice both within and outside the classroom.

Considering the presence of these items in an assessment task requires asking the following questions:

- *Cultural knowledges are valued*—To what degree are non-dominant cultural knowledges valued?
- *Group identities*—To what degree does the assessment item support the production and positive recognition of difference and group identities?
- *Active citizenship*—To what degree is the practice of active citizenship encouraged in the assessment item?

The structure of the coding scale for the element *cultural knowledges* is shown in Figure 3.8.

Figure 3.8 Cultural knowledges coding scale

TO WHAT DEGREE ARE NON-DOMINANT CULTURAL KNOWLEDGES VALUED?

Cultures are valued when there is explicit valuing of their identity represented in such things as beliefs, languages, practices and ways of knowing. Valuing all cultural knowledges requires more than one culture being present, and given status, within the curriculum. Cultural groups are distinguished by social characteristics such as gender, ethnicity, race, religion, economic status or youth. Thus, their valuing means legitimising these cultures for all students, through the inclusion, recognition and transmission of this cultural knowledge.

Curriculum knowledge that is constructed and framed within a common set of cultural definitions, symbols, values, views and qualities, thus attributing some higher status to it, stands in contrast to this.

Note: Linked closely to knowledge presented as problematic, this dimension goes on to recognise the social construction and hence conflicting nature of knowledge, and explicitly values that knowledge associated with sub-group cultures.

KNOWLEDGE VALUES ALL CULTURES

Only high-status culture		Multiple cultural knowledges
	1 . . . 2 . . . 3 . . . 4 . . . 5	

1 = Students are not expected to show any explicit recognition or valuing of other than the dominant culture in assessment expectations.

2 = Students are expected to show some inclusion of others' cultures, with weak valuing, through simple reference to a particular feature(s) of them or their existence.

3 = Students are expected to show stronger valuing in curriculum knowledge, by acknowledgment and recognition of multiple cultural claims to knowledge, and perhaps some activity based on an aspect of this, though still within the framework of a dominant culture.

4 = Students are expected to show others' cultures, as explicitly valued through equal inclusion and use of the knowledge/perspective of the group, alongside the dominant culture.

5 = Students are expected to show different cultures as equally valued, so that the concept of a dominant culture is excluded in both its content and form.

The example in Figure 3.9 illustrates the element *cultural knowledges are valued*: in this case, youth images and identities are given visual expression. The task was given to us at a school where we were conducting a workshop on assessment. The task asked Year 9 students to use an event in their lives as an entry point for working with symbolic representation and visual expression.

This task is explicit in its valuing of image and identity and thus explicitly values youth culture. The *working with and valuing difference* in this assessment is aimed at providing an environment where young people feel valued and supported and are thus more likely to engage in the academic

Figure 3.9 Year 9 Art

Year 9 Unit 5 'Image and Identity' Making Task
Development Folio

Date Started: 3 February Date Due: Week Beg. 31 March

Concepts: *Self, culture and place*

Way of Responding: *Towards an Aboriginal symbolic and communicative, visual langauge*

Media Areas: *Drawing, Block print, Text art, Ceramic vessel*

Conditions: *6 weeks, teacher directed, school time with some home time*

The tasks

1. Select an event or place that has had a significant impact on you from the graph of your life's highs and lows.

2. Describe by writing about it: (i) Its specialness; (ii) its impact on you; (iii) The way it made you feel; (iv) The relationship you have with it now and things associated.

3. Explore the ideas in 2, through the following processes and media: (a) Drawing (b) Lino Block print (c) Text art (d) Clay vessel.

   Tips: Develop organic/geometric pattern.

   Write/print the description of your event/place as an art/design work.

   Develop focus points, placement and size of the letters/words and the development of tone, writing over the top of other words to create darks etc., to reflect qualities of your experience.

   Develop the form of your vessel as well as the surface. Develop a symbolic expression of the impact of your event/place on you as a vessel – 'containment' versus 'access', 'versatility and adaptability', 'individuality', 'specialness', 'feel to touch, to use, to hold' eg. spiky, delicate, smooth.

4. Present your description in 2, and the made items in 3, in an interesting *series*. Your art is your experience made visible and must reflect an evolved visual expression that makes meaning to you. How well your visual expression communicates meaning, will determine the longevity and interest your personal story has to a wider audience. The work will be considered for showing at the Arts 'Identity' Exposition night.

curriculum. What is interesting about this assessment task, in relation to *productive assessment*, is that despite its obvious commitment to *working with and valuing difference*, the three other dimensions are also clearly represented. There is a clear requirement that students demonstrate an intellectual engagement with the task, in that they have to engage in higher-order thinking to consider their 'identity' and how their identity has been constructed through a particular event in their life, and that they have to communicate this through both an artform and a piece of extended writing. Connectedness is present in the focus on their existing knowledge of themselves, the presentation of a problem for them to solve in terms of how best to represent a significant event in their life through a piece of art, and that this art may well be presented to an audience beyond the classroom at the Arts 'identity' exposition night.

Analysing assessment tasks in the Productive Pedagogies Research

In the Productive Pedagogies Research, small teams of experienced teachers applied structured assessment and performance measures to code a whole class set of student work samples and their associated assessment task for each teacher we observed. The teachers who undertook the coding did not teach in the case-study schools. Those teachers who participated in the study were asked to select a task that reflected their best practice. It is important to note that the practical requirements of transporting and handling these tasks may have placed some limits on what was selected. Most of the student work samples were submitted on standard-sized paper. Any associated performances or tasks completed using other media were not included. These limitations may have contributed to the predominantly summative nature of the tasks: most were intended to be viewed by the classroom teacher only; many simply required students to engage in rote learning or simple manipulation of information; and they generally held limited legitimacy beyond school classrooms.

Further analysis compared the tasks with teachers' stated pedagogical goals on a survey. The results suggest that a strong misalignment was apparent between assessment and the stated pedagogical goals of most of the teachers participating in the study (QSRLS 2001). Unfortunately, the large-scale nature of the study suggests that these types of practices are widespread—perhaps endemic even—in a system that is recognised nationally for its long-term and innovative approaches to teacher-moderated school-based assessment (Cummings & Maxwell 1999). One could speculate on what the findings might be in those educational systems with more constraining testing regimes imposed on schools, as in England and in most states of the USA.

At the same time, we acknowledge that schools are complex and busy places where teachers face increasing demands, and that assessment processes provide a limited and partial view of classroom practices. We also acknowledge that assessment tasks must be read within the context of the curriculum, the school and its community. However, it is important to consider how assessment processes position students in relation to knowledge, how these processes are linked to outcomes and the stratifying effects of schooling. As Teese (2000: 5), in an argument cognate with that of Bourdieu and Passeron (1977), explains:

> Language facility, attentiveness, achievement motivations, self-confidence in learning, personal organization and self-direction, capacity to learn for intrinsic satisfaction rather than extrinsic interest—these elements of the scholarly disposition are fundamental to success in the more academic areas of the curriculum. But they are linked closely to an educated lifestyle and arise from the continuous and informal training given by families rather than explicit and methodical instruction in school.

Critical analysis of assessment tasks must therefore consider the contexts in which these processes are developed, and must take into account the degree to which they assess access to codes of power and lifestyle as distinct from learning.

Occasionally we encountered attempts by teachers to enhance the relevance of tasks by tapping into students' interests and cultural experiences, but sometimes the trivial nature of these tasks and the low expectations reflected in them undermined any such good intentions. For example, a Year 8/9 Studies of Society and the Environment exam asked students to match endangered animals with football teams (Figure 3.10).

Figure 3.10 Year 8/9 Studies of Society and the Environment

12.   Match the animal to the sporting team.

Eels	Brisbane Rugby League
Broncos	Balmain Rugby League
Sharks	Parramatta Rugby League
Tigers	Canterbury Rugby League
Bulldogs	Cronulla Rugby League

/10

13.   What two animals support the shield in our Coat of Arms?

1._____

2._____

/2

While a strong football culture exists in many schools, this test does little to challenge students intellectually, it provides no opportunity for higher-order thinking, and there is no requirement to demonstrate depth of knowledge about endangered species. This kind of test is indicative of the presence of deficit ways of thinking about students who traditionally underachieve, or who have been sorted into the 'bottom' streams of classes. The pervasiveness of low expectations for Indigenous students came up in our interview with the principal of the Indigenous community school in our study, when he complained about attitudes in the educational bureaucracy:

[They've] got limited expectations of what the school should be achieving . . . they were saying when they came out to tell

me about how to set benchmarks . . . well other schools do
this, but you wouldn't be worried about that . . . I didn't say
anything at the time and, in fact, even [the District Director]
said to me once . . . in the operational plan you've put State-
wide, is that being a bit ambitious? I said no, that's what we're
going for, that's what the community wants.

Another important aspect of the schooling context to take
into consideration when analysing assessment tasks is the
professional background and experience of the teachers
developing the task. It emerged in our interview with the
teacher who developed the task in Figure 3.10 that she was
teaching outside her area of professional expertise because of
a system of rotating students among teachers teaching set
topics. Darling-Hammond (1997) has emphasised the importance of teachers having an intellectual understanding of the
subject matter they are teaching—what she has more recently
referred to as 'threshold knowledge'. She has argued that the
compliance model of teacher reform—high-stakes testing
and monitoring, heavy use of commodified curriculum,
standardisation of teaching approaches—does not have the
capacity to address the question of whether teachers have
the necessary threshold knowledge to engage with specific
fields of knowledge (Darling-Hammond 2000). To achieve
the levels of intellectual demand required to improve
student outcomes requires sufficient baseline and threshold
knowledge of a field's operational concepts, assumptions,
histories and procedures. Martino, Lingard and Mills (2004)
have similarly shown in research on teacher practices in relation to girls and boys that teacher threshold knowledge about
gender and research on gender and schooling is necessary
for effective pedagogies for both boys and girls. Darling-
Hammond also argued, and utilised evidence to support the
position we have taken, that progress demands concentration
on the professionalism and professional development of
teachers, with a specific emphasis on pedagogies and
building learning communities, as opposed to a top-down
standardised testing approach.

We also stress that teachers require certain threshold knowledge about their students' cultural and community backgrounds. For instance, we witnessed a teacher covering a unit on 'Aboriginal Culture' teach a lesson on '*the* kinship system'. The class consisted of many students who were from isolated Indigenous communities and who, unlike many urban Indigenous people, still had access to their traditional languages. When an Indigenous student explained the system to the teacher, the teacher corrected the student using a textbook definition of the system. There is clearly a need for teachers working with students from diverse backgrounds to have an understanding of diverse cultures, pedagogies and critiques of contemporary schooling practices. Without a certain threshold of knowledge about these topics, the education provided to, for example, Indigenous students is likely to be irrelevant, patronising, based on populist assumptions about Indigenous cultures, students and their families, and to consist of socially unjust practices.

The equity implications of reforming assessment regimens, along with the pedagogical ones, are captured well by Hargreaves (1989: 165) when he stresses the need for all students to experience a connected *and* challenging curriculum:

> If improved educational equality or increased educational opportunity are among our chief educational goals . . . this will require a curriculum which helps to *redefine* what is to count as cultural capital, which recognizes and rewards practical, aesthetic, and personal and social achievements, as well as intellectual and academic ones, and which combines rigour and relevance in the curriculum for *all* pupils, instead of offering rigour for some and relevance for others.

Our research demonstrates that when students are provided with assessment tasks that are connected to their experiences, are intellectually challenging and mediated by supportive classroom practices, they are far more likely to remain engaged in learning. They are also more likely to learn more and thus to achieve better outcomes. Furthermore, we contend that in order to meet many of the social outcomes of schooling indicated in Chapter 2, assessment tasks need to be cognisant of difference and provide students with opportunities to value difference and to contribute to the diverse communities in which they live.

Commentary on the degree of productive assessment

As we were visiting schools during the Productive Pedagogies Research, we encountered a number of assessment tasks during our classroom observations that exemplified varying aspects of *productive assessment*. In this section we describe the classroom settings and pedagogies associated with these tasks. Generally speaking, all of the tasks were integrated with classroom teaching practices, extended over a period of time, and allowed multiple opportunities for feedback and development. It is also interesting to note that many of these tasks were associated with low-status and low-stakes areas of the curriculum. This suggests that perhaps teachers in these areas are more prepared to take risks and to find innovative ways to engage students in learning. Some examples of these tasks follow.

Year 11 Multistrand Science: Creating a creature

In a rural school, Year 11 students were studying Multistrand Science (a subject that draws on basic concepts in a number of scientific disciplines including biology, geology and chemistry). They were nearing the completion of an extensive study of the ecosystem of the town's river. This task was closely connected to the students' world beyond the classroom because of the river's importance to the local area's economy, culture and environment. Previous work included a substantial amount of in-class and fieldwork activities that engaged the students in disciplinary processes through the application of such techniques as using classification systems and water quality monitoring, and in disciplinary knowledge through studying the impact of flood and industry along the river. The performance of this task involved developing the students' understanding of the ecosystem of their local river. Through higher-order thinking and the consideration of alternatives, the students were asked to create a creature adapted to the conditions of the river ecosystem. They were required to draw the creature and describe its physical and behavioural adaptations. The completion of this problem-based task was dependent on the students having a thorough knowledge of the topic.

Year 12 Art: Designing a 3-D installation

A Year 12 Art class worked collaboratively on a submission to design a 3-D installation for a public space with a youth theme. This theme allowed for the explicit valuing and exploration of youth culture. The collaborative and problem-based nature of the task required extended dialogue between students and the teacher to develop shared ideas, concepts, themes and design elements. Links with the world beyond the classroom were strong because the installation was planned for a public space. Local government officers were also consulted. The students demonstrated complex understandings of each stage of the project and related disciplinary processes by working through the specifications of the design brief, negotiating the time frame of the project and sourcing materials. The preparation of the application required elaborate written and technical information. The final proposal was supported by reasoned and creative explanations of its aesthetic and functional appeal. In the class we observed very little teacher direction. Students were clearly engaged in the project in ways that demonstrated their deep understanding of what was expected of them. They were able to provide a thorough artistic explanation of their work.

Year 6 Social Studies: Theme park design

In a Year 6 Social Studies class, the children worked in small groups over a number of lessons to design a theme park. This topic was strongly connected to the students' world beyond the classroom because the school is located close to a number of major theme parks. As well as having visited these parks, some of the children knew park employees, and the parks featured large in the community's psyche. Along with designing themes, rides and attractions, the children were required to consider a range of other issues such as profit margins, marketing, integration with other local industries and services, facilities for people with special needs, personnel issues and pricing. The groups gave regular reports to the class and were required to respond to questions posed by the teacher and other students. A feedback cycle of researching, developing and presenting the theme park designs was well established in the class when this observation was made. A local theme park manager was invited to a final presentation of the proposals and to comment on each design.

Year 8 Health and Physical Education: Coordinated performance

A Year 8 Health and Physical Education teacher was working on a unit with a class about building a raft. This was one of the few group tasks we observed that required a coordinated performance. An initial teacher directed discussion established the scope of the tasks, identified the skills the students would need to build the raft and negotiated the agreed outcomes from the exercise. The students suggested that if they were going to build a raft, they needed to learn how to effectively work in groups. In response to that, the teacher had the students play a game in the gym where they were allowed to throw balls in all directions, with the aim of the game being to keep the balls in perpetual motion. There was frenetic movement of balls around the class. The teacher stopped the game and asked how it could be modified to work more effectively. There was extensive discussion about rules. Much of this discussion was extended to take in questions of rules in society—questions of who created them, why, whether they were able to be negotiated, whether everyone had the same opportunity to create the rules and so on. The game continued under different sets of rules. Students were able to construct rules, argue why these were appropriate and look at their effects. This one lesson was not treated as an isolated incident but as focusing on the development of one skill needed in order to solve the larger problem. We saw a number of other interesting lessons conducted by this teacher. All of these were designed in ways that sought to build on the skills and knowledges which the students and the teacher had deemed necessary to solve the larger problem of the construction of a raft.

Findings of the Productive Pedagogies Research associated with productive assessment

Generally speaking, tasks such as those described in the previous section tended to be the exception rather than the rule. A substantial number of tasks we coded had very low demands in relation to the intellectual quality dimension of *productive assessment.* These tasks occupied the students with 'busy work' and often demanded routine repetitive procedures. The teachers who coded the tasks speculated that many seemed to have been designed to meet parental demands for 'authoritative'-looking homework, but that this type of work required little intellectual challenge. Recall of knowledge was most often the focus of assessment. It was generally felt that the tasks demonstrated what the students could reproduce rather than being used as an instrument for stimulating and guiding learning.

However, as we have noted, in the Queensland data the assessment practices tended to be better at Year 11 (the highest year level researched and the penultimate year of secondary schooling), reflecting the fact that teachers have ownership there over a very professionalising school-based system of assessment. This respect for teacher professional judgments is supported by a state-wide system of teacher moderation. The conversations between teachers about assessment regimens and their alignment or otherwise with syllabus purposes, along with teacher involvement in the moderation of student work, seem to work as a very effective mode of professional development for teachers encouraging sophisticated assessment literacy. Our own experiences in providing professional development on these matters for teachers around Australia would confirm the highly sophisticated forms of assessment literacy among many senior teachers in Queensland schools. This also confirms the point of the significance of systemic assessment policies.

Even so, within the entire research sample, tasks appeared to substantially underestimate students' intellectual abilities. This was especially the case in Year 8 (the first year of secondary school in the Queensland system), given what some 'good' Year 6s were achieving. Generally, students were not required to think deeply. Most tasks did not draw on the students' experiences beyond the classrooms, and when they did they were rarely embedded in intellectually demanding activities. In a number of cases, assessment tasks focused on process rather than a product. For example, we received a number of tasks that assessed students' note-taking abilities. Teachers tended to comment often on appearance and 'the look' of work, rather than on student performance. Criteria were often unfocused and often did not match the task. In some instances very little care was taken with assessment as a means of learning. For example, in some instances students received no written feedback on how to improve their extended pieces of writing (only ticks were used), and in others students might receive ticks for the same answers for which others received crosses.

School differences

In many instances there appeared to be links between expectations of assessment items and the school's socioeconomic status. The higher the socioeconomic status of the school, the greater were the expectations of the assessment task. Expectations contained within tasks in the same subjects for the same year levels differed greatly between schools. There were some assessment items that enabled students to demonstrate high levels of *productive performance*. Examples of these were: a Year 6 task on critical multiculturalism, which required students to research a country and present the contributions of people from that country to Australia; and a Year 8 task, which required students to provide a detailed justification for studying ancient Egypt.

The Productive Pedagogies Research showed no systematic alignment between teachers' pedagogies and assessment practices. However, we argue that *productive assessment* should be characterised by a strong and transparent connection between school-level goals and classroom-level assessment. This connection ensures that the student outcomes desired by the whole-school community, which are ideally negotiated and explicitly stated, are reflected in classroom assessment tasks.

An understanding of the relationship between learning and assessment varied greatly among the teachers we interviewed. When their assessment tasks were compared with their responses on a questionnaire, we found no apparent alignment between the type of assessment tasks they developed and their stated pedagogical goals (QSRLS 2001). Ideally, one would expect a relationship to exist between these factors, but the assessment tasks teachers designed did not appear to reflect the outcomes from teaching that they most commonly identified as being important for their students. In Chapter 4, we argue that a negotiated and shared vision for learning is aimed at establishing a foundation for pedagogical action that is not only aligned with community expectations but is also aligned with assessment.

Practical applications of productive assessment

Increasingly in schools there is a recognition that quality teaching and learning are mediated by integrated assessment tasks, and that the development of appropriate and challenging assessment is dependent on the 'assessment literacy' of the teachers involved in constructing assessment items. We believe that the application of *productive assessment* to the analysis of student work samples can help teachers develop this literacy. We have worked with numerous schools and teachers to consider how assessment can be used to further teacher professional learning and, in turn, student learning. Informed by agreements on how to conduct professional dialogue, such as those provided by the protocols developed by the Coalition of Essential Schools (McDonald et al. 2003), we usually begin by analysing a common piece of assessment. This involves a consideration of how well the task meets the criteria of the various elements of *productive assessment*, as well as the goals of the school, the outcomes of the syllabus and the learning need of the students. Taking these considerations into account, we ask teachers to code each item of *productive assessment* according to its coding rubric (QSRLS 2001). They then explain their codings to each other and work together to reach a consensus. It is this dialogue that serves to develop assessment literacy. There is normally significant discussion about how an item can be improved and what specifically needs to happen to it in order for this to occur. The Productive Pedagogies Research also demonstrated how such professional dialogue was a part of the culture of successful schools and a focus of effective leadership within them (Lingard et al. 2003; Hargreaves 2003; Hayes et al. 2004).

What is always interesting in the discussion around these tasks and the *productive assessment* rubric is that it leads into conversations about curriculum and pedagogy and what needs to happen in the classroom in order to enable students to complete the task successfully. Another related professional development activity is to examine student performances on an assessment task to reflect on the pedagogy needed to improve such performances.

Conclusion

Productive pedagogies has provoked widespread interest, particularly among teachers and schooling systems throughout Australia but also elsewhere around the globe. However, the concept of *productive assessment* has been somewhat ignored and the findings of the Productive Pedagogies Research on the misalignment of much assessment with curriculum goals and pedagogical practices also largely neglected. There are a number of possible reasons for this. For instance, *productive pedagogies* was first raised in an interim report of the study, and was subsequently taken up and advocated by Education Queensland (the state department of education in Queensland) as an idealised form of pedagogy prior to the completion of the study. Also, due to the nature of the research, assessment items and related student work were stored until a substantial number had accumulated to warrant preparing teachers as coders. For this reason, the assessment and performance findings were not reported to Education Queensland until the final report. This meant that there was not a sustained focus on this form of assessment until a much later date than the focus on the *productive pedagogies* framework. Furthermore, the Queensland New Basics project, which was acquiring significant national attention and was launched prior to the completion of the study, used the *productive pedagogies* framework while employing the notion of Rich Tasks as its preferred form of assessment. This also meant that *productive pedagogies* gained far greater exposure than *productive assessment*. It was not until Education Queensland set up its Productive Pedagogies Unit that *productive assessment* received widespread systemic and teacher attention in Queensland.

We have been noticing a renewed interest in professional learning related to assessment and a drive by many schools to get assessment 'right' in Australian systems. To some extent, it seems to us, this increasing concern with assessment has been driven by an increasing focus on curriculum and pedagogy, the discussions about which inevitably lead to discussions about assessment. This point is well captured by Torrance (1995: 55):

> Teachers have engaged with changes in assessment most enthusiastically and effectively when these changes have derived from, or developed in parallel with, clearly understood changes in the curriculum. But changes in assessment *per se*

run the risk of being interpreted within a traditional 'testing paradigm' rather than a 'pedagogical paradigm' and so confounding the best intentions of those developing new forms of assessment. Thus, rather than thinking of authentic assessment 'driving' instruction, it might be more helpful to think of it as providing a new framework for the discussion and development of instruction.

This is what we have found to be the case with the *productive assessment* framework. When we have had discussions with teachers, and other educators, about what constitutes good assessment we invariably engage in conversations about the aims of the curriculum and forms of pedagogy that can align with such assessment practices in order to produce the kinds of outcomes indicated in Chapter 4. However, we are not naïve about what teachers are able to achieve alone, particularly in systems replete with standardised testing and heavy technical surveillance of teachers through other accountability mechanisms, such as in England and in some states of the USA (Apple 2000b). Mobilisations around those matters are necessary. Nonetheless, it is our considered view, and one backed by the findings of the study, that more intellectually demanding assessment practices as outlined in this chapter are a necessary element of good classroom practice. Teachers located within different educational systems and different policy frameworks have varying degrees of autonomy to pursue such practices. We believe that assessment needs to be rearticulated and pulled back into teachers' professional dialogue. The alignment of curriculum, pedagogies and assessment is central to the enhancement of teacher effects on student learning and indeed, when complemented by appropriate whole-school culture and leadership practices, necessary to enhancing whole-school effects so that schools can make a difference. This is an important social justice issue, particularly given the significance of schooling to life opportunities for students from disadvantaged backgrounds. We turn to the framework of *productive performance* in Chapter 4, thus completing our discussion of the three-messages system of schooling.

4 Productive performance

The enduring concern to improve students' outcomes from schooling is often seen as a problem of improving standards. While there are few people that would argue against improving standards, there are also few people that are able to suggest how to define and address these issues in effective ways. Improving classroom practice is clearly a key factor. Here we agree with Black and Wiliam's (1998: 148) argument, that 'standards can be raised only by changes that are put into direct effect by teachers and pupils in classrooms'. A complicating factor is that issues of standards are linked to questions of how the goals and purposes of schooling are understood, and these understandings are always politically contested. In this chapter we frame the issue of improving students' outcomes through a consideration of the nature and purposes of schooling as well as improved classroom practice. Although understandings of the nature and purpose of schooling are often articulated by policy makers and politicians, we contend that locally developed and rearticulated understandings should inform the pedagogical and assessment work of teachers in schools, as they attempt to meet the day-to-day demands of preparing young people for changing and challenging futures. We hope here to inform this important aspect of teachers' work by putting forward a broad set of indicators of the types of outcomes we believe students should achieve through participation in schooling. We call these outcomes *productive performance*.

This chapter is the third of three in which we look at classroom practices, particularly assessment practices. As we proposed in *Leading Learning*, schooling at its best is about creating learning environments that help students to understand their world in ways that will enable them to change it for the better, both for themselves and others. Ideally, schooling needs to open opportunities for *all* young people: opportunities for meaningful work, for intellectual, personal, cultural and social life, for decent relationships, and for forming and reforming a society in which they and others would want to live. Located in these broad goals and purposes of schooling is a specific commitment to the intellectual and social outcomes that students achieve through schooling. If these outcomes are to be valued, they need to be reflected in classroom practices, in terms of both the assessment tasks where students demonstrate them and the pedagogies that support their development. This chapter outlines the framework of *productive performance* that encapsulates such outcomes, and illustrates these performances with examples of students' work. It builds on the previous two chapters on *productive pedagogies* and *productive assessment*, which we suggest should be aligned with *productive performance* in classroom practices.

Productive performance and the goals of schooling

The concept of *productive performance* evolved out of the Productive Pedagogies Research. 'Productive' here as a descriptor of performance, as with 'productive pedagogies' and 'productive assessment', underscores the fact that schools produce outcomes, both intended and unintended. While in some ways Connell's (1985) argument that teachers' work is a labour process without a product is correct, in another sense teachers' work does produce outcomes—some better than others. Schools play a part in constituting society through the preparation of certain sorts of people and certain types of citizens, as well as individuals with particular cognitive and social dispositions. In this way, teachers' work *is* clearly productive work.

Productive performance contains both silences and amplifications about the types of student performances that are valued and pursued in schools. Desired outcomes from schooling are articulated at one level by broad systemic statements in relation to content, opportunities, and the sorts of persons and citizens schooling ought to produce. Such statements are, as with most educational policy, settlements of a particular kind between the multiple stakeholders of schooling. However, the translation of these statements into pedagogical experiences, assessment practices and collective action at the school level is by no means a straightforward process. Education systems are multilayered, and policies are seldom implemented as envisaged. Meanings shift and slide as they are differently interpreted by multiple actors, including those ultimately responsible for what happens in classrooms—teachers and students in specific places. Local contexts have concerns of their own, and are also important mediators between national policies and what happens in classrooms. McConaghy & Burnett (2002) suggests, for example, that rural and remote parts of Australia have different socio-spatial dynamics from urban centres. They have different experiences of global restructuring, particularly in terms of power relations, emergent identities, and flows and movements of people, ideas and resources. The significance of place, and of movement across places, suggests the need for a more situated understanding of the goals of schooling. Under the contradictory and contested conditions heightened by globalisation, we argue that local communities need a voice to formulate their own purposes of schooling, in engagement with broader goals. It is appropriate and necessary that local concerns about what counts as educational goals and indicators of learning should be actively negotiated and articulated, alongside national and global concerns and interests. Community and teacher participation in discussions around such goals are important in enhancing whole-school effects on student performance and for creating networks of social capital around schools (see Baron, Field & Schuller 2000).

In taking performance as our focus, this chapter does not specifically engage with debates on the form and nature of the curriculum, apart from recognising the need for informed public debate on school curricula. However, two assumptions drawn from sociology of education underpin our answer to the classic question: What knowledge is of most worth? The first assumption is that the curriculum as a selective tradition is closely related to social and cultural patterns of power (Young 1971; Apple 1990). What count as valued knowledges, skills and dispositions to be taught by schools reflect configurations of the state, civil society and the economy as well as a range of social and cultural interests. That said, we note the observations of Bernstein (2001) and others such as Connell (1985) about the powers of abstraction in knowledge. For example, drawing on Durkheim, Bernstein contends that there is a 'fundamental similarity in the very structuring of meaning' across all societies. Knowledge is structured around two types: the material, everyday world, and the immaterial, transcendental world. Whereas the content of these knowledge categories may change historically and culturally, the demarcation remains, as does the form of the knowledge within each of the categories (see Singh 2002). Thus, our second assumption is that one of the purposes of schooling is to decode and transmit immaterial, abstract knowledges, alongside material and everyday knowledges. How these different forms are best represented and balanced within the curriculum is an underlying point of contention in curriculum debates.

From the perspective of 'making a difference', we would argue that it is important to acknowledge the power/knowledge nexus and make it more visible. Delpit (1995: 28–9) has eloquently explained how power, and we would add knowledge, remains in the hands of those who have it when the liberal middle-class values and aspirations of teachers shape the curriculum and culture of schools:

> Many liberal educators hold that the primary goal for education is for children to become autonomous, to develop fully who they are in the classroom setting without having arbitrary, outside standards forced on them. This is a very reasonable goal for people whose children are already participants in the culture of power and who already have internalised its codes. But parents who don't function within the culture often want something else. It's not that they disagree with the former aim, it's just that they want something more. They want to ensure that the school provides their children with the discourse patterns, interactional styles, and spoken and written language codes that will allow them success in the larger society.

At issue here is not just what is taught but how it is taught, what is assessed and how it is assessed. Delpit emphasises the need for teachers to teach the codes of power explicitly to those children who would otherwise be denied access to them and their benefits. Similarly, the French sociologist Bourdieu (see Bourdieu & Passeron 1977) has argued that if the implicit cultural code of schooling is not made explicit, then schools will continue to reproduce social inequalities under the guise of meritocracy. In Bourdieu's analysis, schools and their curricula draw heavily on the cultural capital and ethos of the middle classes. Students whose home backgrounds match the school are likely to be more at ease with the expectations and activities required by the academic curriculum than those whose backgrounds are different. For students with middle-class backgrounds, schools may be experienced as an extension of home in terms of cultural capital; for them, social heritage becomes scholastic achievement. Students whose home backgrounds do not provide the cultural and linguistic capital of the school need to make great effort to *acquire* what other students are *given* by their home backgrounds. In these circumstances, failure to achieve is often interpreted as 'lack of ability'; inversely, success is often 'a *social* gift treated as a *natural* one' (Bourdieu 1976: 110).

In writing about the curriculum, Bourdieu is clear that it is 'absolutely necessary to give priority to those areas where the objective is to ensure that fundamental processes are thoughtfully and critically assimilated. These processes—the deductive, the experimental, the historical as well as the critical and reflective—should always be included' (1990: 309). As well as these 'fundamental ways of thinking', Bourdieu proposes the methodical transmission of 'the technology of intellectual enquiry', giving as examples the use of dictionaries, the rhetoric of communication, the preparation of a manuscript and the reading of numerical and graphical tables. In his words (1990: 309):

> If *all* pupils were given the technology of intellectual enquiry, and if in general they were given rational ways of working (such as the art of choosing between compulsory tasks and of spreading them over time), then an important way of reducing inequalities based on cultural inheritance would have been achieved.

Explicitness, then, of goals at all levels from the systemic to the school, classroom, work programs and individual assessment items is one necessary factor in working towards socially just practices. This is in accordance with both of the sociological observations we have made about curriculum: its relationships to broader social, cultural and economic patterns of power; and the importance of students having access to the powers of abstract knowledges as well as everyday knowledges.

As currently structured, schooling systems are an exemplar of modernism, with their standardised approaches to teaching and learning, their lockstep categorisations and classifications of people and subjects, and their unmistakable architecture of classrooms. Seddon (2001: 308) sums up the modernist project of the curriculum as follows:

> The history of modernist education indicates that state provided education, structured by a public curriculum and realised by a teaching workforce trained in appropriate principles of teaching, was a key instrument for managing

populations within national jurisdictions. Curriculum served as a means of regulation, an instrument of control and construction, wrapped up in nation-building rhetoric, which welded and organised 'the people' into a collective productive force to advance the nation, consolidate national identity, and realise national density.

These modernist assumptions have been challenged in a range of ways, particularly as the project of the nation-state is shifting under globalisation, together with the nature of work in knowledge economies and the construction of knowledge itself. State systems are driven more by concerns of economic competitiveness than by nation-building, and neoliberal ideologies promote individualism and market choice above collective concerns for a public 'common good'. Curriculum is increasingly influenced by interests at supra- and sub-national as well as national levels. Under these circumstances, the desirable relationship between the state systemic and the local in the educational policy cycle is a pressing concern for educational policy. In some cases, this takes the form of state attempts to control teacher practices through detailed prescriptions for practice and standardised testing. This is very evident in England, for example, in the tension between a call for teacher professionalism and a de-professionalising of teachers through a regulation of their practices (Mahony & Hextall 2000; Jeffrey & Woods 1998; Ball 2004). Pressures that emphasise the 'calculable and measurable' aspects of teachers' work (Smyth 1998: 193) produce a narrowing of teaching practices and reduce the complexity of curriculum debates at the school level to the selection of content. In other cases, a measure of autonomy is devolved to schools and local communities, accompanied by state regulatory frameworks, reporting procedures and standardised testing. At issue here is the desirable mix between centralised and devolved powers. This affects the degree to which schools can and are likely to work collectively through community consultations and professional dialogue towards school-level statements of goals, bearing in mind that pressures for control at systemic level will potentially reduce the desired outcomes of curriculum in practice.

Without common and agreed goals, teachers are forced to work in isolation, acting on what they consider to be important learning goals. Under these circumstances, they rely on their own professional and personal experiences to inform their actions, but their experiences and values may be vastly different from those of their students and the communities in which they work, as illustrated by the example from Delpit quoted above. The central importance of co-constructing a shared vision for learning is that it provides a foundation for coordinated action, but there is no simple formula for such action, and the tendency for power and competing political agendas to play out in these processes at all levels should not be underestimated. As Schofield (1999: 13) reminds us: 'Discrepancies occur between what the official stated aims are and those actually pursued by teachers and students. This reinforces the argument that aims have to be accepted by the teaching profession as well as the community if they are to find their way into the actual practice of schooling'. We often see a gap between policy hope in terms of systemic goals and actual policy happenings expressed as teacher practices in schools (Kenway et al. 1997). As McLaughlin (1987) insightfully demonstrated some time ago, effective policy implementation in education depends on the smallest unit, in this case the teacher and the classroom. Achieving desired changes through the many levels of the education system is no simple matter; experience in 'policy implementation' suggests that policies are seldom put into practice as envisaged by policy designers, particularly when they are at a distance from classrooms and teachers. In this sense, policy is palimpsest. Teachers are the most important players in the policy cycle, as they and their students form the smallest unit, but they are often not constructed as such within educational policies. Policy production at systemic level and teacher practices in classrooms operate within different logics of practice. Alternatively, in some cases where policy makers recognise this, they may consequently seek to control teacher practices through constraining policy frames. Despite both policy takes, teachers remain the most significant educational factor in relation to the production of student outcomes, a finding confirmed by the Productive Pedagogies Research.

The need to build a shared vision of student performance linked to pedagogy and assessment was well illustrated by the results of our survey of teachers whose classrooms were also observed as part of the Productive Pedagogies Research (QSRLS 2001). What was evident to the researchers was a misalignment between teachers' stated pedagogical goals and the types of assessment tasks they set. Although teachers claimed in survey responses that they valued the pedagogical goals of higher-level thinking skills, citizenship and academic excellence, these goals were not reflected in the assessment tasks they submitted for coding by the research team. In their survey responses, teachers ranked the teaching of basic literacy and numeracy skills as the most important goals of schooling, more important than citizenship and intellectual and academic purposes. This prioritising and valuing probably reflect the policy fetish of contemporary govern-ments for literacy and numeracy—an example of how policy discourses may constitute practices. The testing regimens often associated with such a focus can also have the effect of drawing teacher practices away from intellectually demanding pedagogies and assessment practices. What this illustrates is the need to align elements of the systemic policy ensemble with the support of good classroom practices and student performance at the school level.

The distinction made by Bruss and Macedo (1985) between a 'pedagogy of the answer' and a 'pedagogy of the question' is a most useful one here. The former is reflected in some contemporary policy attempts to regulate teachers' work, as well as in so-called 'teacher-proof' curriculum packages, which conceive of teachers as passive implementers of decisions and theories developed elsewhere. By contrast, a pedagogy of the question sees space for teachers to rearticulate macro-goals through professional dialogue into goals and pedagogical and assessment practices at the school level. This is not to say that the teacher in the classroom ought to be an autonomous professional deciding what is to be taught and how—rather that teachers have to be involved in the collective conversations at multiple levels over the goals of schooling and curricula, with some space to recontextualise these through professional 'reading' of their own classes and school communities.

In his Reith lectures, Anthony Giddens points out that globalisation 'has come from nowhere to be almost everywhere' (1999: 1), and its pushes and pulls are complex and contradictory. In relation to purposes of schooling, one manifestation of globalisation may be seen in the move towards supranational agreements about schooling, for example within the OECD member countries (Henry et al. 2001) and in Europe (Novoa 2000; Lawn & Lingard 2002). However, these recent education policy communities are not to be confused with the pressures for policy convergence in education experienced for many decades by poorer countries through the funding policies of the World Bank and International Monetary Fund. Global policy convergence can also be seen in developments throughout the world to more school-based management (Whitty, Power & Halpin 1998). Again, however, this policy move is unequally experienced by different countries and by different local groups, depending in large measure on the resources, both material and symbolic, available to school communities. Thus it is important, when reading the complex pushes and pulls of globalisation referred to by Giddens, to resist homogenising these.

The reconfigurations of globalisation, as the work of Castells (1997, 2000) convincingly illustrates, bring with them double logics of wealth and poverty, inclusion and exclusion. Along with extraordinary creativity and innovation, globalisation has brought increased inequalities in almost every country, both developed and developing. At the same time as the 'space of flows' brings inclusion in global networks to those who are linked, it radically excludes those who are not. As Castells observes, 'education, technological literacy and research and development are extremely unevenly distributed in the world' (2001: 18). Major efforts—supported by the World Bank, the United Nations and other international agencies—to increase the numbers of children attending school in poorer places, do not necessarily mean improved educational experiences for these children. It may mean little more than 'warehousing' them, as Castells evocatively suggests. One of the challenges of globalisation is that its creativity and innovation, and its jagged configurations of wealth and poverty, inclusion and exclusion, are experienced differently *within* countries and regions, as well as between them. This brings enormous challenges for an agenda of equity in education.

Curriculum frameworks developed at state, national and international levels provide a means by which local plans can be articulated with broader social concerns. There is a way, though, despite the effects of an emergent global policy space, and despite the experiences of participants in them and the capacities of new technologies to break this local containment, that schools remain very local institutions. However, as has been suggested here, and as was articulated in Chapter 1, while teachers and their pedagogical and assessment practices are centrally important in the attempts to have outcomes match such aspirations, substantial responsibilities also lie with school leaders, policy makers and the governments that make policy and fund educational systems. Thus while we are concerned in this book for a positive thesis about schools, we also recognise the responsibilities that lie beyond teachers and classrooms and the inhibiting and negative effects of much contemporary educational policy (Ball 1994; Apple 2001).

In thinking about goals for schooling, and the role these might play in linking classroom performance to national and supranational ideals, it is useful to begin by looking at examples of existing statements of goals: the Jomtien *World Declaration on Education for All* (UNESCO 1990) as an instance of global goals; and Australia's *Adelaide Declaration on National Goals for Schooling in the Twenty-First Century* (MCEETYA 1999), which was agreed to by all state and territory schooling systems in Australia and supported by the non-government sector. Both declarations affirm the importance of education for the future of young people as individuals, for the societies of which they are part, and for the world as a whole. Both affirm the importance of education for participation in and development of knowledge economies. Both have values statements as preambles, and both set out a series of goals. The first article of the Jomtien Declaration makes a very broad ambit claim for education:

1. Every person—child, youth, adult—shall be able to benefit from educational opportunities designed to meet their basic learning needs. These needs comprise both essential learning tools (such as literacy, oral expression, numeracy, and problem solving) and the basic learning content (such as knowledge, skills, values and attitudes) required by human beings to be able to survive, to develop their full capacities, to live and work in dignity, to participate fully in development, to improve the quality of their lives, to make informed decisions, and to continue learning. The scope of basic learning needs and how they should be met varies with individual countries and cultures, and inevitably, changes with the passage of time.

2. The satisfaction of these needs empowers individuals in any society and confers on them a responsibility to respect and build on their collective cultural, linguistic and spiritual heritage, to promote the education of others, to further the cause of social justice, to achieve environmental protection, to be tolerant towards social, political and religious systems that differ from their own, ensuring that commonly accepted humanistic values and human rights are upheld, and to work for international peace and solidarity in an interdependent world.

3. Another and no less fundamental aim of educational development is the transmission and enrichment of common cultural and moral values. It is in these values that the individual and society find their identity and worth.

4. Basic education is more than an end in itself. It is the foundation for lifelong learning and human development on which countries may build, systematically, further levels and types of education and training.

In similar vein, the Adelaide Declaration in Australia, agreed to by all ministers for education, is structured around a preamble and a statement of national goals consisting of two parts: an outline of the 'talents and capacities' that all students should have developed by the time they complete schooling; and a statement of what socially just schooling entails. Thus the preamble states:

> Australia's future depends on each citizen having the necessary knowledge, understanding, skills and values for a productive and rewarding life in an educated, just and open society. High quality schooling is central to achieving this vision.

Both documents elaborate on their broad vision statements: while the Jomtien Declaration provides an 'expanded vision' and fuller clarification of what basic education for all might entail, the Adelaide Declaration outlines its goals for a system of 'school education to year 12 or its vocational equivalent'. As a national document, it is able to elaborate further on the capacities that schooling should develop, the curriculum areas it should address, and the social justice goals it should promote in the Australian context.

It is striking how much convergence there is about the goals of schooling in these two statements, representing both a developed country and poor countries operating under the aegis of the United Nations and other world bodies. Read in the most positive light, declarations such as these provide a common 'foundation for action', as the Adelaide Declaration notes. The Jomtien Declaration, written in the context of decades of failed development initiatives, notes the importance of looking at 'whether people actually learn as a result of [educational] opportunities' and the importance of 'political commitment and political will backed by appropriate fiscal measures and reinforced by educational policy reforms and institutional strengthening'. It also notes the need for learners to receive 'nutrition, health care and general physical and emotional support'.

To some extent, statements of goals such as these may be helpful in thinking of what *productive performance* might look like at classroom level. Indeed, it is our argument that they may be translated into classroom practices through *productive performance* practices. In saying this, however, we also recognise that they have important limitations. First, statements of goals by themselves achieve little unless they are owned and actively engaged with by schools, teachers and local communities. Our earlier example of teachers ranking basic literacy and numeracy skills above the citizenship and intellectual and academic purposes of schooling is pertinent here. It shows how the lofty ideals of the Adelaide Declaration may be shifted aside at school level in a policy and media environment that stresses performative rankings and test scores. Second, statements of goals give no indication of the different starting points of schools and the different distances schools would need to travel to meet them. For some schools, achieving the goals of the Jomtien or Adelaide declarations would take no extra effort, while for others it would require little short of transformation. Third, statements of goals generally give little indication of the resources required to meet them. A clear example is to be found in the education goals of post-apartheid South Africa, which affirm the right to basic education for all, as well as the right of equal access to educational institutions, protection from unfair discrimination, and rights to language, culture and religion.

In practice, the state does not have the resources to provide free basic education for all, and deep historical patterns of inequality have proven extremely difficult to shift. Implicit in the Adelaide Declaration are adequate resources to meet its goals of 'further strengthening schools as learning communities . . .', 'enhancing the status and quality of the teaching profession', and supporting students to 'attain high standards of knowledge, skills and understanding through a comprehensive and balanced curriculum'. In spite of its explicit commitment to social justice and equity for Australia's Indigenous students, inequalities are profound in practice. Broad statements of goals, even when explicitly recognising the values of equity and social justice, are seldom able to address the multiple ways in which schooling itself produces and reproduces inequalities.

While recognising the limitations of statements of goals, we nonetheless recognise their importance, not least in providing a common basis for action. Goals set in the Adelaide Declaration are compatible with the intellectual and social outcomes of *productive performance* and may be useful as a framework for teachers and school communities to engage with in addressing local conditions. In addition, the 'four pillars of education' set out in the UNESCO report *Learning: The Treasure Within* (Delors 1996) have been picked up in a number of places: learning to know, learning to do, learning to live together, and learning to be.

Global, national and local interests and concerns shape the notion of *productive performance* that we detail below. We emphasise that it is not value-free; it should not be treated as an ideal form; and it should not replace local discussions about the purposes of schooling, as these are necessary in order to inform schooling practices and in particular the practices of teachers. A core contribution of concepts such as *productive performance* is to facilitate and support conversations about the purposes of schooling. The findings of the Productive Pedagogies Research in relation to teachers' values, their classroom practices and their approaches to assessment suggest an urgent and widespread need for teachers to engage in sustained professional dialogue with each other about how to translate agreed purposes of schooling into performances. That research also indicated the pressing need for professional discussions on the goals of schooling. Teachers need time for such illuminating or 'edifying' conversations, to use Stephen Ball's (1997a) term, which he sees as necessary to teacher development.

Productive performance

The notion of *productive performance* is based on the premise that if particular intellectual and social outcomes are valued as goals of schooling, these should be evident in classroom practices, in terms of both pedagogies and assessment. In developing the notion of *productive performance*, the research team began with Newmann and Associates' concept of authentic achievement. This was reworked and expanded into a student performance scale which included social as well as academic outcomes. The elements of 'analysis' and 'disciplinary concepts' were renamed *higher-order thinking* and *depth of understanding* respectively, in order to create a more transparent link between student performance and the pedagogies and assessment practices described through the Productive Pedagogies Research classroom observation and assessment scales. *Elaborated communication* remains as in the Newmann and Associates study. We included *problematic knowledge* as a reflection of the need to provide students with a sense of the ways in which knowledge is a social and political construct. Collectively, these elements comprised the academic outcomes that were looked for in student work samples. We also sought to encapsulate the broader goals of schooling by introducing into our framework a number of elements that would look for social outcomes. These included *cultural knowledges, connectedness to the world beyond the classroom, responsible citizenship* and *transformative citizenship*. The last element is linked to change and transformative aspirations of schooling.

The coders evaluating the assessment tasks were asked to consider the following questions related to academic outcomes in the *productive performance* framework:

- *Problematic knowledge*—To what degree is knowledge presented as constructed?
- *Higher-order thinking* (analysis)—To what extent do students use analysis?
- *Depth of understanding* (disciplinary concepts)—To what extent do students demonstrate an understanding of important disciplinary concepts?
- *Elaborated communication*—To what extent is elaborate communication present?

The coders evaluating the assessment tasks were asked to consider the following questions related to social outcomes in the *productive performance* framework:

- *Connectedness to the world beyond school*—To what extent does the student make connections between the task and the world beyond the classroom?
- *Cultural knowledges*—To what degree are non-dominant cultures valued?
- *Responsible citizenship*—To what degree do students demonstrate responsible citizenship?
- *Transformative citizenship*—To what degree is the practice of transformative citizenship evident?

The elements of *productive performance* that seek to identify academic outcomes in student work samples draw on theories of constructivist learning that encourage students to construct new knowledges through use of complex reasoning skills, such as hypothesising, synthesising and evaluating (see Vygotsky 1978; Cole 1996; Renshaw 1998; Daniels 2001). The development of these skills within tasks that have value and meaning beyond school can be traced through the authentic assessment movement that is generally acknowledged as originating with the work of Archibald and Newmann (1988), and is also evident in Sizer's 'assessment by exhibition'. This movement grew out of a concern for learning and assessment to be both contextualised and meaningful for students (Cumming & Maxwell 1999). It has also strongly emphasised an academic curriculum that helps 'students gain experience with the ways of thinking and speaking in academic disciplines' (Shepard 2000: 7).

Cormack et al. (1998) make the point that in Australia such kinds of learning have often been restricted to gifted and talented programs and rarely extended to students who come from traditionally marginalised groups within schools. Newmann and Associates (1996) in the USA argued students from disadvantaged backgrounds are often further disadvantaged by the absence of such learning. This is central to our argument that the intellectual quality of pedagogies and assessment practices is a social justice issue. Our position would be that much of the very good and demanding pedagogical and assessment work done in programs for the gifted and talented should be available to all students, because they are necessary in order to achieve the kinds of outcomes from schooling that are now prerequisites of most post-school pathways.

In an information-rich world, being able to access, select and apply knowledge forms a core skill set in most occupations. Being able to make connections, value a wide range of cultural experiences and act responsibly are generally also taken-for-granted features of most workplace cultures. These approaches add weight to earlier calls for 'concrete' or contextualised forms of knowledge (e.g. Connell et al. 1982) to improve the performances of students from disadvantaged backgrounds. Classroom practices that are relevant (connected) may well improve all students' performance, but this is likely to be even more true of students from sociocultural backgrounds who have traditionally not done as well with the more decontextualised forms of curriculum commonly found in conventional classrooms. As noted already, such contextualisation needs to be complemented by explicitness.

The *productive performance* scale is thus composed of eight elements. In the *productive pedagogies* research, the degree to which each of these elements was reflected in student performances was coded on a four-point scale—1 being the lowest-quality indicator and 4 being the highest-quality indicator. The structure of the element *knowledge is presented as problematic* is reproduced in Figure 4.1; all the other elements are structured in a similar way.

Figure 4.1 Knowledge is presented as problematic

TO WHAT DEGREE IS KNOWLEDGE PRESENTED AS CONSTRUCTED?

Presenting *knowledge as problematic* involves an understanding of knowledge not as a fixed body of information but rather as being constructed, and hence subject to political, social and cultural influences and implications.

Knowledge as given sees the subject content within the assessment item represented as facts or as a body of truth. The transmission of the information may vary but is based on the concept of knowledge as being static and able to be handled as property, perhaps in the form of tables, charts, handouts, texts, and comprehension activities.

Note: For the purposes of scoring this dimension, the focus is on the content of the assessment item and a judgment as to the proportion of the presented knowledge that is problematic.

KNOWLEDGE AS PROBLEMATIC

None   1 . . . 2 . . . 3 . . . 4   Substantial

1 = Student performance treats no knowledge as problematic. All knowledge is presented in an uncritical fashion.

2 = Student performance treats minimal amounts of knowledge as problematic—interpretations are linked/reduced to a given body of facts.

3 = Student performance treats moderate amounts of knowledge as problematic. Different knowledges are often presented as having equal status, and are equally accommodated and accepted.

4 = Student performance treats substantial amounts of knowledge as problematic. Knowledge is seen as socially constructed, with conflicting implications and social functions producing resolution and/or conflict.

In the study, the *productive performance* framework was applied to student work samples that were selected by teachers participating in the study. The only constraints placed on this selection process were that we received whole-class sets of student work that had been conducted in the year of the study with a class observed during the study. We encouraged teachers to choose samples that illustrated favourably their approaches to assessment. It was assumed that in order for students to perform highly, the assessment tasks should encourage such performances (see Chapter 3). However, teachers were not made aware of the criteria by which the tasks and students performances would be analysed. In the following section we detail the items within the two broad categories: academic performance and social performance. While there is clearly a degree of arbitrariness between these two categories, a focus on social performance clearly indicates the importance of not isolating schools from the broader social agenda, nor of treating the curriculum as value-free knowledge.

Academic performance

In detailing what we consider to be essential academic performances for young people entering adult life in the first decade of the twentieth century, we are both looking backwards and into the future. The inclusion of elements of higher-order thinking, depth of understanding and elaborate communication recognise the core skills and dispositions required to access and participate in disciplinary knowledges. Disciplines such as history, mathematics, science and geography are fields of knowledge with their own groups of experts and knowledge-producing practices. They are powerful knowledges reflected in the location of their experts in universities and in the strict monitoring of their rules of reproduction and participation.

As well as these enduring performances, we include the element of problematic knowledge, which recognises the need to be able to understand how knowledge is constructed and influenced by various processes such as cultural editing, whereby people and cultures construct the world in particular ways. This inclusion reflects the growing recognition of a futures-oriented perspective in education that considers different ways of knowing, different values and epistemologies

(Slaughter 1995), and how these produce effects of power. Futures-oriented outcomes in education recognise that the knowledge required in new economies is different from that which has occupied traditional education and training programs: 'Today, thinking about knowledge emphasises knowledge constructed as practical, interdisciplinary, informal, applied and contextual over knowledge constructed as theoretical, disciplinary, formal, foundational and generalisable' (Chappell 2003: 6). Additionally, this 'new knowledge' is high in use value for organisations, it is context-specific, its usefulness may be short-lived, and it is constructed through collaboration and networks.

It is for these reasons that the academic performance elements in *productive performance* reflect the importance of providing students with the opportunities to engage productively with their lives, both now and in the future. The pressing need for active citizenship, a productive workforce and a creative population requires that young people acquire the abilities to critically engage with knowledge, to demonstrate that knowledge is something that is constructed and that they can play a role in its construction. In order to engage with knowledge in such ways, young people need to learn to demonstrate an ability to think in complex, collective and creative ways. For instance, students need to be able to look at old and new problems from a variety of angles in order to find creative solutions where past ones may not be working. Some of the important questions facing our society, in what has sometimes been referred to as 'new times', include environmental, ethical, political, economic and social issues that operate across a range of scales, from the local to the global.

Productive performances may be demonstrated when students are asked to engage in substantial problems requiring the application of disciplinary knowledges and problem-solving skills. An increasingly important dimension of these tasks is that they involve communicating, networking and negotiating with others (see Chapter 3). For example, students might be asked to host and organise a science and ethics conference.

This is one of the Rich Tasks developed for Years 7–9 within the New Basics project (Education Queensland 2004). In such an assessment task students would not have to demonstrate teacher specified scientific knowledge; rather, they would have to demonstrate specific in-depth scientific knowledge about a particular issue chosen by them, and which may be different from that of other members of the class, while demonstrating knowledge about the nature of science in relation to social issues. This task is described in the following terms (Education Queensland 2004):

> Students will identify, explore and make judgments on a biotechnological process to which there are ethical dimensions. They will identify scientific techniques used, along with significant recent contributions to the field. They will also research frameworks of ethical principles for coming to terms with an identified ethical issue or question. Using this information, they will prepare pre-conference materials for an international conference that will feature selected speakers who are leading lights in their respective fields.

Communication is increasingly taking place in virtual workplaces among workers who may occasionally, or never, meet face-to-face. Even the day-to-day interactions in our personal lives are mediated by call centres (sometimes based in other countries) and online transactions. Thus *productive performances* are ideally demonstrated through a variety of media. These might include the construction of web pages, the making of films, the presentation of artwork, presentations at public conferences, public exhibitions, and putting into operation business plans, alongside the more traditional report writing, creative essays and scholarly papers. In such performances, the individual work is sometimes subsumed within group processes where the focus is on students being able to communicate and collaborate well with colleagues, rather than on individualised demonstrations of knowledge and skills.

Within the *productive performance* framework, students' levels of academic performance were determined in relation to the extent to which they conformed to the following descriptions of *problematic knowledge, higher-order thinking, depth of understanding* and *elaborated communication.*

Problematic knowledge involves students demonstrating an understanding of knowledge not as a fixed body of information but rather as being constructed, and hence subject to political, social and cultural influences and implications. This is opposed to where students represent knowledge as facts or as a body of truth.

Higher-order thinking occurs when students manipulate information and ideas in ways that transform their meaning and implications. This transformation occurs when students combine facts and ideas in order to synthesise, generalise, explain, hypothesise or arrive at some conclusion or interpretation. When students manipulate information and ideas through these processes, they solve problems and discover new (for them) meanings and understandings. This dimension is thus concerned with the extent to which students use higher-order thinking in their assignment work.

Depth of understanding occurs when students demonstrate an understanding of important disciplinary concepts, when they use concepts, ideas, theories or principles from the discipline to make connections with other disciplinary concepts or other disciplines, or when they use concepts, ideas, theories or principles to interpret and explain specific, concrete information or events. Instead of being able to recite only fragmented pieces of information, students develop relatively systematic, integrated or holistic understandings. Mastery is demonstrated by student success in producing new knowledge by discovering relationships, solving problems, constructing explanations and drawing conclusions.

Elaborated communication is present in a student's performance when the response to the assessment item demonstrates a coherent communication of ideas, concepts, arguments and/or explanations. This form of communication is rich in detail, qualifications and argument.[1]

---

[1] For the purposes of the research, this element was restricted to written communication.

Social performance

The four elements of social performance in the Productive Pedagogies Research spell out the types of performances that we believe students need to be able to demonstrate in order to make a contribution to society and to ensure that all graduates from school have the capacity to be active and informed citizens. Thus we draw on a range of literature that argues for students to be made aware of their citizenship obligations within a multicultural and ever-changing society (Rose 1995; Apple & Beane 1999; Quicke 1999; Arnot & Dillabough 2000; Freire 2001). Rose (1995), in his telling study of successful government schools in the USA, speaks of the distribution of authority in effective multicultural classrooms and the related respect for difference he found in such classrooms. These performances also reflect a set of commitments that society makes to its young people—to actively connect them to the world beyond school, to value their cultural knowledges, to provide for their participation in democratic processes, and to support their imaginings and efforts to create the kind of society they want. These social performances are thus reciprocal and reflect the rights of young people embedded within a relationship of mutual responsibility with society. In Australia, this relationship was formalised in *Stepping Forward—Improving Pathways for All Young People*. In this commitment, the Ministers for Education, Employment, Training, Youth Affairs and Community Services (2002) agreed to develop 'practical ways to increase the social, educational and employment out-comes of Australia's young people including those who are at risk, disconnected or in vulnerable circumstances'. The emphasis in this commitment is on what society has to offer young people, whereas the emphasis in curriculum frame-works tends to be on what society wants and needs from its young people in the future. The notion of *productive performance* recognises both these emphases.

The *connectedness to the world beyond the classroom* item of *productive performance* corresponds to the goal of making schooling relevant to the individual and social needs of students and their communities (Rose 1995; Quicke 1999; Freire 2001). Thus, *productive performance* is also concerned with the extent to which students are able to make links between their work and contemporary public situations and issues. In Australia, as in many other places, providing students with skills and knowledges to live productively within a diverse society is a measure of the relevance of schooling to a world increasingly concerned with 'difference'.

Assessment of student performance should therefore take into account the ability of students to see the world from multiple perspectives—that is, to demonstrate an under-standing of knowledge as a cultural construct. The inclusion of students' explicit valuing of cultural knowledges within the notion of *productive performance* thus recognises the ways in which education can contribute to the development of a socially just society that recognises concerns raised through various politics of difference and of representation (Connell 1993; Rose 1995; Quicke 1999; Arnot & Dillabough 2000; Gale & Densmore 2000; Benhabib 2002; Ladson-Billings & Gillborn 2004).

Addressing matters of social justice within student perform-ance is tied into the citizen goals of schooling. Citizenship is a primary concern of schooling throughout most Western countries and is one that needs to be thought about carefully in the context of globalisation, with its complex reconfigur-ations of the nation-state (Appadurai 1996) and related need for a (provisional) global humanism and respect for all persons (Said 2004; Gilroy 2004). In this context, active citizenship must be extended to recognise those without citizenship, such as refugees who have no rights and no rights to rights. In our conception of *productive performance*, citizenship has two aspects. Responsible citizenship involves students demonstrating a political literacy regarding the rights and responsibilities of citizens. Transformational citizenship goes beyond this, and integrates matters of social justice and cultural knowledges with attempts to change society for the better. We would expect that students demonstrating *productive performance* would show an understanding of both of these forms of citizenship, and an understanding of how citizenship itself actively includes some while excluding others.

The extent to which the elements of social performance were demonstrated in student work was determined on the basis of the following understandings of *connectedness beyond the classroom, cultural knowledges, responsible citizenship* and *transformative citizenship.*

Connectedness beyond the classroom occurs when students treat the assessment as having value and meaning beyond the classroom, and clearly is dependent on teacher construction of the assessment task. Two areas in which student work can exhibit some degree of connectedness are: (a) a real world public problem (i.e. students confront an actual contemporary issue or problem, such as applying statistical analysis in preparing a report to the city council on the homeless); and (b) students' personal experiences (i.e. the student performance focuses directly or builds on students' actual experiences or situations).

Cultural knowledges are valued when students explicitly value such things as non-dominant cultures' beliefs, languages, practices and ways of knowing. Cultural groups are distinguished by social characteristics such as gender, ethnicity, race, religion, economic status or youth. Thus, their valuing means students legitimise these cultures, through the inclusion, recognition and transmission of this cultural knowledge. The valuing of all cultural knowledges requires more than one culture being present and given status in the student performance. Knowledge that is constructed and framed within a common set of cultural definitions, symbols, values, views and qualities, thus attributing some higher status to it, stands in contrast to this.

Responsible citizenship is demonstrated when students display an awareness of the importance of creating positive human relationships and of respecting individuals. Responsible citizenship may also involve recognising the impact of individuals on their community and environment. It involves students accepting that a harmonious and 'good' society relies on its members respecting and exercising individual rights and responsibilities.

Transformative citizenship occurs when students acknowledge that in a democratic society all individuals and groups: have the right to participate in all of the democratic practices and institutions in that society; have the right to engage in the creation and transformation of that democratic society; have the responsibility to ensure that no groups or individuals are excluded from these practices and institutions; and have the responsibility to ensure that a broad definition of the political includes all relationships and structures throughout the social arrangement. In the age of globalisation, these matters stretch to citizenship issues beyond the local and the national. Transformative citizenship is present in any assessment item in any subject domain when the student elaborates on the meaning of such citizenship.

Thus, the outcomes that constitute *productive performance* involve students being able to: recognise the socially and culturally constructed nature of knowledge; demonstrate high-level analysis or higher-order thinking skills; show an in-depth understanding of a topic; use elaborate communication, in both written and non-written media, in order to demonstrate such understandings; make connections between new knowledges and the world beyond the classroom; and demonstrate a commitment to both responsible and transformative citizenship ideals.

Examples of productive student performance

The medium by which students demonstrate their achievements will vary according to the intended audience and purpose of the assessment task. The more connected the performance is to the world beyond the classroom, the more likely it is to be presented to an audience beyond the school. Exhibitions such as those developed by the Coalition of Essential Schools in the USA and the National Schools Network in Australia, and encouraged by the New Basics reform in Queensland, illustrate these kinds of performances. However, our primary interest in this section is to discuss the message rather than the medium of student performances. We believe that this message should convey to students that the tasks they are asked to perform have meaning and value beyond school, that the criteria by which they are judged are worthwhile and explicitly articulated, and that their performances will be enhanced through feedback and practice.

In the Productive Pedagogies Research, the logistics associated with handling and coding thousands of student work samples limited the type of student performances analysed to easily manageable written tasks. Student performances in Years 6, 8 and 11, in English, Mathematics, Social Science and Science classes, were considered. We observed around 150 primary school teachers and just over 300 secondary teachers. We collected from most of these teachers one whole-class set of student work and coded in excess of 5000 work samples. Many tasks tended to limit students to low levels of performance. Interestingly, at times, work of high intellectual quality was presented by the students but not demanded by the task. For example, students occasionally stepped outside the requirements of the task to comment critically or to present analysis. There was also little valuing of difference present in any of the student performances, as this was generally not demanded of assessment tasks. Ironically, in some instances, students' valuing of difference was commented on critically by the teacher for stepping outside the scope of the task or representing 'incorrect' views. In some schools, assessment tasks appeared to have the potential to demand high-quality academic and social performance but students appeared not to have had appropriate preparation to achieve high intellectual outcomes. It is thus important to acknowledge that students' performances are heavily dependent on what is asked of them in the assessment task, as well as the pedagogies they experience. Another significant factor here is the extent of scaffolding provided by the teacher for the task. The forms of pedagogies and assessment practices that help to produce such performances were discussed in Chapters 2 and 3. Here we examine some examples of student work that illustrate particular elements of productive student performance. These are actual tasks; we have not altered them in any way except to conceal names and places. We have included samples of each student's task to convey something of their actual performance. The first is a Year 5 persuasive writing essay, the second a Year 11 film review and the third a Year 8 Science project. In all three cases, the students had to demonstrate that they had:

- researched the topic thoroughly;
- grasped the form of the text type they were using;
- produced a 'polished piece' of writing that incorporated feedback received during earlier drafts; and
- addressed the criteria for the task that were made explicit in a rubric or through a detailed description of what was required.

Year 5 persuasive writing essay

This task was developed by teachers who had a commitment to the introduction of philosophy for children throughout the school (we have written extensively about this school in *Leading Learning*). One feature of this commitment was that students were regularly engaged in discussion about difficult and complex issues. In this task, the students were required to select a controversial issue and craft a piece of persuasive writing through a number of drafts. At the time, the construction of a beach volleyball stadium on Bondi beach for the 2000 Olympic Games in Sydney was an issue that generated national interest. The student had taken a 'straw poll' of other students on whether or not the stadium should be built and received some feedback from the teacher on notes of a draft essay. The student opened the essay with the paragraph shown in Figure 4.2.

The essay goes on to outline a number of reasons why the stadium should not be built: the loss of amenity for residents and visitors, the environmental impact, and the students'

Figure 4.2 Year 5 persuasive writing essay

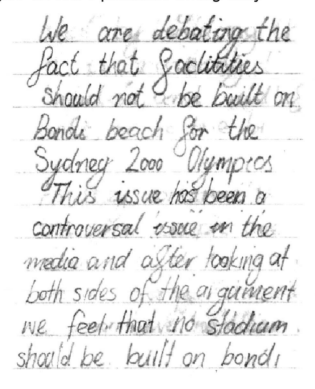

We are debating the fact that facilities should not be built on Bondi beach for the Sydney 2000 Olympics. This issue has been a controversal issue in the media and after looking at both sides of the argument we feel that no stadium should be built on bondi

poll that came out strongly against the construction. A description was also given of a protest at the beach and of the perceived lack of consultation of local residents and those opposed to the construction. The student's work reflects high levels of most indicators of social performance:

- It is connected to an issue of public concern; it makes substantial connections between classroom knowledge and situations outside the classroom; it explores these connections in ways that create personal meaning and significance for the knowledge.
- The inclusion of the results of a survey of peers demonstrates moderate reference to transformative citizenship by acknowledging that in a democratic society all individuals and groups have the right to

participate in all of the democratic practices and institutions in that society.

- The performance demonstrates moderate levels of responsible citizenship by arguing that as many beachgoers have protested against the construction it should not proceed. Responsible citizenship involves students accepting that a harmonious and 'good' society relies on its members respecting and exercising individual rights and responsibilities. In this performance, responsible citizenship would have been more strongly reflected if the student's arguments had been more persuasive and encompassing of opposing views, but it is important to remember that this was a Year 5 student, who was about ten years old.

- The student did not assume the dominant view at the time, which portrayed the protesters as disgruntled party spoilers. The intense pressure to get the city ready for the Olympics generally mobilised public opinion against the concerns of residents and environmentalists. Thus the student demonstrated a valuing of non-dominant concerns.

While we offer this assessment of the student's performance in terms of the *productive performance* measures, we also emphasise that the degree to which such a work sample demonstrates local agreements about the broader purpose of schooling can only be fully assessed within the context in which the task is produced, set against an understanding of the nature of what the task required, the syllabus requirements, and age-level expectations. Therefore, generally speaking, we can say that elaborate written communication is present in minimal to moderate levels, because the student's performance demonstrates a coherent communication of ideas, concepts, arguments and/or explanations through the process of writing. There are also moderate amounts of higher-order thinking, as the student combines facts and ideas in order to synthesise, generalise, explain, and arrive at the conclusion that the volleyball stadium should not be built.

Year 11 film review

This Year 11 film review stemmed from a unit of work in English exploring the theme of tolerance and the way prejudice and discrimination affect individuals and society. Students were required to put themselves in the role of a journalist assigned the task of writing a feature article on a film they had just previewed—in this case, *Mississippi Burning*. Their brief was to examine the 'issues of discrimination represented in the film and the social and political background that provides its context'. The first few paragraphs of the task are shown in Figure 4.3. In the remaining part of the essay the student provides an overview of the plot and its location with a particular historical context. Methods of cinematography are commented on and some scenes are described in detail.

The nature of this task requires the student to demonstrate a range of *productive performance* elements detailed in the task description. These include highlighting discrimination and the historical contexts in which people have been denied dignity, freedom and the right to achieve their potential; treating knowledge as problematic and subject to political, social and cultural influences; and considering complex issues of establishing ethical values and attitudes as an individual with a social responsibility. The achievement of a well-structured film review also relies on the performance of high levels of language proficiency through elaborated written communication, higher-order thinking and depth of understanding. The student has responded to these criteria in the following way:

- Through a description of how Klansmen are portrayed in the film, the student exposes racism as the result of political, social and cultural influences that can be captured and highlighted through techniques of cinematography: '. . . what the director chooses to capture on camera, and the characters are used to create a powerful impact'.
- The student's review demonstrates a sustained recognition of the impact of racism in the USA in the 1960s

Figure 4.3 Year 11 film review

A Cage for Life...

Alan Parker's newly released film
"Mississippi Burning" recreates the
segregation and hatred experienced by the
Black Americans during the early 1960's.
The film focuses strongly on discrimination
and aims to shock.

How do we classify people? By their job,
their colour, their money? If they are lower in a
hierarchy, does this mean they are less important?
Should differences of colour or race, be treated
differently? Why do we categorize people at all?

Unborn babies do not have the choice of
which family they are born into, or where they are
to be born. The colour of their skin is not their
choice, and their backgrounds are not of their
making.

Alan Parker's movie *"Mississippi Burning"* is
a forceful condemnation of racism and the evils of
discrimination. This is an extremely powerful
motion picture that uses many different methods to
ensure that the message is correctly conveyed to the
audience. It focuses on discrimination in ways that
have never been done before.

The plot of the movie revolves around the
disappearance of three civil rights workers. When
they are reported missing, two FBI agents, Allan
Ward (Willem Dafoe) and Rupert Anderson (Gene

and how this was powerfully conveyed in the film. The power of the dominant culture and its insidious infiltration of the police and court system is recognised, acknowledged and challenged in the review.

- The review applies appropriate analysis to an assessment of the film and its impact. This includes explaining techniques and hypothesising about the response of audiences.
- A number of disciplinary concepts are mentioned, and these include character portrayal and the use of music as a powerful tool.
- Elaborated written communication is demonstrated in the final product. This involved the writing of numerous drafts and the incorporation of student teacher feedback.
- The task is strongly connected to the world beyond the classroom, and the student reflects on differences between the society portrayed in the film and the student's own social milieu.

We are not suggesting that this is an exemplary task or student performance, but that the task does allow the student to develop and demonstrate *productive performances*. The opportunity for feedback, as well as opportunities to practise these performances, are critical to supporting their development. This is especially useful when students are involved in identifying the performances to be developed; when these are justified according to their value beyond school; when the criteria by which the performances will be assessed are made explicit; and when classroom practices and processes that support the development of these performances are also developed through consultation between the teacher and students.

Year 8 Science project

This final example of a student performance is not taken from the Productive Pedagogies Research but it is included here because it provides a good illustration of 'elaborated written communication' in a Science task. The students were asked to create an enclosure for a new zoo opening in their country town. The enclosure was to reflect an eco-system. We focused on this task in an earlier chapter but here we consider the quality of one student's performance. Prior to the final report, two progress reports had to be submitted. The requirements for each report were made explicit in a rubric. To add to the authenticity of the task, the progress reports and the teacher's response took the form of letters from a designer to their supervisor. The letter constituting the first progress (Figure 4.4) and the supervisor's response are shown below.

According to the task description, this progress report was intended to provide a plan for the ecosystem, suggest possible organisms, identify potential problems and describe why the enclosure was a worthwhile investment. This student goes beyond the ecosystem proposal to also outline the benefits for the town and community. Their progress report reflects *productive performance* in the following ways:

- The student is using persuasive arguments about the benefits of the proposal to local tourism and employment that demonstrate an understanding that the worth of the proposal will be assessed according to political, social and cultural influences and implications.

- The report demonstrates substantial amounts of analysis in order to formulate a proposal that creates an innovative solution to the problem set in the assessment item.

- The creation of an ecosystem goes beyond the application of isolated disciplinary concepts such as food chains. The task requires that the student create new knowledge by discovering relationships between the design constraints of a zoo and a sustainable habitat containing a number of organisms.

- The elaborated written communication has already been noted. As well as the progress reports the students were required to submit plans and food webs.

Figure 4.4 Year 8 Science project

Dear Miss G (Zoo manager)

This letter will explain the enclosure that I planned, which can be profitable for everyone in many ways, if it is a part of your New Zoo.

Before drawing out the plan, I have considered many things:
- ✓ The habitat/climate of which the animals will suit
- ✓ The cost of building the enclosure
- ✓ The cost of maintaining the enclosure
- ✓ The benefits of building it
- ✓ The problems for building it.

The habitat is suited to the plants and animals that I have chosen. All the animals and plants are native to Australia, which means that there isn't the need to build a costly special habitat for the species.

Money might be a problem, but the only building required is a secure fence which surrounds the area, and maybe artificial river. Both of these are not overwhelmingly expensive. There is a low cost for maintaining the enclosure, because only 2 of the 12 different types of species, need feeding.

There are a great number of benefits of building this enclosure. Tourism is the first problem that the zoo can change. Tourism in the area isn't the greatest at the moment, but building the enclosure will attract many visitors. More tourists mean more business for the community, which ends up helping everyone.

Although we live in the outback country, many people do not know where and how animals live. The enclosure will attract and teach visiting schools from around the district/community and adults a bit more about the animals in the enclosure.

The employment rate is very low. The zoo can help the rate rise because of the many jobs it will create. No matter what type of person you are, you can still apply for a job at the enclosure.

Another problem is the training of the birds. They must be trained to be tame and not fly away, otherwise it may easily fly away and attack other people.

I hope you will deeply consider using my plan for the enclosure. The enclosure is natural, beneficial, and educational. It is exactly what you need to solve your problem.

Yours Sincerely,

- The task has explicit value and meaning beyond the school. In other tasks such as this with direct application to the local community, outside experts have been consulted during the planning and assessment phase. This highlights the value of the task and performance beyond the school.

While many elements of *productive performance* are required by each task described above, none of them demands high levels of each element. We do not claim that this should be a requirement of each task, but that students have the opportunity to regularly practise each of these performances. This requires that teachers monitor and assess the nature of performances demanded of students across the subjects and year levels in order to identify imbalances and to monitor students' progress. For example, findings in the Productive Pedagogies Research suggest that there is a widespread absence of the requirement that students demonstrate a valuing of other cultural knowledges. We suspect that one reason for such an absence is the lack of time for sustained professional dialogue that was commonly reported by teachers during interviews in the study.

A core assumption underpinning this discussion is that a pause in activities is necessary in order for those who work in schools to make explicit how schools function *and* for them to function as places of learning. Schools need to be places of teacher learning as well as of student learning, and indeed there ought to be a close relationship between the two (Young 1998). As the old saying goes, 'Who dares to teach must never cease to learn!'. Not all schools set aside time within the school day or even week for teachers to meet for professional dialogue. Opportunities for sharing ideas, collective problem solving and planning must compete with the other demands and pressures on teachers' time. More often than not, this time is squeezed off the agenda or reduced to a minimum by these competing concerns. In the absence of opportunities for collective reflection, schools tend to become busy places, where a lot happens and where learning relies on the capacity of individual teachers in classrooms, the capacities and cultural capital of students, rather than on the planned alignment across the school of the effects of curriculum, pedagogy and assessment.

Bernstein (1973: 228) conceptualises formal educational knowledge as being realised through these three message systems; he states that 'curriculum defines what counts as valid knowledge, pedagogy defines what counts as a valid transmission of knowledge, and [assessment] defines what counts as a valid realisation of this knowledge on the part of the taught'. We argue that the primary purpose of pausing, and placing how schools function under scrutiny, is to align these systems in ways that support the learning outcomes of both students and teachers: the effects of curriculum, pedagogy and evaluation need to be continually monitored and negotiated at the local level though a *shared understanding* of each system, a *common language* for discussing them and a *mechanism for aligning* their purposes.

Correlations between classroom practices and social and academic outcomes

A question of central interest in the Productive Pedagogies Research was how teachers' pedagogical and assessment practices influenced student outcomes. The study attempted to examine the relationship between productive pedagogies and students' academic and social performance in each of the 24 schools in the study. The correlations between averages for the dimensions of productive pedagogies determined at the school level, and students' academic and social performance, were detailed in the study's final report (QSRLS 2001).

A significant positive correlation was evident between intellectual quality in the classroom and students' academic performance. In other words, in classrooms where students had opportunities to perform intellectually demanding tasks, they also demonstrated intellectual outcomes through their

assessment tasks. Moreover, supportive classroom pedagogies were positively correlated with students' academic
performance at a similar level to intellectual quality in the
classroom. This finding suggests that students' ability to
perform intellectual tasks was enhanced by a supportive
classroom environment. The connectedness of pedagogies to
the world beyond the classroom was also correlated with
improved academic performance, but to a lesser degree than
intellectual quality and social support.

These findings are important in that they show the
centrality of intellectual demand, supportiveness and
connectedness for academic outcomes. While there was
no significant correlation between pedagogies that value
difference and students' academic performances, we suggest
that this does not detract from the importance of these
practices—rather, that most teachers do not know how to
deal effectively with difference in classrooms. There are
significant system and school professional development
responsibilities here. The valuing-of-difference dimension
of productive pedagogies was significantly correlated with
social outcomes, as were connectedness and supportiveness.

In terms of the argument of this chapter, these findings
suggest, among other things, that classroom assessment practices often do not provide the opportunity for students to
display intellectual and other sorts of desired outcomes; and
that the purposes of schooling are not generally translated
into creative and demanding assessment practices. The
examples provided in the sections above are the products of
some teachers' attempts to translate the broader purposes
of schooling into student performances.

An overall conclusion of the Productive Pedagogies
Research was that if students are to demonstrate the richer
outcomes of schooling, indicated by *productive performance*,
they need to be doing work of this kind in the classroom.
This way of thinking places the planning of outcomes ahead
of the planning of classroom practices. This somewhat counter-
intuitive way of thinking, or backward mapping, was
developed by Richard Elmore (1979/80) as an alternative

form of policy implementation to the more familiar forward mapping, but it has been taken up as an effective way of planning and aligning curriculum, assessment and pedagogy in some schools (Hayes 2003). There are multiple ways in which backward mapping may be operationalised in schools in relation to teaching and learning, but a fundamental starting point is to ask the question upfront: What do we want students to be able to know, value, understand and do? Answering this question makes assessment integral to teaching because it requires a consideration of how such performances will be taught, achieved and measured. In addition, this approach emphasises the importance of professional and broader community dialogue that generates shared understandings of the nature and purposes of schooling. Such understandings help mobilise pedagogies in support of assessment and, more importantly, in support of the achievement of certain performances. This approach builds coherence by requiring that teachers understand how these performances develop across all learning programs, not just at the level they teach. A key set of questions for teachers becomes: What can students do? What am I responsible for teaching them? How will I know when they can do these things?

Conclusion: alignment for productive performance

In this chapter we have highlighted the importance of linking concerns about student performance to schooling goals that are cognisant of the needs of people living in a complex and increasingly globalised world. These goals are both academic and social; they are both individual and collective; and, while they are backward-looking about preserving some traditions and knowledge forms, they are also futures-oriented. These demands require that students develop their capacities for engaging in critical analysis, for producing and handling information, for communicating, and for working together in ethical ways. Given the explosion of knowledge and the notions of the 'knowledge society', 'knowledge economy' and 'learning society' (see Hargreaves 2003), *productive performance* also requires that students develop and demonstrate an understanding of the nature of knowledge. Such an understanding requires that knowledge be understood in depth rather than superficially. This depth would require less content to be taught, in the spirit of Ted Sizer's (1987, 1992, 1994) much-quoted 'less is more' philosophy. It is this philosophy that also underpins the New Basics reform in Queensland. Indeed, a central finding of the Productive Pedagogies Research, outlined throughout this book, is that a crowded curriculum is likely to result in teachers' fast coverage of extensive material, rather than the pursuit of in-depth intellectual quality. This suggests the danger that 'coverage' is being valued over quality. And we would add that speed of coverage is a factor advantaging those students who bring to school the requisite cultural capital and disadvantaging those who do not.

This tension varies across educational systems and reflects differences in forms of curriculum and accountability. The Queensland system in which the study was conducted has not had public examinations for about three decades. The form of teacher-moderated school-based assessment in the senior school in Queensland encourages a considerable degree of teacher professional judgment framed by moderation from colleagues. At the same time, there are emergent pressures for more system-wide testing for accountability purposes at global, national and state levels, along with other constraining curriculum pressures (Apple 2001). Such standardised testing has been endemic in US schooling for a long time, as have packaged curricula, while standardised testing has also been in place in England since the late 1980s. Thus teachers have varying degrees of control over curriculum pacing. We would note that fast pacing and an emphasis on coverage inevitably favours those students who bring to school a specific form of cultural capital and related dispositions (Bourdieu 1984, 1986, 1994) which are attuned to those embedded in the formal and informal practices of schooling.

Just as considerations of explicitness in assessment practices are necessary for schooling to function in more socially just ways, so too are considerations of curriculum coverage, pedagogical pacing and intellectual quality.

In the current information age, it is also necessary that all students develop the communication skills required to nego-tiate its demands. This will require students being able to demonstrate an ability to communicate in elaborate ways through qualification, justification and coherent communication of ideas via a variety of media. This requires an emphasis on multiliteracies (New London Group 1996). In the Queens-land New Basics project such multiliteracies include: 'Blending traditional and new Communications media; Making creative judgments and engaging in performance; Communicating using languages and intercultural under-standings; and Mastering literacy and numeracy' (Education Queensland 2000). Another critical aspect of living in new times is that students learn to value difference and to be able to critically engage with the complexities of life in ways that reflect a concern with social justice. This also raises knowledge issues, in that students should be required to demonstrate an understanding both of non-dominant knowl-edges and of how some knowledges have acquired particular kinds of hegemonic status.

Within classroom practices that are designed to promote students' understandings of social justice, it is important that students be presented with opportunities to explore and understand the citizenship goals of schooling. This clearly will entail students making connections between what they do in the classroom and the broader society. This is the *con-nectedness* element of classroom practices as developed by the study. It is such views about the purposes of education that have contributed to our understandings about the particular academic and social performances that need to be promoted through the schooling process.

We reiterate that the concept of *productive performance* outlined in some detail in this chapter was developed as part of the research design of the Productive Pedagogies

Research. We are not saying that these performances should be taken up by all schools and all teachers, irrespective of systemic location and traditions. Rather, we have outlined our approach to emphasise the need to align performance with *productive pedagogies* and *productive assessment*, which were detailed in earlier chapters. We stress here that the types of student performances that are valued in schools should be identified, and agreed to, at the local level through community and professional dialogue. Such considerations need then to be layered into practices at all levels, from the broadest to the individual classroom level. We would also argue that teachers and community, including disparate voices, need to be involved in systemic considerations of goals for schooling and their rearticulation. In terms of the social and citizenship outcomes from schooling, we affirm Rose's (1995: 430) somewhat poetic question derived from the thinking of the American educational philosopher John Dewey: 'How does the mind reflect back on itself and its attendant social structures in ways that foster democracy in the ongoing flow of classroom life?'. Such considerations, we suggest, would go a long way towards the alignment of the message systems of schooling—curriculum, pedagogy and assessment—towards achieving improved academic and social outcomes for *all* students.

5 Schools can make a difference

> In fact, to penalize the underprivileged and favour the most privileged, the school has only to neglect, in its teaching methods and techniques, and its criteria when making academic judgments, to take into account the cultural inequalities between children of different social classes. In other words, by treating all pupils, however unequal they may be in reality, as equal in rights and duties, the education system is led to give its *de facto* sanction to initial cultural inequalities. (Bourdieu 1976: 113)

The message systems of schooling—curriculum, pedagogy and assessment—are not abstract concepts. They are enacted within specific schools and specific societies at specific times. Earlier chapters of this book have looked at forms of classroom practices that might contribute to more equitable student outcomes and improve learning for all students. This chapter focuses on schools as contexts for learning. In what ways might individual schools and the education system more broadly enhance opportunities for learning? What kinds of whole school practices contribute to more equitable student outcomes, and support teachers as they work in classrooms to improve learning for all students? We look here at how school organisation, teacher professional communities and school leadership may support and spread good classroom practices across the whole school. We also consider the importance of broader policy frames and funding support for schools to achieve equitable learning outcomes. A central concern here is the need to work with the different logics of practice of systemic policy frames, school leadership and the daily life of classrooms.

Schools as places of learning

Schools are public places, shared by many people, as well as places of unique personal experience and memory. Schools have been set up around the world as designated spaces with the same common purpose and intention—to provide systematic, structured learning opportunities for young people. Schools around the world tend to look much the same in their outward forms; indeed, it would be rare to come on a school and not know it as such. Schools have designated places for work and play; they have classrooms that divide students up into age and subject groupings; they have timetables that divide the day according to clock time and regulate movements within the schools; they have roles and expectations for students, teachers and parents; they have sporting teams and school choirs; and so on. World institution theorists such as John Meyer and colleagues (1979, 1992) argue that schooling as an institution has a life of its own, and that Western ideas and forms of organisation have jumped across national boundaries to become a symbol of modernity in all countries, rich and poor alike.

Alongside their obvious 'sameness', schools are very different from each other. Each is a specific place, with its own unique 'feel' and its own ways of doing things. Though schools have common practices and organisational forms, these spell out differently in different schools. The micropolitics of schools mediate the common forms of staffrooms and classrooms to produce very different school-specific experiences. Schools around the corner from each other, with similar parent and community bodies, may be very different in culture and overall effectiveness, as Christie's (1998, 2001) studies of dysfunctional and resilient schools in South Africa illustrate. Classrooms and corridors may be bleak, but they may also be bright; students and teachers may be disaffected and overcome by low morale, but they may also be enthusiastic and motivated; rhythms of teaching and learning may be disrupted and shallow, but they may also be consistent and fulfilling; school may be experienced as a place of failure, but it may also be experienced as a place of success. Usually, these sorts of differences are evident between schools, but sometimes they are evident within a single school. The Productive Pedagogies Research found this to be the case in some of the large secondary schools in the study. For example, a mathematics department in one of the larger secondary schools was creative, vital, researching and theorising its own practices, reforming its pedagogies and so on to very good effect, while other departments in the same school were staid and more traditional in orientation.

With their stable and recognisable patterns, schools as social institutions appear to have predictable levers for improvement—and for contributing to social change. At the same time, the differences that exist between schools have led social researchers and educationists to question the extent to which schools themselves might be able to control their patterns of student engagement and achievement. How to change schools to improve student achievement and achieve greater equality of outcomes has been a major concern for educationists and social reformers.

Schools and social inequality

A perennial problem for sociology of education is that schools produce unequal outcomes for students of different social and cultural backgrounds. Achievement in school is closely linked to socioeconomic background and (in Australia) command of English and Indigeneity. In 1966, the Coleman Report on *Equality of Educational Opportunity*, commissioned by the US Congress, was one of the first research studies to challenge social reformers by arguing that schools did not reduce social inequality. Through large-scale survey research, James Coleman and colleagues produced compelling evidence to show that personal and family characteristics overrode the effects of schooling in influencing students' life chances. In their words, 'the inequalities imposed on children by their home, neighbourhood and peer environment are carried along to become the inequalities with which they confront adult life at the end of school' (Coleman et al. 1966: 325).

Nearly 40 years later, Richard Teese and John Polesel's (2003) study of Australian secondary schooling confirmed what others in the intervening years had found: that children (both boys and girls) of manual workers and the unemployed are the students most likely to achieve poorly at school, to leave early or fail to gain a place in tertiary education, to be unemployed after school or find low-paid, low-skill jobs. Almost all paths to economic advancement in Australia (and similar countries) are linked to secondary education, and achievement in schooling is closely tied to patterns of economic success and marginalisation. Moreover, individual schools are so predictably positioned in relation to each other in terms of student achievement that, according to Teese and Polesel, 'which schools the best students represent is a matter of near certainty' (2003: 2). Their careful comparison of achievement patterns across schools shows consistent differences between schools serving rich and poor communities. Schools serving rich communities—whether private or state schools—show concentrations of material and symbolic advantage leading to high achievement in the academic curriculum; they are 'fortified sites', which are comparatively rich in resources of all kinds to support student success. Schools serving poor communities are 'exposed sites', which achieve poorly in comparison (Teese & Polesel 2003: 123):

> It is not cultural advantage that is pooled at these sites, but multiple disadvantage—poor language skills, fragmented family lives, poverty, low levels of parental education, lack of facilities, leisure that is distracting rather than supportive of school. These are indeed 'exposed sites' in which effective

learning depends very largely on the capacity of teachers to make up for the gap between what the academic curriculum assumes about students and who students really are.

For over 30 years, sociologists of education have probed why and how schools produce and reproduce social inequalities across generations. Different definitions of 'the problem' have led to different 'solutions' or interventions being proposed as remedies. Where 'the problem' is defined in terms of deficiencies in family background and income levels, 'the solution' is seen to lie in compensating for these deficits through providing additional resources and compensatory programs. Where 'the problem' is defined in terms of students' access to the curriculum, 'the solution' is seen to lie in enhancing student learning and improving teacher pedagogical practices. Typically, 'the problem' has proven difficult to pin down and define, and impossible to 'fix' in a sustained way. And we would note that the sociology of education has been better at providing the critical accounts of how schools reproduce social inequality than any positive thesis about what might be done (Young 1998).

In this chapter we suggest that the complex mix of practices that make up schools—and their relationship to the broader society—are not easy to disentangle and reconstitute. Discourses of schooling offer points of engagement that enable us to work both with and against the practices of schooling and their effects. We consider here a number of school-level and systemic interventions proposed by researchers and policy makers—specifically, notions of school organisational capacity, teacher professional learning communities, and leadership for learning. We suggest that instead of approaching these as 'solutions', it is more useful to engage with them as ways of foregrounding the most important work of schools, namely learning.

Before exploring these discourses, it is useful to frame the question of schools and social inequality within a classic sociological formulation of the relationship between social structure and human agency. In his well-known essay on the *Sociological Imagination*, C. Wright Mills (1959/2000) argues that individuals can make sense of their lives only when they understand the times in which they live and the circumstances of other people like themselves. We need to understand the patterns and structures of our societies, our historical times and how they are changing, as well as how individuals like ourselves are shaped and formed in social patterns. On this basis we are best able to assess our life chances, and to tell the difference between our personal troubles (problems that have to do with ourselves alone) and social issues (problems that have to do with broader social patterns and opportunities). At the intersection of individual biography, social structures and the 'push and shove' of history lie the possibilities for engaging with change.

Whether a student succeeds or fails at school may well be a result of personal effort: it may reflect individual capacities and choices. But it may also be the result of structures of opportunity that lie beyond the control of single individuals: what school individuals attend, the curriculum and pedagogies they experience, where they live, how well versed they are in English, what cultural and material resources they have at home. To what extent individual lives are determined by social structure, and to what extent they are shaped by free choice and human agency, is a matter for careful consideration. While recognising the seemingly enduring nature of social patterns, it is important to recognise also that they are (and have been) changed by human action. On the one hand, it is important to avoid an approach in which individuals and whole groups have no choice but to live out their predetermined social fate. On the other hand, the inverse approach overemphasises the power of human agency and free will, and runs the risk of 'blaming the victim' by holding individuals responsible for circumstances that are beyond their control. Both positions need to be held in tension. It needs to be recognised that individuals and their actions are able to make a difference, but they alone cannot change entrenched social patterns.

Applying this analysis to schools, it is possible to read the findings of Coleman et al. and others as implying that schools make no difference to students' social and academic outcomes. Yet this reading oversimplifies the complexity of what happens in schools, and easily becomes part of the perpetuation of inequalities. Indeed, having low expectations of students in disadvantaged communities is a sure way of contributing to poor outcomes for these students. Moreover, closer reading shows that the findings of the Coleman Report are in fact more nuanced and challenging than this, and the logic of their argument provides important spaces for intervention.

The Report begins with the premise that an important focus of schooling is to 'teach certain intellectual skills such as reading, writing, calculating, and problem solving' (Coleman et al. 1966: 20)—skills that are measured by standard achievement tests. As the Report notes (1966: 20):

> These tests do not measure intelligence, nor attitudes, nor qualities of character. Furthermore, they are not, nor are they intended to be, 'culture free'. Quite the reverse: they are culture bound. What they measure are the skills which are among the most important in our society for getting a good job and moving up to a better one, and for full participation in an increasingly technical world . . .

Statistical analyses of a large sample of test results found that 'variations in family background account for far more variation in school achievement than do variations in school characteristics' (1966: 218). Moreover, significant differences were found in the educational achievements of 'minority groups and whites', and these grew cumulatively as students moved through school. The Report notes that (Coleman et al. 1966: 22):

> Whatever may be the combination of nonschool factors— poverty, community attitudes, low educational level of parents—which put minority children at a disadvantage in verbal and nonverbal skills when they enter the first grade, the fact is the schools have not overcome it.

Importantly, however, the Report goes on to explore possible differential effects of schooling. It found that characteristics of schooling—facilities, curriculum and teachers —made the most difference for low-achieving students and those who came to school least prepared in terms of the demands of schooling. The implication was clear: 'it is for the most disadvantaged children that improvements in school quality will make the most difference in achievement'. Furthermore, the feature of schooling found to have the most important effect on achievement for all students was good teachers. Again, their effect was greatest on children whose backgrounds were most educationally disadvantaged. And again, the Report states a clear implication: 'a given investment in upgrading teacher quality will have the most effect on achievement in underprivileged areas' (1966: 317).

Two other factors were found to have differential effects on students' achievement (1966: 23, 321):

> . . . [A] pupil attitude factor, which appears to have a stronger relationship to achievement than do all the 'school' factors together, is the extent to which an individual feels that he [sic] has some control over his [sic] own destiny.

> . . . [M]inority pupils . . . have far less conviction than whites that they can affect their own environments and their futures. When they do, however, their achievement is higher than that of whites who lack that conviction.

And (1996: 22):

> Finally, it appears that a pupil's achievement is strongly related to the educational backgrounds and aspirations of other students in the school.

However the Coleman research is judged, it needs to be noted that it did not propose simple determinism as an adequate analysis of educational inequality. Nor did it attempt to explore what schools might do in anything but the broadest terms. That said, its findings do point to a number of spaces for intervention, which subsequent research has supported. Schools do make a difference for disadvantaged students, albeit not an overwhelming one. Provision of good teachers and upgrading of teacher quality are likely to improve student achievement in disadvantaged areas. And education systems can make a difference through supplying well-prepared teachers to disadvantaged schools and supporting them to do their work.

This is not to say that good teachers alone can redress systemic inequalities; arguably, these need to be addressed at systemic level. Even if individual teachers can make a difference to student outcomes, no single teacher—or even groups of teachers—can fully redress the patterns of inequality of the broader society and the ways in which these play out through schooling. The same is true for individual schools. So the pedagogies and related assessment practices we have documented throughout this book can make a difference, but not *all* of the difference.

There are patterns of performance among schools that are largely predictable—what Teese and Polesel (2003) refer to as 'the institutional geography' of the schooling system. Though single schools may go against the inevitability of their institutional geography to jump out of line in terms of student achievement, this is unlikely to lead to systemic change in patterns of inequality related particularly to social class and cultural background. That said, all schools do have a central mandate to address the learning of young people in systematic and structured ways. Maintaining a focus on this mandate—albeit under unequal social circumstances—is an important goal for the work of teachers and students.

Thus we acknowledge the arguments of the reproduction theorists (Bowles & Gintis 1976; Bourdieu & Passeron 1977) who suggested that schools reproduced and legitimised social inequalities in a fairly deterministic fashion. However, our position is a more nuanced one, drawing on the important insights of the Coleman study. We seek to work with a positive thesis about what schools and teachers can achieve, while acknowledging the constraints. Teachers and schools *can* make a difference, but this is limited and framed by the structure of the broader society, the effects of social, economic and cultural power, and the impact of educational policies and practices (Lippman 1998; Thrupp 1999). The capacity of teachers and schools to make a difference is also enabled or inhibited by broader economic and political changes, and thus the capacity to have positive educational and social justice effects has a specific temporal component. Michael Apple (2000a) has acknowledged the possibilities of critical pedagogies such as the *productive pedagogies* model, but also notes the need for caution and wariness of romanticism in current educational policy contexts, given the savage inequalities that now exist in many societies in these times of globalisation and neoliberal policy dominance.

This book and the research on which it is based trace their lineage in some ways to an influential Australian sociological study of schools, families and social division, *Making the Difference* by Bob Connell and his colleagues (1982), which went beyond structuralist reproduction theory. That study provided an account of how social class, interwoven with gender, related to school achievement and questions of educational opportunity, with some suggestions for what schools and teachers could achieve, given extant structural social inequalities around social class and gender. (See Connell 2002; Yates 2002; Thrupp 2002; and Arnot 2002, for contemporary accounts of this study and its applicability to the twenty-first-century schooling, as well as Thrupp 1999 and Thomson 2002.) This book seeks to provide a realistic account, grounded in research evidence, of how schools and teachers can make a difference through a focus on classroom, school and system level reforms, while also recognising the limitations of school-based reform alone.

The findings of the Coleman Report stimulated a wave of educational research from different theoretical and political perspectives. One theoretical strand was the so-called reproduction theory mentioned above. Another of the most important empirically based strands was research on school effectiveness (e.g. see Creemers 1994; Edmonds 1979; Rutter et al. 1979; Scheerens 1992; Scheerens & Bosker 1997). Initially, researchers in this tradition attempted to refute the Coleman findings by comparing schools and attempting to pinpoint what the features were of schools that were more 'effective' in terms of student achievement. Thus, they turned the focus from social context on to school-level factors in an attempt to determine what features made a difference. Large-scale quantitative studies varied in design and results, as they attempted to establish causal relationships between different 'inputs' and school-level factors affecting achievement. Numerous research studies came up with a largely common set of features: strong leadership with a curriculum focus; clear goals and high expectations of staff and students; an emphasis on quality of teaching and learning; a supportive school environment; a culture of monitoring and evaluation; and parental involvement and support.

Initially, researchers in the effectiveness tradition assumed that these sorts of variables applied across schools in all contexts and could be used as 'levers' for improving schools and their effectiveness. Over time, researchers developed more sophisticated analyses of 'school effects' and more complex modelling of interlocking variables affecting school effectiveness (see McBeath & Mortimore 2001; Teddlie & Reynolds 2000; Townsend, Clarke & Ainscow 1999). Research has investigated not only whole-school effects but also classroom and teacher effects, as well as subject and department effects. Differential effects have been explored in relation to school composition, and the effects of race, gender, ethnicity and so on. While the bulk of the research has concerned the USA, the UK and The Netherlands, a body of literature has developed in countries across the world. Research in the school effectiveness tradition has highlighted differences between developing and industrialised countries, finding that school effects are greater in the former (Heneveld & Craig 1996). In addition to the list of factors identified in richer countries, studies in developing countries identified the importance of adequate material resourcing and pedagogical support, the language of instruction, and the health of students.

That said, it remains the case that socioeconomic context overwhelms school-level effects, which account for only a small percentage of the variance in student achievement.

According to Townsend, the variance attributable to schools is around 5%–10%—though the variance attributable to classroom effects can be 35%–55% (2001: 119). Hallinger and Heck (1996) have found that the variance attributable to school principals is mediated rather than direct, although leadership is recognised as a variable in all effectiveness studies. In other words, schools do have an effect, but it is not large; classrooms have a greater effect, and individual teachers the greatest—but these are not the determining effects in student achievement.

School effectiveness research has been strongly and consistently criticised by researchers who do not share its theoretical and methodological assumptions. The points at issue between supporters and opponents of this research are well illustrated in special issues of the journal *School Effectiveness and School Improvement* (2001). The most powerful criticism is that this approach leaves largely unaddressed the relationships between schools and the inequalities of broader social, political and economic contexts. By foregrounding school effects, it backgrounds the structural inequalities that are the larger determinants of student outcomes (see Thrupp 1999; Slee & Weiner with Tomlinson 1998; Fleisch & Christie 2004). It also has little to say about the cultural features or micropolitics that differ so markedly from school to school. In spite of debates about the nature of 'effectiveness' and what might make a school 'effective', this research tradition has little to say about school change and what sorts of things schools might do to improve the learning experiences of a range of different students in vastly different circumstances. Moreover, the focus on 'large-lever' factors cannot identify or address the very different ways these play out in different contexts. For example, Bruce Fuller (1991) has used world institutional theory to show that schools in developing countries may have the same outward forms of schools in industrialised countries, but in fragile states schools and their predictable forms may serve more as symbols of modernity than as indicators of learning. In a similar vein, Heather Jacklin's (2004) study of South African township schools highlights the aridity of many classrooms, where the outward rhythms of pedagogy may signify nothing but repetitive behaviour, with no substantive teaching and learning taking place.

Partly in response to the quantitative, large-scale, large-lever nature of school effectiveness research, school improvement researchers such as Fullan (1982, 1993, 1997, 2001), Hargreaves (1994, 1997, 2003), Hopkins et al. (1994) and Stoll & Fink (1996) have generated a different tradition of research, which tends to be qualitative, smaller in scale, and focused on processes within schools and how these might be improved. This research addresses the complexities of day-to-day activities in schools and does not attempt to establish causal links between measurable inputs, school-level factors and outcomes. Other research on the micropolitics of schools (e.g. Blasé 1991) and on the politics of education policy (Gewirtz 2002; Gewirtz, Ball & Bowe 1995) has countered the overtly non-political stance of school effectiveness research. And a number of studies have confirmed that practices within schools may have considerable effect on student learning outcomes, while at the same time confirming the overwhelming influence of social context on learning outcomes. As a result of this research, a lot more is known about different dimensions of schools that influence student achievement—as well as the limitations of schools in achieving improved student outcomes.

The position we take in this book is that although the field of schooling is an unequal one, it *is* possible for all schools to focus on learning, and for schools to make a difference to students' learning experiences and outcomes. As Hayes has argued elsewhere, 'The illusory and seductive desire to make the world a better place by fixing educational problems and dilemmas should not be confused with the day-to-day rhythm of teaching and learning in schools' (2003: 243). The challenge for teachers, administrators and other educators is to make sure that schools are places of learning, so that learning is one of the effects of schooling. To labour the point made throughout this book, the quality of pedagogies is an important social justice matter. Such quality includes intellectual demand and working with and valuing difference, in addition to supportiveness and connectedness. Given that the message systems of curriculum, pedagogy and assessment take place in institutional contexts as well as social contexts of relative wealth and poverty, it is important to recognise the influence of these environments—in terms of both possibilities and constraints. Different sites of practice in education have different logics: the logics of the message systems at classroom level; the logics of leadership, management and teachers' work as professionals at the school level; the logics of structural and policy reform at systemic level. The challenge is to engage with these different logics as well as with social contexts, with the purpose of foregrounding learning.

School organisation as a context for learning

What kinds of whole-school practices contribute to more equitable student outcomes, and support teachers as they work in classrooms to improve learning for all students?

The organisation of schools, with their separate classrooms, age and subject groupings, and departmental configurations, form the physical and social architecture for teachers' work. The individualistic nature of teachers' work in their 'egg crate' classrooms has been noted in almost all studies of teachers' work (e.g. Lortie 1975; Connell 1985; Lawn 1996; Acker 1999). Many—if not most—teachers operate in professional isolation behind their classroom doors, without having substantive conversations with colleagues about their core tasks: about the goals of schooling; about curriculum and the nature of knowledge; about how students learn and what may be expected of them; about effective pedagogy and assessment. In these key dimensions of their professional work, most teachers work alone. This situation represents the pressures on teachers' work, class sizes, the workloads, the architecture of schools, and so on. The possibility that the organisation of schools and, more specifically, professional communication with colleagues could make a difference to teachers' work with students has been explored in a number of different studies on teacher professional communities. A central assumption that was tested in both the CORS research and the Productive Pedagogies Research was that school organisation, and specifically teacher professional communities, would influence student learning. What is entailed in the notion of teacher professional community, and how might it affect student performance?

Professional learning communities

The concept of the teacher professional community was given prominence by an important study by Talbert and McLaughlin in the mid-1990s on the work of high school teachers in the USA. Through grounded analysis, these researchers investigated the culture and institutional forms of teachers' work. They found that different departments created 'fundamentally different settings for teaching and learning—even within the same school' (2001: 47). Strong professional communities at the department level, they argued, play an important role in establishing 'norms for teaching' and expectations for student performance. Analysing what they termed the 'three legs of the classroom triangle'—subject matter, beliefs about students in the class, and notions of effective pedagogy—they identified two types of strong professional communities: those that emphasised the traditional curriculum and teacher-centred pedagogies; and those that emphasised shared responsibility for the development of innovative, student-centred curriculum and pedagogy. (They found very few of the latter.) In contrast to these strong professional communities, and often alongside them in a school, departments with weak communities tended to operate as collections of independent teachers, who did not share ideas about teaching and learning or have a shared sense of responsibility for student learning. Some communities of practice, they found, believed that all students could achieve high standards, whereas others held deficit views about non-traditional students and what they could achieve.

Talbert and McLaughlin were able to show that the different ways in which teachers worked with colleagues affected what and how they taught in classrooms, how they understood their work with students, and what they expected of each other and of students. Teacher community, they proposed optimistically, could be 'a primary unit for improving education quality' (2001: 12). However, that would depend on the culture, values and norms of teaching espoused by the community, as the communities of practice they found varied not only in terms of strength and weakness but also in the expectations of teachers and students. Moreover, as they pointed out, communities depend on the experience of shared goals and common work; without this, teachers might interpret pressures to build communities as a form of what Hargreaves (1994) has termed 'contrived collegiality'.

A compatible but somewhat different notion of teacher professional communities was developed in the work of Louis, Marks and Kruse (1996; see also Louis, Kruse & Marks 1996), which formed part of the CORS project and was picked up by the Productive Pedagogies Research. Drawing on US research on school effects, the CORS research built a quantitative model of 'school organizational capacity' including the concept of 'teacher professional communities', which both CORS and the Productive Pedagogies Research found to have a positive influence on pedagogy and on student learning outcomes.

Research on school-wide professional communities by Louis and colleagues began with the assumption that teachers' interactions with each other outside classrooms affected the impact they had on their students. Sustained professional contact with colleagues, they argued, was important in 'increasing teachers' sense of craft' and building their commitment in 'increasingly difficult and demanding' work contexts (Louis, Marks & Kruse 1996: 758). In particular, they postulated that school-wide professional communities would influence or be influenced by the extent to which teachers considered their students to be capable of successful learning, and themselves to be responsible for student learning. To investigate this, they drew up a framework and statistical model for school-wide professional community, and tested its dimensions as well as its relationship to teacher responsibility for student learning. The model developed by Louis, Marks and Kruse was made up of the following:

- five *elements of practice*: shared norms and values; a collective focus on student learning; collaboration to foster sharing of expertise; deprivatised practice, including peer coaching and team teaching; and reflective dialogue;
- alongside these elements of practice, a range of *structural conditions* affecting the design of a school as a work setting: size; staffing complexity; scheduled planning time for teachers within the school day; and flexible governance arrangements which enabled 'teacher empowerment';
- as well as these structural conditions, a factor termed *human and social resources*, which would enhance school-wide professional community: supportive leadership focused on school improvement; openness to innovation; respect in terms of honouring the expertise of others; feedback on instructional performance; and professional development;
- two other features of school organisation: *school level* (primary or secondary) and *gender*.

Through empirical investigation, Louis and colleagues established, among other things: that school-wide professional communities as set out in their model do exist, but vary considerably between schools; that they are more likely to be present in primary than in secondary schools; and that school size—to their surprise—did not make a significant difference. Their study showed that providing opportunities for teachers to work collaboratively and to participate in decision making are significant factors associated with the quality of teachers' school life; and that there is a strong relationship between professional community and teachers' sense of responsibility for students' learning which, in turn, would be 'likely to be a cause or a consequence of improvements in student performance' (1996: 786). Similarly, the Productive Pedagogies Research was able to establish a link between professional community and teacher responsibility for student learning, and a partial link between this and teachers' pedagogies as mapped against the elements of productive pedagogies.

From this description, it is apparent that the notion of teacher professional community developed by Louis, Marks and Kruse and replicated in the Productive Pedagogies Research is a complex research construct designed for statistical testing of variables and their interrelationships. It provides a good example of how quantitative research on school effects builds its knowledge base, in this case, by being able statistically to establish relationships between professional community (as defined in the model) and teachers' sense of responsibility for student outcomes, with a tentative link being proposed between this and improvements in student performance. This approach assumes that schools are composed of features that can be described, measured, compared and manipulated, and in these terms the research is able to 'prove' that the way in which schools are organised influences student learning (see Gamoran, Secada & Marret 2000). The research was able to use notions of professional community to argue for the importance of sustained professional contact between teachers, and to show that in schools where this occurred, teachers were more likely to take shared responsibility for student learning.

At the same time, it is apparent that this research approach—building and testing a quantitative model of 'school-wide professional community'—cannot illustrate the texture of daily life and experience in schools. As Little (2003) points out, research of this type does not examine 'the specific interactions and dynamics by which professional community constitutes a resource for teacher learning and innovations in teacher practice', nor does it show how classroom practices 'come to be known, shared, and developed among teachers through their out-of-classroom interactions' (2003: 913). Not only are complex issues of culture and identity easily washed out of the picture as part of daily school experience; politics and ideology are also likely to be casualties.

Given that professional communities can support diametrically different 'norms of teaching' (from traditional to innovative) and expectations for students (from high to low), it is important to look beyond whether or not they exist and to examine what they do and what they value. This is particularly important if professional communities are seen as a tool for school reform—as is suggested in the extensive literature on learning communities that developed during the 1990s. This literature is replete with suggestions on how to reconstruct schools in order to move them towards learning communities (Butt 1999), build communities of learners (McCaleb 1994), transform schools into learning communities (Retallick 1999), and meet the challenge (Johnson 1999).

However, as Westheimer (1999: 5) points out, 'the dominance of reform rhetoric around professional community camouflages important distinctions' between such communities. Glossing over substantial differences can result in schools appearing to be similar because they measure up favourably against indicators of professional communities, while in practice they provide very different learning experiences for their students. This is well illustrated by Marneweck's (2002) study of curriculum implementation in a cluster of rural schools in post-apartheid South Africa. Strong teacher professional communities were in evidence—shared norms and values, deprivatised practice, and reflective dialogue around improving students' learning—but what was shared was limited in terms of subject content and pedagogical knowledge, with the result being poor classroom practice. Ironically, the strong sense of professional community masked this from the teachers, who had no doubts about the quality of their work.

In focusing attention on organisational issues, there is always a danger of form replacing substance. We support Lippman's observation (1998: 296) that:

> Reliance on organizational and governance changes, without giving full weight to ideological and political aspects of schools, may lead reformers to substitute the conditions of reform for the goals. Teacher empowerment, shared governance, collaboration, professional development and more time for reflection may become ends in themselves, divorced from the goals of transforming students' educational experiences.

Whether or not the creation of teacher professional communities can actually be used as a reform strategy is called into question by another approach to learning communities, namely the concept of 'communities of practice', developed by Lave and Wenger (1991) and Wenger (1998). Drawing on Vygotskian sociocultural learning theory, these authors propose that learning takes place as people actively participate in the practices of social communities. People construct identities in relation to their communities, in which they make sense of their experiences and give meaning to what they do. In this approach, 'agent, activity and the world mutually constitute each other' (Lave and Wenger 1991: 33). People belong to many communities of practice—fluid and informal groupings in which they learn, informally, all the time. Communities of practice are the places where 'real work' happens, as informal, invisible and everyday practices rest on formal, visible and official practices. Wenger (1998: 6) describes communities of practice at work as follows:

> Workers organize their lives with their immediate colleagues and customers to get their jobs done. In doing so, they develop or preserve a sense of themselves they can live with, have some fun, and fulfill the requirements of their employers and clients. No matter what their official job description may be, they create a practice to do what needs to be done. Although workers may be contractually employed by a large institution, in day-to-day practice they work with—and, in a sense, for—a much smaller set of people and communities.

Students go to school and, as they come together to deal in their own fashion with the agenda of the imposing institution and the unsettling mysteries of youth, communities of practice sprout everywhere—in the classroom as well as on the playground, officially or in the cracks. And in spite of curriculum, discipline, and exhortation, the learning that is most personally transformative turns out to be the learning that involves membership in these communities of practice.

In his early work, Wenger was clear that communities of practice could not be 'legislated into existence'. They could be 'recognized, supported, encouraged and nurtured', but not 'designed', in the sense of being systematically planned. As he noted (Lave & Wenger 1991: 243), 'The challenge is to support rather than displace the knowledgeability of practice'. Further (Lave & Wenger 1991: 229):

> Practice itself is not amenable to design . . . One can design visions, but one cannot design the allegiance necessary to align energies behind those visions. One can design work processes, but not work practices; one can design a curriculum but not learning. One can attempt to institutionalize a community of practice, but the community of practice itself will slip through the cracks and remain distinct from its institutionalization.

It is quite clear that this analytical approach is very different from the quantitative modelling used by Louis and colleagues to investigate school-wide professional communities —though it is compatible with the approach taken by Talbert and McLaughlin (2001), who use the term 'communities of practice'. As originally conceived of by Lave and Wenger, communities of practice cannot be imposed on or designed into existence in schools—though the Productive Pedagogies Research suggests they should be. They are not formal structures but informal contexts of shared work, where people engage with colleagues in day-to-day work practices. Arguably, one of the best ways to encourage and nurture communities of practice for teachers is to provide time for professional exchanges as part of the school day and normal work of teachers, thereby according them value in the symbolic economy of the school. Such practices, of course, have funding implications.

Moreover, it is necessary to recognise that concepts like 'teacher professional communities' and 'schools as learning organisations' have the potential to operate as forms of control. Furthermore, each of the concepts that constitutes these notions is open to contestation over definition. 'Building professional communities' and 'communities of practice' may be used to press for values consensus in ways that are undemocratic and override legitimate differences in teachers' views. They may be used to serve a management agenda without concern for teacher interests. Similarly, it is problematic to assume that schools are 'learning organisations' simply because they are places of institutionalised learning for young people (Hayes et al. 2004; Young 1998). In practice, most schools have a low capacity for problem solving, for learning from their experiences and their environments, and for changing themselves accordingly, which are all features of learning organisations in the broad sense of the term as developed by Argyris and Schon (1978) and Senge (1990). Uncritically using the term may have the effect of masking the work that schools need to do if they are to be places of organisational and individual learning.

We conclude this discussion on teacher professional community with a wry perspective on the nature of 'community' provided by the sociologist Zygmunt Bauman (2001). Bauman suggests that 'community' is a 'feel-good' word that conveys a warm, comfortable and safe place. However, the communities of our dreams bear little resemblance to communities that really exist. Really existing communities are places of dissent and discord rather than comfort and harmony; instead of unity of interest, they hold a variety of different, often competing, interests. They are places of insiders and outsiders, where safety comes at the cost of conformity, and freedom is traded for security. Dreams of community are dreams of 'paradise lost', of 'the kind of world which is not, regrettably, available to us' (2001: 3). This perspective is a good counter to idealised notions of teacher professional learning communities (see Renshaw 2003).

This section has illustrated that different—and sometimes incompatible—assumptions may be embedded in commonly used terms. Conceptual clarity is important in understanding complex notions—in this case, the relationship between school organisation and student learning. A relationship can be shown to exist, but it is not a simple one. In using the concept of learning communities, we have shown that it is important that reforms at an organisational level are not viewed as 'solutions' that become ends in themselves. It is important also to consider, in this case, the norms of teaching they support and the kinds of learning experiences they provide to students, which may be very different. In addition, in focusing on the organisational level, it is important not to lose sight of the broader political, social and economic contexts within which schools operate, and the possibilities and limitations these bring.

In providing a critical reading of the concept of teacher professional communities, our goal has been to show the importance of working both with and against the common discourses of schooling. Discourses indicate the types of statements and claims that can be made about schools; the types of questions that can be asked; the status of subjectivities; and what counts as legitimate knowledge. They function in ways that go beyond reflecting and describing what is, by also constituting possibilities and marking limits of what may be said and done. Discourses of schooling offer points of engagement to work with and against the practices of schooling. In *Leading Learning* (Lingard et al. 2003), we used two processes in deconstructing discourses, dis/solving and disembedding. *Dis/solving* involves working against tendencies to settle the meanings of categories and, instead, continuing to keep them in play. This brings into focus what has slipped from view, such as student experiences and teacher ideologies. Dis/solving involves pursuing tensions and unsettling observations that do not quite fit, and prompts us to ask different sets of questions. *Disembedding* challenges us to pull apart concepts that have blended and blurred in meaning. It helps us to work against idealised notions of schools and teacher communities, and to recognise that schools are not infinitely malleable but are complex institutions that are difficult to change.

We return, then, to what we have identified as the central challenge for teachers, administrators and other educators: how to make sure that schools are places of learning, so that learning is one of the effects of schooling. What contexts matter for teachers and teaching? How might good practice be spread and supported across schools?

Supporting and spreading good practice across the school

Research on school change, from a range of theoretical perspectives, is replete with suggestions for intervention. The approach we have taken in this chapter is to resist defining 'problems' in ways that suggest obvious 'solutions' in an attempt to 'fix' schools. Instead, we have argued, schools are a complex mix of practices that are not easy to disentangle and re-form. Their 'sameness' in outward appearance as world institutions goes together with a uniqueness of experience as specific places. The broader social, political and economic contexts in which individual schools are situated provide their institutional geography in which common patterns of experience and expectations are predictable— though not, we have argued, inevitable. Teese and Polesel (2003: 188) outline the contrasting circumstances of schools as follows:

> Where a school fits within the institutional geography of the school system is a major issue for the morale of teachers, their expectations of students, the kind of support they receive from parents, and the economic inducements they can offer students to work hard. Where favourable conditions are met, staff cohesion and purposive leadership are much more likely to occur. Where, on the other hand, there is a concentration of

disadvantage, the tensions experienced by both teaching staff and students as they grapple with the curriculum may weaken cohesion and shared sense of purpose, depress expectations, and lead to persistent behavioural problems . . . In general, the lower the level of attainment in a school, the lower the level of student motivation and the weaker the rapport between students and teachers.

At an institutional level, disadvantage often translates into high turnover in staff, high numbers of beginning teachers and first-time leaders, high student mobility, and increasing numbers of students with special needs. Schools in poor countries are often inadequately resourced; teachers are not well qualified or properly paid; there are health problems related to poverty that impede learning (including HIV/ AIDS); and communities may not have the will to invest financially or psychologically in schooling. In many parts of the world, schools contend with contexts of violence, geno-cide and armed conflict, and face added challenges in being places of care, safety and psychological containment for staff and students.

Yet within the predictability of broad social patterns both within and between countries, each school makes its own history, shaped by the actions of individuals within it. In working to build schools as places of learning, the insights offered by research and experience have much to contribute, but they do not provide one-size-fits-all solutions, no matter how appealing this may be. What we have argued in this chapter is that discourses of schooling offer not solutions but opportunities to engage with institutional practices in order to foreground the most important work of schools, namely learning. In what follows, we suggest a number of points of engagement to build schools as places of learning: a focus on learning; teacher professional activity; alignment and pro-gram coherence; and leadership.

Focus on learning

The daily lives of schools bring time, space and activities into rhythms of learning, both formal and informal, structured and unstructured. Formal, structured learning is the object of curriculum and pedagogy. Informal, situated learning takes place in the distributed practices of fluid communities. Building habituated practices of learning into the school day is one way of supporting learning; supporting and encouraging the learning of communities around teachers' professional practice is another way.

Maintaining a focus on learning as the central purpose of the organisation is a way of ensuring that its substantive work is attended to. As Christie's (1998, 2001) work in dysfunctional and resilient schools in rural and township schools in South Africa illustrates, maintaining a strong sense of purpose is itself a source of resilience for schools in contexts of hardship, as is having a sense of agency and ability to act even when circumstances appear overwhelming. Our observation is that schools in economically and socially disadvantaged communities are more likely to focus on providing socially supportive environments for students, rather than having high expectations of them in terms of learning outcomes. Yet it is even more important for these particular students that their schools do provide learning of sound intellectual quality; research since Coleman has consistently found that schools make a greater difference to the learning outcomes of these students than they do for more advantaged students. If schools focus on learning as their primary goal, the four dimensions of productive pedagogies provide a good framework for both individual and institutional learning.

Institutional learning happens, as does individual learning, in planned and formal ways, as well as in fluid situated practices. Opportunities to reflect on goals, practice and performance need to be formally structured as part of organisational operation, as do opportunities to build shared understandings, and to develop joint capacity for addressing problems and learning from experience. An organisational culture of learning needs to be fostered as well as structurally built.

Our lived experience in organisations speaks against overly rational approaches in organisational analysis. Schools as organisations are infused with emotions, intrigue and micropolitics, and it is useful to recognise this in analysing the work of schools. Using a psychoanalytic approach, Abraham Zaleznik (1989) draws a distinction between the 'real work' of organisations and the 'psychopolitics' of their unconscious group processes. Working together on joint tasks generates complex emotions for individuals, as they deal with aversions as well as affinities, anxieties as well as containment, and a tussle between cooperation and control. These feelings and energies generated in social interactions need to be channelled into the substantive work of organisations—in the case of schools, into teaching and learning. It is all too easy for organisations to lose their focus, resulting in psychopolitics taking a disproportionate amount of energy in complex organisations and uncertain times; too much emphasis on keeping relationships smooth, avoiding conflict and 'greasing the wheels of human interaction' (Zaleznik 1989: 160) may take necessary energy away from the substantive task of the organisation. Zaleznik's position is that complex emotions should not be suppressed but channelled —which may be difficult but rewarding: 'aggressive energy channelled into real work is the one sure route to a sense of mastery, to the pleasure that comes from using one's talents to accomplish things' (1989: 61). This perspective is useful in bringing into view the unconscious and non-rational dimensions of organisational work, which remind us that achieving a focus on learning is not a simple and straightforward task for schools.

Teacher professional activity

A focus on learning is not sufficient in itself if teachers do not have the necessary knowledge and skill in terms of both subject content and pedagogical repertoire. Ensuring that teachers have the necessary threshold knowledges, skills and dispositions is an important basis for teacher professional activity. Opportunities for professional development are a key aspect of teacher capacity building and, according to the

Productive Pedagogies Research, both internal and external professional development bring significant effects for schools. As McLaughlin's (1987) influential analysis of implementation points out, both capacity and will are needed for teachers to change classroom practices, and change generally requires a strategic balance of pressure and support. This is not to suggest a behaviourist approach to teacher development—rather to point to the importance of professional engagement with teachers for the improvement of classroom practice. We concur with Elmore, Peterson and McCarthey (1996: 149), who note:

> Changing practice is primarily a problem of teacher learning, not a problem of organization ... School structures can provide opportunities for the learning of new teaching practices and new strategies for student learning, but structures, by themselves, do not cause learning to occur ... School structure follows from good practice but not vice versa.

Given the competing demands on teachers' time, it is all too easy for collective reflection to be squeezed out of the day or reduced to a minimum. Providing opportunities for professional dialogue and substantive work with other teachers during the school day is a way of valuing teacher professional engagement with each other, both structurally and symbolically. Building a shared understanding and common language around learning and student achievement entails sustained and substantive professional conversations, which take time. Providing opportunities and expectations for teachers to work with each other across the space and time divides of conventional classroom practice acknowledges the structural and cultural challenges of spreading good practice from isolated pockets of individual classrooms across the school.

Providing opportunities for formal learning for teachers and for informal interactions of situated learning does not, in itself, guarantee that learning takes place, or that teacher professional communities will spring up. In this sense, high expectations of teachers and a sense of shared responsibility for students' learning need to be part of the professional capacity built at school level. While the notion of teacher professional communities, particularly its use as a reform tool, needs to be treated with care, the elements suggested by Louis and colleagues do have value, as does the insight of Talbert and McLaughlin on shared norms for teaching and expectations of students' work. Building the structural and cultural conditions for shared norms and values and for deprivatisation of practice are likely to support teacher professionalism. Pressure in the form of accountability for outcomes needs to accompany support.

That said, we are mindful of power relations in organisations, and recognise that teacher communities with shared norms may operate as forms of control, which stifle significant and legitimate points of disagreement among teachers. We are mindful of the need not to wash power and ideology out of organisational analysis, and this is true for teacher professional activity and capacity building.

Hargreaves's (2003: 165) observation about contrived collegiality is worth quoting in detail:

> Collaborative cultures can also create problems when they are hijacked by hierarchical systems of control . . . Contrived collegiality is collaboration imposed from above about what to plan or learn, with whom to plan or learn it, and where and when to undertake the planning and learning. Contrived collegiality is more than a scaffold of structures and expectations that promotes and supports collaboration. It is a prison of micromanagement that constrains it.

Hargreaves goes on to point out that these forms of control may actually undermine opportunities for teachers to take 'bottom-up' professional initiatives. While being cognisant of the dangers of micromanagement and overcontrol, it remains a challenge to work against privatised practice, to harness professional expertise in joint tasks, and to align the work of teachers around a common focus on learning.

Alignment and program coherence

Hayes (2004) suggests that one of the ways to support and spread learning across schools is to focus school organisation around learning, and to work continuously towards a common focus for practitioners at various sites in schooling where teaching takes place. These include classrooms, but they also include other sites where teachers work professionally with each other: teaching teams; department groups; the school executive and formal leadership; the practices of district and systemic support teams beyond the school. Each of these constitutes what Hayes has termed 'sites of pedagogical practice'. Building coherence across these different sites, or 'bringing alignment to scale', is a way of developing shared understandings of teaching and learning as core activities within the school. Just as students' classroom learning is the primary site of teachers' pedagogical practice, so teachers' learning may be viewed as the site of pedagogical practice for department heads and teacher leaders. In the same way, the professional learning of department heads and teacher leaders is conceptualised as the pedagogical practice of senior executive; and the professional learning of senior executive is conceptualised as the pedagogical practice of principals.

This approach also casts district and system personnel beyond the school in pedagogical roles, and challenges them to conceptualise their work with schools as primarily pedagogical in nature. In contrast to the tendency of systems to put downward pressure on schools, this approach provides a mechanism by which students' learning needs can be translated up through systems. Hence, it focuses district and system personnel on their pedagogical practices; at the district level these practices are related to the learning needs of those working in schools, while at the system level these practices are related to the learning needs of those working in districts. This is a point we return to later.

Leadership

In addressing leadership as a means for supporting learning in schools, it is useful to distinguish briefly between leadership, management and headship as three interrelated concepts. Leadership is the exercise of influence over others towards achieving goals; as such, it can take place outside as well as inside organisations, and can be exercised throughout organisations, at most levels and in most activities. Management is primarily concerned with structures and processes by which organisations meet their goals and purposes; it tends to happen inside rather than outside organisations and is often tied to formal positions. Headship (or principalship) is a structural position, carrying with it responsibilities and accountabilities. Ideally, schools should be replete with leadership spread throughout the organisation; they should be well managed in unobtrusive ways that support their central purposes and the substantive work of teachers and students; principals should integrate leadership and management functions and possess skills in both; they should disperse leadership as much as possible, and delegate management appropriately with adequate support and accountability. Such idealisations of school leadership and management are—like the communities of our dreams—rarely found in practice.

Discourses of leadership commonly emphasise individuals rather than social relations, and idealise leaders in heroic, often masculinist terms. Discourses of schooling tend to conflate the positional power of the principal with leadership and management, thereby reinforcing hierarchical structural relations and the centrality of the person as leader. Where leadership is portrayed as transformational, inspirational and visionary, leaders are elevated above the communities they are part of which, by implication, lack or need these attributes. In this book, we resist the power of these discourses. While recognising the importance of individual leaders, including principals, and the importance of goals and ideals in leadership, we argue that it is possible to lead from the centre rather than the top, and to stretch and disperse leadership across people and functions. Like Lambert, we believe that 'leadership needs to be embedded in the school community as a whole [because] leadership is about learning together, and constructing meaning and knowledge collectively and collaboratively' (2000: 3). We also recognise that leadership entails power and ethics, and that it may not always be 'good', positive or effective—all notions that slip easily from view in dominant discourses.

In *Leading Learning*, we set out the normative notion of 'productive leadership', suggesting that good leadership from the position of the principal requires 'habits of reflexive self-monitoring' (Brubacker 1993: 214), a moral preparedness 'to do the right thing and cause the right change' (Said 1994: 75), and the capacity to deal with the wholeness of the school. This dispositional approach (using Bourdieu's concept of habitus) is somewhat different from approaches that foreground activities in leading learning. For example, reflecting on instructional leadership in schools, Southworth (2002: 87) supports the need for school leadership to have 'high levels of knowledge and understanding of curricula, pedagogy, student and adult learning'. In the schools he studied, heads used modelling, monitoring and professional dialogue, including classroom visits and discussions, as strategies to improve the quality of teaching and learning. In our somewhat different but complementary approach, we would support the dispersal of these sorts of leadership activities across the different pedagogical sites of practice in the school.

Decentring the prominence of the individual principal as leader does not mean that there is no need for leadership from the position of the principal. Indeed, as Louis, Kruse and Marks (1996) point out, the principal is in the best position to deal with conflict and to negotiate structural changes to support learning. Working with others on vision building, creating networks, negotiating boundaries, aligning tasks and ensuring that accountabilities are addressed remains the responsibility of the principal, together with ongoing organisational and management work to support teaching and learning. While leadership may be spread, it remains the case that a lot of leadership activity is needed for schools to thrive. The same is true for management.

A key issue in current debates on educational leadership is the extent to which school-based management, particularly in large secondary schools, draws leadership away from pedagogical concerns to the many tasks of management—marketing, budgeting, reporting, human resource management and so on. There is every indication, we believe, that this is the case, and that management tasks may absorb energy without adding to the improvement of learning. This is not an inevitable consequence of school-based management, but it is one that needs to be recognised and resisted. In the face of complex competing demands on the time of the principal, we have no doubt that it is all the more important to foreground learning as the central focus of the school and to disperse leadership so that learning becomes the responsibility of as many people as possible.

Current trends in school reform and restructuring have highlighted changes in the relationship of schools to external constituencies—the state; parents and communities; businesses and other organisations. Not only are schools more evidently accountable to external constituencies and located in market relationships; it is also the case that they need to network across their boundaries to access knowledge, people and material resources. Leadership faces the challenge of positioning schools locally within the framework of state policies and establishing collaborative relationships with their local communities. An important task is to filter competing and often contradictory demands from outside the school, and to work towards coherence in the school's relationship to its community as well as central education departments. This entails developing more permeable boundaries and establishing external relationships, while keeping learning as a central focus.

Dispersal of leadership, finding different ways of working and developing permeable boundaries do not reduce the accountability of leadership for achieving the goals of the school. No matter what strategies, structures and cultures are developed, those with designated responsibility in an organisation are accountable for its operations and outcomes. Structures and processes of accountability need to be established for schools and school leadership, and, we would suggest, these need to foreground learning.

Systemic supports

It now remains to map back from schools and their organisational forms to the systems of which they are part, and to engage with systemic logics of practice around their central mandated task—supporting schools in providing socially just and structured learning opportunities for young people. In what ways might education systems enhance opportunities for learning, and support schools and teachers in their work to improve learning experiences and outcomes for *all* students?

The Productive Pedagogies Research (QSRLS 2001: 144–151) presented Education Queensland with a picture of itself as a system lacking alignment, and proposed three focal points around which it might coordinate policy, practice and funding:

1. It suggested a *focus on pedagogy and assessment* as a key nodal point for innovative change, school renewal and curriculum reform. Shifting the concerns of the system from a neoliberal emphasis on performance and accountability to the core business of teaching and learning would provide a basis on which to engage with more fine-grained specifications about pedagogical change.

2. It suggested the *development of school leadership* focused on pedagogical leadership, 'whereby restructuring, change agency, management of emotional economies, creating a demanding culture of care, and use of hot knowledge is focused on the core business of schools: productive pedagogies and productive outcomes'. This emphasis would counter the emergence of a managerially focused leadership 'focusing on restructuring, on micro-management, on systems development and implementation, even on outward management of school/community relationships' while neglecting pedagogy.

3. Finally came *investment in teachers*, including the development of teacher professional learning communities

with a focus on aligning pedagogy, curriculum and assessment. With regard to this, the Productive Pedagogies Research advocated both out-of-school and in-school professional development, linked to school professional learning communities and focused on issues related to pedagogy and assessment, as well as on teachers' threshold knowledges in specific fields, including curriculum knowledge ('their operational concepts, assumptions, histories and procedures').

The Productive Pedagogies Research argued strongly against a 'compliance model of teacher reform' (Darling-Hammond 2000)—high-stakes testing and monitoring, heavy use of commodified curriculum, and standardisation of teaching approaches. Instead, it advocated a concentration on professionalism (QSRLS 2001: 149):

> In terms of professional development, there is evidence here that the investment in teachers' social capital and their intellectual capital is both necessary and, where targeted effectively in combination with particular enabling approaches to school leadership, sufficient for improved pedagogy and outcomes. The good news is that many positive achievements are possible with the appropriate levels of school and systemic support and targeting for teacher professional development.

We support these suggested foci for systems to support schools and align their policies, practices and funding and, in line with the approach developed so far, we suggest that these be approached as nodal points for active engagement rather than as 'solutions' to the 'problems' identified.

Education systems tend to be complex and multilayered, and the types of misalignments identified by the Productive Pedagogies Research are common: the operation of 'silos' in schools as well as district and central offices; different goals and priorities in different parts of the system; lack of coherence in timelines, philosophies and advocated practices between different branches; and lack of alignment between systemic agendas and the priorities of schools. No single set of interests drives education systems: there are multiple providers and stakeholder groups; there are multiple expectations of schooling systems, multiple mandates, and multiple accountabilities to be addressed. Funding is a mix of public and private; and treasury allocations are politically driven. Even where systems have strategic visions and specific performance goals, these may not be adequate to guide schools on a day-to-day basis.

Moreover, bureaucracies have their own organisational logics, and these of necessity mediate relationships with schools. Since the 1990s, 'new public management' in Australia and elsewhere has resulted in what Limerick, Cunnington and Crowther (1998) term 'neo-corporate bureaucracies'—hybrid organisations, which hold on to hierarchy while simultaneously moving to decentralise and achieve efficiencies. Current bureaucracies tend to be headed by managers rather than expert professionals, and their organisational cultures and practices are increasingly managerial rather than collegial (see Yeatman 1990, 1993). According to Limerick and colleagues, neocorporate bureaucracies have 'delayered' by cutting middle management, with the result that the work of professional knowledge workers in the middle has intensified. While apparently decentralising decision making, they have proliferated systems and reporting procedures, including performance indices and performance management at the operational level, so that there is little room for discretionary action. Under these conditions, attention turns inwards to a preoccupation with procedures and reports at the expense of service delivery, and decision avoidance is common practice. The overall result, according to these authors, is a highly politicised system and culture, with little space for professional identity. If this analysis is correct in relation to the bureaucratic systems responsible for schooling, it is unlikely that a simple call for alignment could bring coherence of support for schools.

In addition, the closer systems concerns come to political agendas, the less likely they are to connect to the day-to-day imperatives of schooling. Political cycles are short, certainly much shorter than the cycles of educational change; and they are more likely to be preoccupied with the logics of 'observables', 'deliverables' and 'vote winning' than with the logics of supporting student learning. As with other discourses of schooling, discourses at systemic level are a complex mix of practices. Bringing coherence and alignment within the system requires active engagement, rather than hopeful expectation.

In endorsing the focal points for systemic policies identified by the Productive Pedagogies Research—pedagogy, leadership and professionalism—we suggest a number of perspectives to guide engagement. These are: building a systemic focus on learning; working with a mix of centralisation and decentralisation to engage local initiatives with broader policy frames; providing the highest possible levels of resources for the work of schools within a redistributive framework; and engaging in robust public debate about schooling and its purposes.

First, in building a systemic focus on learning, it is useful to recognise how difficult it is for the hierarchy of education systems to engage with their smallest unit—teaching and learning in classrooms. Decades of research on education reform and the implementation of change reiterate that the core of educational practice is not easily changed: teachers' understanding of curriculum and the nature of knowledge; how students learn and what may be expected of them; and effective pedagogy and assessment. Changes to the norms of teaching, including teachers' expectations of students, cannot be mandated centrally by education systems; they are significantly mediated by context, as well as by the values and beliefs of individuals through the system. Building a shared vision for learning involves engaging the many layers of the system. Here, Elmore's (1979/80) backward-mapping approach is a useful heuristic; given that changes to the core are related to teacher capacity and will, this needs to be addressed from context to context by combinations of pressure and support; by incentives coupled with expectations; by opportunities for learning and accountability for outcomes; and by changes to norms and expectations backed up through the system. Additionally, the heuristic of viewing district- and system-level work in terms of pedagogical sites of practice offers a means for focusing the system on learning as a first principle.

Second, for the system to support classroom practices that improve student learning, we suggest that it is important to stimulate local initiative within broad policy guidelines. A strategic combination of centralisation and decentralisation enables local initiatives and agency to be explored within systemic frames of accountability. Here, it is important to avoid forms of devolution that intensify control through overstipulating operational procedures and inhibit expressions of difference while appearing to encourage them. Allowing local concerns to be articulated and building shared visions with local communities and teachers enables schools to move away from standardised 'one-size-fits-all' approaches. Rather than seeking to replicate good practice through imitation, regardless of context, we suggest that local variation is more likely to meet local conditions and harness local agency. With systemic support of this nature, school-based management offers opportunities for pedagogical leadership, rather than simple micromanagement. Providing frameworks that enable local agency while building accountability is one way in which systemic policy may support the work of schools.

A third perspective entails providing resources for the work of schools. Given the disparity of resources between schools in terms of the communities they serve, it makes sense to acknowledge the correlation between socioeconomic status and achievement. As the statement from Bourdieu at the start of this chapter indicates, to provide equal treatment to students in unequal circumstances is in fact a way of sanctioning initial inequalities. In terms of first principles of equity, we support the point made by Teese and Polesel: 'The total resources available to a child at school should be relative to the educational effort which must be made on behalf of the child. Where more teaching is needed more resources should be provided' (2003: 218). How these equity principles are given expression in specific funding models and institutional practices may well be a point around which local initiatives and agency are harnessed.

Fourth, in times of neoliberal performativity it is important to stimulate robust public debate about the forms and purposes of schooling, as well as of education more broadly. Concerns with effectiveness and efficiency, performance indicators and publication of results are easily amenable to minimalist definitions and quantitative measures of success and failure. Education systems are called to account by political pressure and public concern, and it is all too easy in current times for performance and accountability to be defined in terms of basic skills, high-stakes testing and standardised approaches to monitoring teaching. Our concern is not to oppose accountability, effectiveness and efficiency—rather to enrich the terms in which they are defined, in ways that reflect the deeper educational and moral purposes of schooling (Rose 1995). While the logic of schooling calls for attention to be focused inwards, the broader goals of education and equity call for attention to focus outwards as well, in terms of social engagement with an enriched debate about the possibilities and limitations of schooling. Indeed, we would argue for a robust definition of educational accountability, which would include vertical accountability upwards and downwards within educational systems, as well as horizontal accountabilities within schools and with their communities. We would also suggest the significance of temporal accountability, given the significance of schooling to the creation of the imagined community which is the nation. Reconciliation with Indigenous Australians is one pressing temporal accountability for Australian schools. So too is the production of global citizens committed to humanistic values on a global as well as local scale.

Conclusion

Schools and the classrooms by which they are constituted signify wealth differentials through their resource patterns, principles through their organisational processes, power through their curriculum, values through their assessment procedures, and beliefs through their pedagogical forms. Perhaps more than hospitals, armies and other institutions, they tell us how societies understand and reproduce themselves. As such, they can simultaneously nurture learning and understanding while ruthlessly stratifying and dividing. They can operate as the communities of our dreams while being the instruments of our fears. They are saturated with meaning and yet sometimes seemingly lack any soul. In this book we have attempted to stay open to the multiple effects of schooling, while maintaining an unashamed belief in the hope made possible through curriculum, assessment and pedagogies of a particular kind.

In this final chapter we have located our interest in teaching and learning in classrooms within the contexts of schools. Just as we argued in earlier chapters that teachers matter, here we have argued that so do schools. Individual schools and teachers may mediate the predictability of social reproduction and interrupt broader social patterns of inequality, but they cannot re-form them. Indeed, the interplay between the micro-contexts of schools and the macro-contexts within which they are located predictably produces both sameness and difference. Differently textured experiences mark the individuality of each school, at the same time as the warp and weft of these experiences are stretched across a largely consistent frame. Given the predictability of the institutional geography of schools— the well-recognised correlation of academic achievement with material and symbolic advantage—what is remarkable is the extent to which this goes unchallenged. This situation is an instance of what Bourdieu (2001: 1) terms the 'paradox of doxa':

> . . . that the established order, with its relations of domination, its rights and prerogatives, privileges and injustices, ultimately perpetuates itself so easily, apart from a few historical accidents, and that the most intolerable conditions of existence can so often be perceived as acceptable and even natural.

The known and savage inequalities of schooling—in terms of differing resources, experiences and outcomes—are a good example of the 'paradox of doxa' and the way we accord respect to the order of things as we find them. Inequalities are normalised in discourses of schooling in a number of ways: they are naturalised so that their social construction slips from view; they are individualised so that their social patterns are not acknowledged; their meanings are settled so that change seems impossible; alternatives are so idealised in utopian visions that what is achievable becomes devalued. Speaking against the normalisation of inequalities is an ethical and political move with which we engage as we work with and against these discourses to address what we have identified as the central challenge for teachers, administrators and other educators: how to make sure that schools are places of learning, so that learning is one of the effects of schooling.

Our intention was to take up the challenge to speak to teachers about their work, while also speaking to a broader audience of principals, parents, policy makers, social democratic politicians and others about how to provide equitable and just schooling for all. The detailed descriptions of productive performance, assessment and pedagogy in earlier chapters were designed to identify important elements of these practices, while also providing some suggestions about how to achieve these in classrooms. The Productive Pedagogies Research has provided a unique and rare insight into some teachers' classrooms that we hope will inform and enrich other teachers' practices. For policy makers too, the scale and findings of this large study provide a source for reflection on how best to support teachers and schools to improve students' learning.

Underpinning our efforts has been a desire to support professional dialogue about classroom practices and their effects. Despite our familiarity with schools and classrooms, having spent large chunks of our lives in such places, we are generally not good at talking about what goes on there. Exacerbating this problem is a lack of time for sustained dialogue in schools among teachers. Simply put, time to talk about the frameworks described in this book is likely to influence practice, whereas isolated classroom practice is likely to perpetuate the inequities that are long-standing and well documented in schooling. Such time needs to be resourced to allow teachers professional space away from the 'gritty materialities' of their classrooms.

Throughout, we have stressed our concern to contribute to more equitable, improved outcomes for all students. This is based on the belief that the quality of teaching and learning experienced by students is a critically important social justice issue for schools today, and one that must be addressed at all levels of schools and society. Our focus has been to examine the three message systems of schooling through an analysis of numerous pieces of student work, assessment tasks and classroom observations in diverse school settings. While we acknowledge that teachers and schools alone cannot bridge the gap between what students bring to school and what we desire for them, we should not lose sight of the fact that they *do* matter and they *can* make a difference.

Bibliography

Acker, S. 1999, *The Realities of Teachers' Work*, Cassell, London.

Anderson, B. 1983, *Imagined Communities*, Verso, London.

Anderson, R.C. 1994, 'Role of the reader's schema in comprehension, learning and memory', in *Theoretical Models and Processes of Reading*, 4th edn, R. Ruddell, M.R. Ruddell & H. Singer (eds), International Reading Association, Newark, NJ, pp. 469–82.

Anyon, J. 1981, 'School knowledge and social class', *Curriculum Inquiry*, vol. 11, no. 1, pp. 3–42.

Anyon, J. 1995, 'Race, social class, and educational reform in an inner-city school', *Teachers College Record*, vol. 97, no. 1, pp. 69–94.

Appadurai, A. 1996, *Modernity at Large: Cultural Dimensions of Globalization*, University of Minnesota Press, Minneapolis, MN.

Apple, M. 1990, *Ideology and Curriculum*, 2nd edn, Routledge, New York.

Apple, M. 1996, *Cultural Politics and Education*, Open University Press, Buckingham, UK.

Apple, M. 2000a, 'Can critical pedagogies interrupt rightist policies?', *Educational Theory*, vol. 50, no. 2, pp. 229–54.

Apple, M. 2000b, 'The shock of the real: critical pedagogies and rightist reconstructions', in *Revolutionary Pedagogies Cultural Politics, Instituting Education, and the Discourse of Theory*, P. Trifonas (ed.), RoutledgeFalmer, New York, pp. 225–50.

Apple, M. 2001, *Educating the 'Right' Way: Markets, Standards, God, and Inequality*, RoutledgeFalmer, New York.

Apple, M. & Beane, J. 1999, *Democratic Schools: Lessons from the Chalk Face*, Open University Press, Buckingham, UK.

Archibald, D. & Newmann, F. 1988, *Beyond Standardized Tests: Assessing Authentic Academic Achievement in the Secondary School*, National Association of Secondary School Principals, Reston, VA.

Argyris, C. & Schon, D. 1978, *Organizational Learning: A Theory of Action Perspective*, Addison-Wesley, Reading, MA.

Arnot, M. 2002, 'Making the difference to sociology of education: reflections on family—school and gender relations', *Discourse: Studies in the Cultural Politics of Education*, vol. 23, no. 3, pp. 347–55.

Arnot, M. & Dillabough, J. (eds) 2000, *Challenging Democracy: International Perspectives on Gender, Education and Citizenship*, RoutledgeFalmer, London.

Ashman, A. & Conway, R. 1993, *Using Cognitive Methods in the Classroom*, Routledge, London.

Ashman, A. & Conway, R. 1997, *An Introduction to Cognitive Education: Theory and Applications*, Routledge, London.

Augé, M. 1995, *Non-Places: Introduction to an Anthropology of Supermodernity* (trans. John Howe), Verso, London.

Baker, C.D. 1997, 'Literacy practices and classroom order', in *Constructing Critical Literacies*, S. Muspratt, A. Luke & P. Freebody (eds), Allen & Unwin, Sydney, pp. 243–62.

Baker, C.D. & Freebody, P. 1989, *Children's First Schoolbooks*, Blackwells, Oxford.

Ball, S.J. 1994, *Education Reform: A Critical and Post-Structural Approach*, Open University Press, Buckingham, UK.

Ball, S. 1997a, 'Policy sociology and critical social research: a personal review of recent education policy and policy research', *British Educational Research Journal*, vol. 23, no. 1, pp. 257–74.

Ball, S.J. 1997b, 'Good school/bad school: paradox and fabrication', *British Journal of Sociology of Education*, vol. 18, no. 3, pp. 317–37.

Ball, S.J. 1999, 'Global trends in educational reform and struggle for the soul of the teacher', Paper presented at BERA, 2–5 September, University of Sussex.

Ball, S. 2004, 'Performativities and fabrications in the education economy: towards the performative society', in *The RoutledgeFalmer Reader in Sociology of Education*, S.J. Ball (ed.), RoutledgeFalmer, London, pp. 143–55.

Barnes, M., Clarke, D. & Stephens, M. 2000, 'Assessment the engine of systemic curricular reform?', *Journal of Curriculum Studies*, vol. 32, no. 5, pp. 623–50.

Baron, S., Field, J. & Schuller, T. (eds) 2000, *Social Capital: Critical Perspectives*, Oxford University Press, Oxford.

Bauman, Z. 2001, *Community: Seeking Safety in an Insecure World*, Polity Press, Cambridge.

Benhabib, S. 2002, *The Claims of Culture Equality and Diversity in the Global Era*, Princeton University Press, Princeton.

Berlak, A. & Berlak, H. 1981, *Dilemmas of Schooling*, Methuen, London.

Bernstein, B. 1971a, 'On the classification and framing of educational knowledge', in *Knowledge and Control: New Directions for the Sociology of Education*, M.F.D. Young (ed.), Collier-Macmillan, London.

Bernstein, B. 1971b, *Class, Codes and Control: Theoretical Studies Towards a Sociology of Language*, Vol. 1, Routledge & Kegan Paul, London.

Bernstein, B. 1973, *Class, Codes and Control*, Routledge & Kegan Paul, London.

Bernstein, B. 1996, *Pedagogy, Symbolic Control and Identity: Theory, Research, Critique*, Taylor and Francis, London.

Bernstein, B. 2001, 'From pedagogies to knowledge', in *Towards a Sociology of Pedagogy: The Contribution of Basil Bernstein to Research*, A. Morais, I. Neves, B. Davies & H. Daniels (eds), Peter Lang, New York, pp. 363–8.

Black, P. 2001, 'Dreams, strategies and systems: portraits of assessment past, present and future', *Assessment in Education*, vol. 8, no. 1, pp. 65–87.

Black, P. & Wiliam, D. 1998, 'Inside the black box', in *Phi Delta Kappan*, vol. 80, no. 2, p. 139–48.

Blasé J. (ed.) 1991, *The Politics of Life in Schools: Power, Conflict and Cooperation*, Sage, London.

Boaler, J. 1997, *Experiencing School Mathematics: Teaching Styles, Sex and Setting*, Open University Press, Buckingham, UK.

Boaler, J. 2002, *Experiencing School Mathematics: Traditional and Reform Approaches to Teaching and Their Impact on Student Learning*, Lawrence Erlbaum, Mahwah, NJ.

Bourdieu, P. 1973, 'Cultural reproduction and social reproduction', in *Knowledge, Education and Cultural Change*, R. Brown (ed.), Tavistock, London, pp. 71–112.

Bourdieu, P. 1976, 'The school as a conservative force: scholastic and cultural inequalities', in *Schooling and Capitalism: A Sociological Reader*, R. Dale, G. Esland & M. MacDonald (eds), Routledge & Kegan Paul, London.

Bourdieu, P. 1984, *Distinction: A Social Critique of the Judgement of Taste* (trans. Richard Nice), Harvard University Press, Cambridge, MA.

Bourdieu, P. 1986, 'The forms of capital', in *Handbook of Theory and Research for the Sociology of Education*, J. Richardson (ed.), Greenwood, Westport, CT, pp. 241–58.

Bourdieu, P. 1990, 'Principles for reflecting on the curriculum', *Curriculum Journal*, vol. 1, no. 3, pp. 307–14.

Bourdieu, P. 1994, *In Other Words: Essays Towards a Reflexive Sociology*, Stanford University Press, Stanford, CA.

Bourdieu, P. 2001, *Masculine Domination*, Stanford University Press, Stanford, CA.

Bourdieu, P. & Passeron, J.C. 1977, *Reproduction in Education, Society and Culture*, Sage, London.

Bowles, S. & Gintis, H. 1976, *Schooling in Capitalist America*, Basic Books, New York.

Broadfoot, P. 1996, *Education, Assessment and Society: A Sociological Analysis*, Open University Press, Buckingham, UK.

Brown, P. & Lauder, H. 2000, 'Human capital, social capital, and collective intelligence', in *Social Capital: Critical Perspectives*, S. Baron, J. Field & T. Schuller (eds), Oxford University Press, Oxford, pp. 226–42.

Brown, P., Halsey, A.H., Lauder, H. & Wells, A.S. (1997), 'The transformation of education and society: an introduction', in *Education Culture Economy Society*, A.H. Halsey, H. Lauder, P. Brown & A.S. Wells (eds), Oxford University Press, Oxford, pp. 1–44.

Brubaker, R. 1993, 'Social theory as habitus', in *Bourdieu: Critical Perspectives*, C. Calhoun, E. LiPuma & M. Postone (eds), University of Chicago Press, Chicago.

Bruss, N. & Macedo, D. 1985, 'Towards a pedagogy of the question: conversations with Paulo Freire', *Journal of Education*, vol. 167, no. 2, pp. 7–21.

Butt, R. 1999, 'Towards the learning community: working through the barriers between teacher development and evaluation', in *Learning Communities in Education*, J. Retallick, B. Cocklin & K. Coombe (eds), Routledge, London.

Caldwell, B. 1998, *Linking School Reform to Improved Outcomes for Students: Evidence from Australia*, University of Melbourne, Melbourne.

Castells, M. 1997, *The Power of Identity*, Blackwell, Oxford.

Castells, M. 2000, *The Rise of the Network Society* (2nd edn), Blackwell, Oxford.

Castells, M. 2001, 'The new global economy', in *Challenges of Globalisation: South African Debates with Manuel Castells*, J. Muller, N. Cloete & S. Badat (eds), Maskew Miller Longman, Cape Town, pp. 2–21.

Cazden, C.B. 1992, *Whole Language Plus*, Teachers College Press, New York.

Cazden, C. 1988, *Classroom Discourse: The Language of Teaching and Learning*, Heinemann Educational Books, Portsmouth.

Chappell, C. 2003, 'Changing pedagogy: the changing context', *Working Paper 0313 RP128*, The Australian Centre for Organisational, Vocational and Adult Learning, >http://138.25.185.150/lasso/lassosites/oval/project_detail.lasso?-token.id=33319< [20 June 2004].

Chilisa B. 2000, 'Towards equity and assessment: crafting gender-fair assessment', *Assessment in Education: Principles, Policy, and Practice*, vol. 7, no. 1, pp. 61–81.

Christie, M.J. 1985, *Aboriginal Perspectives on Experiences and Learning: The Role of Language in Aboriginal Education*, Deakin University Press, Geelong.

Christie, P. 1998, 'Schools as (dis)organisations: the "breakdown of the culture of learning and teaching" in South African schools', *Cambridge Journal of Education*, vol. 28, no. 3, pp. 283–300.

Christie, P. 2001, 'Improving school quality in South Africa: a study of schools that have succeeded against the odds', *Journal of Education*, no. 26, pp. 40–65.

Cole, M. 1996, *Cultural Psychology: A Once and Future Discipline*, Cambridge University Press, Cambridge.

Coleman, J., Campbell, B., Hobson, C., McPartland, J., Mood, A., Winefeld, F. & York, R. 1966, *Equality of Educational Opportunity Report*, US Government Printing Office, Washington, DC.

Connell, R.W. 1985, *Teachers' Work*, Allen & Unwin, Sydney.

Connell, R.W. 1993, *Schools and Social Justice*, Temple University Press, Philadelphia, PA.

Connell, R.W. 2002, 'Making the difference, then and now',

Discourse: Studies in the Cultural Politics of Education, vol. 23, no. 3, pp. 319–27.

Connell, R.W., Ashenden, D., Dowsett, G. & Kessler, S. 1982, *Making the Difference: Schools, Family and Social Division*, Allen & Unwin, Sydney.

Connell, R., White, V. & Johnston, K. 1991, *'Running Twice as Hard': The Disadvantaged Schools Program in Australia*, Deakin University, Geelong, VIC.

Cope, B. & Kalantzis, M. (eds) 1995, *The Power of Literacy*, Falmer Press, London.

Cormack, P., Johnson, B., Peters, J. & Williams, D. 1998, *Authentic Assessment: A Report on Classroom Research and Practice in the Middle Years*, ACSA, Deakin, VIC.

Creemers, B.P.M. 1994, *The Effective Classroom*, Cassell, London.

Crowther, F., Kaagan, S., Ferguson, M., Hann, L. & Hargreaves, A. 2002, *Developing Teacher Leaders: How Teacher Leadership Enhances School Success*, Corwin Press, Thousand Oaks, CA.

Cumming, J. & Maxwell, G. 1999, 'Contextualising authentic assessment', *Assessment in Education*, vol. 6, no. 2, pp. 177–94.

Cummins, J. & Sayers, D. 1995, *Brave New Schools Challenging Cultural Illiteracy through Global Learning Networks*, St Martin's Press, New York.

Cushman, K. 1990, 'Performance and exhibitions: the demonstration of mastery', *Horace*, vol. 6, no. 3, March, <http://www.essentialschools.org/cs/resources/view/ces_ res/138> [24 June 2004].

Daniels, H. 2001, *Vygotsky and Pedagogy*, RoutledgeFalmer, London.

Darder, A., Baltodano, M. & Torrres, R.D. (eds) 2003, *The Critical Pedagogy Reader*, RoutledgeFalmer, New York.

Darling-Hammond, L. 1997, *The Right to Learn: A Blueprint for Creating Schools that Work*, Jossey-Bass, San Francisco, CA.

Darling-Hammond, L. 2000, 'Teacher quality and student achievement: a review of state policy evidence', in *Education Policy Archives*, vol. 8, no. 1, pp. 1–45.

Davies, B. 1993, *Shards of Glass*, Allen & Unwin, Sydney.

Delgado-Gaitan, C. 1995, *Protean Literacy*, Falmer Press, London.

Delors, J. 1996, 'Education: the necessary utopia', in *Learning: The Treasure Within*, Report to UNESCO of the International Commission on Education for the Twenty-First Century, UNESCO Publishing, Paris.

Delpit, L. 1995, *Other People's Children: Cultural Conflict in the Classroom*, New Press, New York.

Department of Education (State of Queensland) 2001, *New Basics: Theory into Practice*, AccessEd, Education Queensland, Brisbane.

Department of Education and the Arts 2004, *The New Basics Research Report*, Queensland Government, Brisbane.

Dewey, J. 1916, *Democracy and Education: An Introduction to the Philosophy of Education*, Macmillan, New York.

Dimitriades, G. & McCarthy, C. 2001, *Reading and Teaching the Postcolonial: From Baldwin to Basquiat and Beyond*, Teachers College Press, New York.

Edmonds, R. 1979, 'Effective schools for the urban poor', *Educational Leadership*, vol. 37, pp. 15–27.

Education Queensland 2000, *New Basics: Curriculum Organisers*, The State of Queensland (Department of Education), Brisbane.

Education Queensland 2004, *The Rich Tasks Suite Three: Years 7–9*, <http://education.qld.gov.au/corporate/newbasics/ html/rich-tasks/year9/year9.html> [4 July 2004].

Edwards, R. & Usher, R. 2000, *Globalisation and Pedagogy Space Place and Identity*, Routledge, London.

Eisner, E.W. 1998, *The Kind of Schools We Want*, Heinemann, Portsmouth, NH.

Ellsworth, E. 1989, 'Why doesn't this feel empowering? Working through the repressive myths of critical pedagogy', *Harvard Educational Review*, vol. 59, no. 3, pp. 297–324.

Elmore, R.F. 1979/80, 'Backward mapping: implementation research and policy decisions', *Political Science Quarterly*, vol. 94, no. 4, pp. 601–15.

Elmore, R.F., Peterson, P.L. & McCarthey, S.J. 1996, *Restructuring in the Classroom: Teaching, Learning, & School Organization*, Jossey-Bass, San Francisco, CA.

Epstein, D. & Sears, J. (eds) 1999, *A Dangerous Knowing: Sexual Pedagogies and the Master Narrative*, Cassell, London.

Fleisch, B. & Christie, P. 2004, 'Effectiveness improvement: perspectives from South Africa', *Discourse: Studies in the Cultural Politics of Education*, vol. 25, no. 1, pp. 95–112.

Foucault, M. 1997, *Ethics: Subjectivity and Truth*, P. Rabinow (ed.) (trans. Robert Hurley & others), New Press, New York.

Fraser N. 1995, 'From redistribution to recognition? Dilemmas of justice in a "post-socialist" age', *New Left Review*, no. 212, pp. 68–93.

Fraser, N. 1997, 'Rejoinder to Iris Young', *New Left Review*, no. 223, pp. 126–9.

Freebody, P. 1993, 'Social class and literacy', in *Literacy in Contexts*, A. Luke & P. Gilbert (eds), Allen & Unwin, Sydney, pp. 68–84.

Freebody, P., Ludwig, C. & Gunn, S. 1995, *Everyday Literacy Practices In and Out of Schools in Low Socioeconomic Urban Communities*, Department of Employment, Education and Training, Canberra.

Freire, P. 2001, *Pedagogy of Freedom Ethics, Democracy, and Civic Courage*, Rowman & Littlefield, Boulder.

Fullan, M. 1982, *The Meaning of Educational Change*, Teachers College, Columbia University, New York.

Fullan, M. 1993, *Change Forces: Probing the Depths of Educational Reform*, Falmer Press, London.

Fullan, M. (ed.) 1997, *The Challenge of School Change: A Collection of Articles*, Skylight Training & Pub., Arlington Heights, IL.

Fullan, M. 2001, *The New Meaning of Educational Change*, Teachers College Press, New York; RoutledgeFalmer, London.

Fuller, B. 1991, *Growing-Up Modern: The Western State Builds Third-World Schools*, Routledge, New York.

Gale, T. & Densmore, K. 2000, *Just Schooling: Explorations in the Cultural Politics of Teaching*, Open University Press, Buckingham, UK.

Gamoran, A., Secada, W.G. & Marret, C.B. 2000, 'The organizational context of teaching and learning: changing theoretical perspectives', in *Handbook of Sociology of Education*, M.T. Hallinan (ed.), Kluwer Academic/Plenum Publishers, New York.

Gewirtz, S. 2002, *The Managerial School Post-Welfarism and Social Justice in Education*, Routledge, London.

Gewirtz, S., Ball, S.J. & Bowe, R. 1995, *Markets, Choice and Equity in Education*, Open University Press, Buckingham, UK.

Giddens, A. 1999, *Runaway World: How Globalization is Reshaping our Lives*, Profile, London.

Gilroy, P. 2004, *After Empire: Melancholia or Convivial Culture?*, Routledge, New York.

Gipps, C. & Murphy, P. 1994, *A Fair Test?: Assessment, Achievement and Equity*, Open University Press, Buckingham, UK.

Giroux, H. 1983, *Theory and Resistance in Education: A Pedagogy for the Opposition*, Bergin & Garvey, South Hadley, MA.

Giroux, H. 1989, *Schooling for Democracy: Critical Pedagogy in the Modern Age*, Routledge, London.

Green, B. & Bigum, C. 1993, 'Aliens in the classroom', *Australian Journal of Education*, vol. 37, no. 2, pp. 119–41.

Greene, M. 1998, 'Art imagination, and school renewal: toward a common language', Paper presented at the Fourth International Teaching for Intelligence Conference, 23 April 1988, New York, NY, in *Teaching for Intelligence I: A Collection of Articles*, B. Presseisen (ed.), Hawker, Bownlow Education, Sydney.

Groome, H. 1994, *Teaching Aboriginal Studies Effectively*, Social Science Press, Wentworth Falls, NSW.

Grumet, M. 1988, *Bitter Milk: Women and Teaching*, University of Massachusetts Press, Amherst, MA.

Halliday, M.A.K. 1994, *An Introduction to Functional Grammar*, Edward Arnold, London.

Hallinger, P. & Heck, R. 1996, 'Reassessing the principal's role in school effectiveness: a review of empirical research 1980–1995', *Educational Administration Quarterly*, vol. 32, no. 1, pp. 5–44.

Harding, S. (ed.) 1993, *The 'Racial' Economy of Science: Toward a Democratic Future*, Indiana University Press, Bloomington.

Hargreaves, A. 1989, *Curriculum and Assessment Reform*, Open University Press, Buckingham, UK.

Hargreaves, A. 1994, *Changing Teachers, Changing Times: Teachers' Work and Culture in the Postmodern Age*, Cassell, London.

Hargreaves, A. (ed.) 1997, *Rethinking Educational Change with Heart and Mind*, Association for Supervision and Curriculum Development, Alexandria, VA.

Hargreaves, A. 2003, *Teaching in the Knowledge Society: Education in the Age of Insecurity*, Teachers College Press, New York.

Harris, S. 1990, *Two Way Aboriginal Schooling: Education and Cultural Survival*, Aboriginal Studies Press, Canberra.

Harris, S. & Malin, M. 1994, *Aboriginal Kids in Urban Classrooms*, Social Science Press, Wentworth Falls, NSW.

Hartley, D. 2003, 'New economy, new pedagogy', *Oxford Review of Education*, vol. 29, no. 2, pp. 81–94.

Hasan, R. & Williams, G. (eds) 1997, *Literacy in Society*, Longman, London.

Hayes, D. 2003, 'Making learning an effect of schooling: aligning curriculum, assessment and pedagogy', *Discourse: Studies in the Cultural Politics of Education*, vol. 24, no. 2, pp. 223–43.

Hayes, D. 2004, 'Whole school change that spreads and lasts: a technology of resilience for schools working within adverse conditions', Paper presented to *The Australian Association for Research in Education Conference*, University of Melbourne, 28 November–2 December.

Hayes, D., Christie, P., Mills, M. & Lingard, B. 2004, 'Productive leaders and productive leadership: schools as learning organisations', *Journal of Educational Administration*, November, vol. 42, no. 5, pp. 520–38.

Heath, S. 1983, *Ways with Words: Language, Life, and Work in Communities and Classrooms*, Cambridge University Press, Cambridge.

Heneveld, W. & Craig, H. 1996, *Schools Count: World Bank Project Designs and the Quality of Primary Education in Sub-Saharan Africa*, World Bank, Washington, DC.

Henry, M., Lingard, B., Taylor, S. & Rizvi, F. 2001, *The OECD, Globalisation and Education Policy*, Pergamon, Oxford.

Hill, P.W. & Rowe, K.J. 1996, 'Multilevel modelling in school effectiveness research', *School, Effectiveness and School Improvement*, vol. 7, no. 1, pp. 1–34.

Hill, P.W. & Rowe, K.J. 1998, 'Modelling student progress in studies of educational effectiveness', *School Effectiveness and School Improvement*, vol. 9, no. 3, pp. 310–33.

Hopkins, D., Ainscow, M. & West, M. 1994, *School Improvement in an Era of Change*, Cassell, London.

Hymes, D. 1996, *Ethnography, Linguistics, Narrative Inequality*, Taylor & Francis, London.

Jacklin, H. 2004, *Repetition and Difference: A Rhythmanalysis of Pedagogic Practice*, PhD thesis, University of the Witwatersrand, Johannesburg.

Jeffery, B. & Woods, P. 1998, *Testing Teachers: The Effects of School Inspections on Primary Teachers*, Falmer Press, London.

Johnson, N. 1999, 'Meeting the challenge: becoming learning communities', in *Learning Communities in Education*, J. Retallick, B. Cocklin & K. Coombe (eds), Routledge, London.

Keddie, A. 2004, 'Working with boys' peer cultures: productive pedagogies . . . productive boys', *Curriculum Perspectives*, vol. 24, no. 1, pp. 20–9.

Kenway, J., Willis, S., Blackmore, J. & Rennie, L. 1997, *Answering Back: Girls, Boys and Feminism in Schools*, Allen & Unwin, Sydney.

Ladson-Billings, G. & Gillborn, D. (eds) 2004, *The Routledge-Falmer Reader in Multicultural Education*, RoutledgeFalmer, London.

Laidi, Z. 1998, *A World without Meaning: The Crisis of Meaning in International Politics*, Routledge, London.

Lambert, D. & Lines, D. 2000, *Understanding Assessment: Purposes, Perceptions, Practice*, RoutledgeFalmer, London.

Lambert, L. 1998, *Building Leadership Capacity in Schools*, Association for Supervision and Curriculum Development, Alexandria, VA.

Lambert, L. 2000, *Building Leadership Capacity in Schools*, South Australian Secondary Principals Association, Adelaide.

Lankshear, C., Peters, M. & Knobel, M. 1996, 'Critical pedagogy and cyber space', in *Counternarratives*, H. Giroux, C. Lankshear, P. McLaren & M. Peters (eds), Routledge, London.

Lareau, A. 2000, 'Social class and the daily lives of children: A study from the United States', *Childhood*, vol. 7, pp. 155–71.

Lave, J. & Wenger, E. 1991, *Situated Learning: Legitimate Peripheral Participation*, Cambridge University Press, Cambridge.

Lawn, M. 1996, *Modern Times? Work, Professionalism and Citizenship in Teaching*, Falmer Press, London.

Lawn, M. & Lingard, B. 2002, 'Constructing a European policy space in educational governance: the role of transnational policy actors', *European Educational Research Journal*, vol. 1, no. 2, pp. 290–307.

Lee, V.E. & Smith, J.B. 2001, *Restructuring High-Schools for Equity and Excellence: What Works*, Teachers College Press, New York.

Limerick, D., Cunnington, B. & Crowther, F. 1998, *Managing the New Organisation: Collaboration and Sustainability in the Post-Corporate World*, Business and Professional Publishing, Sydney.

Lingard, B. 2000, 'It Is and It Isn't: Vernacular Globalization, Educational Policy and Restructuring', in N. Burbules & A. Torres (eds), *Globalization and Education Critical Perspectives*, Routledge, New York, pp. 79–108.

Lingard, B. 2001, 'Some lessons for educational researchers: repositioning research in education and education in research', *Australian Educational Researcher*, vol. 28, no. 3, pp. 1–46.

Lingard, B. & Mills, M. 2003, 'Teachers and school reform: working with productive pedagogies and productive assessment', *Melbourne Studies in Education*, vol. 44, no. 2, pp. 1–18.

Lingard, B. & Ozga, J. 2004, 'Educational policy and performativity: causes and effects?', Paper presented to the *Governing by Numbers Workshop*, University of Edinburgh, 27–28 May.

Lingard, B., Hayes, D. & Mills, M. 2002, 'Developments in school-based management: the specific case of Queensland, Australia', *Journal of Educational Administration*, vol. 40, no. 1, pp. 6–30.

Lingard, B., Hayes, D. & Mills, M. 2003, 'Teachers and productive pedagogies: contextualising, conceptualising, utilising', *Pedagogy, Culture and Society*, vol. 11, no. 3, pp. 397–422.

Lingard, B., Hayes, D., Mills, M. & Christie, P. 2003, *Leading Learning: Making Hope Practical in Schools*, Open University Press, Buckingham, UK.

Lingard, B., Martino, W., Mills, M. & Bahr, M. 2002, *Addressing the Educational Needs of Boys*, DEST, Canberra.

Lingard, B., Mills, M. & Hayes, D. 2000, 'Teachers, school reform and social justice: challenging research and practice', *Australian Education Researcher*, vol. 27, no. 3, pp. 93–109.

Lippman, P. 1998, *Race, Class, and Power in School Restructuring*, State University of New York Press, Albany, NY.

Little, J.W. 2003, 'Inside teacher community: representations of classroom practice', *Teachers College Record*, vol. 105, no. 6, pp. 913–46.

Lortie, D. 1975, *Schoolteacher: A Sociological Study*, University of Chicago Press, Chicago, IL.

Louis, K., Kruse, S.D. & Marks, H.M., 1996, 'Schoolwide professional community', in *Authentic Achievement: Restructuring Schools for Intellectual Quality*, F.M. Newmann & Associates (eds), Jossey-Bass, San Francisco, CA, pp. 179–203.

Louis, K., Marks, H.M., & Kruse, S.D. 1996, 'Teacher professional community in restructuring schools', *American Educational Research Journal*, vol. 33, no. 4, pp. 757–98.

Lyotard, F. 1984, *The Postmodern Condition: A Report on Knowledge*, University of Minnesota Press, Minneapolis, MN.

Macdonald, D. 2003, 'Rich Task implementation: modernism meets postmodernism', *Discourse*, vol. 24, no. 2, pp. 247–62.

Mahony, P. 1998, 'Girls will be girls and boys will be first', in *Failing Boys? Issues in Gender and Achievement*, J. Elwood, D. Epstein, V. Hey & J. Maw (eds), Open University Press, Buckingham, UK.

Mahony, P. & Hextall, I. 2000, *Reconstructing Teaching: Standards, Performance and Accountability*, Routledge, London.

Marneweck, L. 2002, Images of a changing curriculum, in *Troubling Practice*, V. Carrington, J. Mitchell, S. Rawolle & A. Zavros (eds), Post Pressed, Brisbane, pp. 123–45.

Marginson, S. 1997, *Markets in Education*, Allen & Unwin, Sydney.

Martino, W., Lingard, B. & Mills, M. 2004, 'Issues in boys' education: a question of teacher threshold knowledges', *Gender and Education*, vol. 16, no. 3, pp. 435–54.

McBeath, J. & Mortimore, P. (eds) 2001, *Improving School Effectiveness*, Open University Press, Buckingham, UK.

McCaleb, S.P. 1994, *Building Communities of Learners*, Lawrence Erlbaum, Mahwah, NJ.

McConaghy, C. 1998, 'Disrupting reproductive and erasive pedagogies. Educational policy processes in postcolonial Australia', *Discourse, Studies in the Cultural Politics of Education*, vol. 19, no. 3, pp. 341–54.

McConaghy, C. & Burnett, G. 2002, *Place Matters: Productive Partnerships for Quality Teaching*, Education NSW, Sydney.

McDonald, J.P., Mohr, N., Dichter, A. & McDonald, E.C. 2003, *The Power of Protocols: An Educator's Guide to Better Practice*, Teachers College Press, New York.

McLaughlin, M.W. 1987, 'Learning from experience: lessons from policy implementation', *Educational Evaluation and Policy Analysis*, vol. 9, no. 2, pp. 171–8.

McNeil, L. 1986, *Contradictions of Control: School Structure and School Knowledge*, Routledge & Kegan Paul, New York.

McNeil, L. 2000, *Contradictions of School Reform: Educational Costs of Standardized Testing*, Routledge, New York.

Mehan, H. 1979, *Learning Lessons: Social Organization in the Classroom*, Harvard University Press, Cambridge, MA.

Meyer, J.W. and Hannan, M. (eds) 1979, *National Development and the World System: Educational, Economic, and Political Change, 1950–1970*, University of Chicago Press, Chicago, IL.

Meyer, J., Ramirez, F.O. & Soysal, Y. 1992, 'World expansion of mass education', *Sociology of Education*, vol. 65, no. 2, pp. 128–49.

Mills, C.W. 2000 (first published 1959), *The Sociological Imagination*, Oxford University Press, New York.

Mills, M. 1996, 'Homophobia kills: disruptive moments in the educational politics of legitimation', *British Journal of Sociology of Education*, vol. 17, no. 3, pp. 315–26.

Mills, M. 1997a, 'Football, desire and the social organisation of masculinity', *Social Alternatives*, vol. 16, no. 1, pp. 10–13.

Mills, M. 1997b, 'Towards a disruptive pedagogy: creating spaces for student and teacher resistance to social injustice', *International Studies in Sociology of Education*, vol. 7, no. 1, pp. 35–55.

Mills, M. 2001, *Challenging Violence in Schools: An Issue of Masculinities*, Open University Press, Buckingham, UK.

Ministerial Council on Education, Employment, Training and Youth Affairs (MCEETYA) 1999, *The Adelaide Declaration*, >http://www.curriculum.edu.au/mceetya/nationalgoals/natgoals. htm< [28 June 2004].

Ministers for Education, Employment, Training, Youth Affairs and Community Services 2002, *Stepping Forward—Improving Pathways for All Young People*, >http://www.mceetya.edu.au/ forward/ourdec.htm< [28 June 2004].

Murphy, R. & Broadfoot, P. 1995, *Effective Assessment and the Improvement of Education: A Tribute to Desmond Nuttall*, Falmer, London.

New London Group 1996, 'A pedagogy of multiliteracies: designing social futures', *Harvard Educational Review*, vol. 66, no. 1, pp. 60–92.

Newmann, F., Secada, W. & Wehlage, G. 1995, *A Guide to Authentic Instruction and Assessment: Vision, Standards and Scoring*, Wisconsin Center for Education Research, Madison, WIS.

Newmann, F.M. & Associates 1996, *Authentic Achievement: Restructuring Schools for Intellectual Quality*, Jossey-Bass, San Francisco, CA.

Novoa, A. 2000, 'The restructuring of the European educational space: changing relationships among states, citizens, and educational communities', in *Educational Knowledge: Changing Relationships between the State, Civil Society, and the Educational Community*, T.S. Popkewitz (ed.), State University of New York Press, New York, pp. 31–57.

Oakes, J., Gamoran, A. & Page, R.N. 1992, 'Curriculum differentiation: opportunities, outcomes, and meanings', in *Handbook of Research on Curriculum: A Project of the American Educational Research Association*, P.W. Jackson (ed.), Macmillan, New York, pp. 570–608.

Ozga, J. & Simola, H. 2004, 'Performativity and performance: teachers in England and Finland', Unpublished paper, University of Edinburgh, Edinburgh.

Presseisen, B. (ed.) 2000, *Teaching for Intelligence I: A Collection of Articles*, Hawker, Bownlow Education, Sydney.

Professional Support and Curriculum Directorate 2003, *Quality Teaching in NSW Public Schools: An Annotated Bibliography*, State of NSW, Department of Education and Training, Sydney.

Queensland Department of Education 2001, *New Basics: Rich Tasks*, Education Queensland, Brisbane.

Queensland School Reform Longitudinal Study (QSRLS) 2001, submitted to Education Queensland by the School of Education, University of Queensland, State of Queensland (Department of Education), Brisbane.

Quicke, J. 1999, *A Curriculum for Life: Schools for a Democratic Learning Society*, Open University Press, Buckingham, UK.

Rawls, J. 1971, *A Theory of Justice*, Belknap Press, Cambridge.

Renshaw, P. 1998, 'Socio-cultural pedagogy for new times: reframing the ZPD and community of learners', *The Australian Educational Researcher*, vol. 25, no. 3, pp. 83–100.

Renshaw, P. 2003, 'Community and learning: contradictions, dilemmas and prospects', *Discourse: Studies in the Cultural Politics of Education*, vol. 24, no. 3, pp. 355–71.

Retallick, J. 1999, 'Transforming school into learning communities: beginning the journey', in *Learning Communities in Education*, J. Retallick, B. Cocklin & K. Coombe (eds), Routledge, London.

Reyes, M., de la Luz 1987, 'Comprehension of content area passages: a study of Spanish/English readers in the third and fourth grade', in *Becoming Literate in English as a Second Language*, S.R. Goldman & H.T. Trueba (eds), Ablex, Norwood, NJ, pp. 107–26.

Rist, R. 1970, 'Student social class and teacher expectations: the self-fulfilling prophecy in ghetto education', *Harvard Educational Review*, vol. 40, no. 3, pp. 411–51.

Rizvi, F. & Kemmis, S. 1987, *Dilemmas of Reform: The Participation and Equity Program in Victorian Schools*, Deakin University Press, Geelong, VIC.

Rose, M. 1995, *Possible Lives: The Promise of Public Education in America*, Penguin, New York.

Rose, N. 1999, *Powers of Freedom Reframing Political Thought*, Cambridge University Press, Cambridge.

Rosenthal, R. & Jacobson, L. 1968, *Pygmalion in the Classroom: Teacher Expectation and Pupils' Intellectual Development*, Holt, Rinehart and Winston, New York.

Rowe, K.J. & Hill, P.W. 1998, 'Modeling educational effectiveness in classrooms: the use of multilevel structural equations to model students' progress', *Educational Research and Evaluation*, vol. 4, no. 4, pp. 307–47.

Rutter, M., Maughan, B., Mortimore, P. & Ousten, J. 1979, *Fifteen Thousand Hours: Secondary Schools and Effects on Children*, Harvard University Press, Boston.

Sachs, J. 2003, *The Activist Teaching Profession*, Open University Press, Maidenhead, UK.

Said, E. 1994, *Representations of the Intellectual*, Vintage, London.

Said, E. 2004, *Humanism and Democratic Criticism*, Columbia University Press, New York.

Scheerens, J. 1992, *Effective Schooling: Research, Theory and Practice*, Cassell, London.

Scheerens, J. & Bosker, R. 1997, *The Foundations of Educational Effectiveness*, Pergamon, Oxford.

Schofield, K. 1999, 'The purposes of education, paper commissioned for 2010', Queensland State Education, Queensland Department of Education, Brisbane.

Seddon, T. 2001, 'National curriculum in Australia? A matter of politics, powerful knowledge and the regulation of learning', *Pedagogy, Culture and Society*, vol. 9, no. 3, pp. 307–31.

Senge, P. 1990, *The Fifth Discipline: The Art and Practice of the Learning Organization*, Random House Australia, Sydney.

Shepard, L. 2000, 'The role of assessment in a learning culture', *Educational Researcher*, vol. 29, no. 7, pp. 4–14.

Shor, I. 1980, *Critical Teaching and Everyday Life*, South End Press, Boston, MA.

Simon, K. 1986, *On Target with Authentic Assessment: Creating and Implementing Classroom Models*, Appalachia Educational Laboratory, Charleston, WV.

Singh, P. 2002, 'Pedagogising knowledge: Bernstein's theory of the pedagogic device', *British Journal of Sociology of Education*, vol. 23, no. 4, pp. 571–82.

Sizer, T. 1984, *Horace's Compromise: The Dilemma of the American High School*, Houghton Mifflin, Boston, MA.

Sizer, T. 1987, *Horace's Compromise: The Dilemma of the American High School*, Houghton Mifflin, Boston, MA.

Sizer, T. 1992, *Horace's School: Redesigning the American High School*, Houghton Mifflin, Boston, MA.

Sizer, T. 1994, *Horace's Hope: What Works for the American High School*, Houghton Mifflin, Boston, MA.

Sizer, T.R. 1998, 'On the habit of informed skepticism', Paper presented at the Fourth International Teaching for Intelligence Conference, 23 April 1988, New York, in *Teaching for Intelligence*

I: A Collection of Articles, B. Presseisen (ed.), Hawker, Bownlow Education, Sydney.

Slaughter, R. 1995, *From Fatalism to Foresight—Educating for the Early 21st Century*, Australian Council for Educational Research, Hawthorn, VIC.

Slee, R. & Weiner, G., with Tomlinson, S. 1998, *School Effectiveness for Whom? Challenges to the School Effectiveness and School Improvement Movements*, Falmer Press, London.

Smylie, M. & Perry, G. 1998, 'Restructuring schools for improving teaching', in *International Handbook of Educational Change*, Kluwer Academic, Dordrecht, pp. 976–1005.

Smyth, J. 1989, 'A "pedagogical" and "educative" view of leadership', in *Critical Perspectives on Educational Leadership*, J. Smyth (ed.), Falmer Press, London, pp. 179–204.

Smyth, J. 1998, 'Finding the "enunciative space" for teacher leadership and teacher learning in schools', *Asia-Pacific Journal of Teacher Education*, vol. 26, no. 3, pp. 191–202.

Smyth, J. 2001, *Critical Politics of Teachers' Work: An Australian Perspective*, Peter Lang, New York, NY.

Southworth, G. 2002, 'Instructional leadership in schools: reflections and empirical evidence', *School Leadership and Management*, vol. 22, no. 1, pp. 73–91.

Sternberg, E. 1998, *Corporate Governance: Accountability in the Marketplace*, Institute of Economic Affairs, London.

Stoll, L. & Fink, D. 1996, *Changing Our Schools: Linking School Effectiveness and School Improvement*, Open University Press, Buckingham, UK.

Talbert, J.E. & McLaughlin, M.W. 2001, *Professional Communities and the Work of High School Teaching*, University of Chicago Press, Chicago, IL.

Teddlie, C. & Reynolds, D. (eds) 2000, *The International Handbook of School Effectiveness Research*, Falmer Press, London.

Teese, R. 2000, 'The age of curriculum', in *Academic Success and Power Examinations and Inequality*, Melbourne University Press, Melbourne.

Teese, R. & Polesel, J. 2003, *Undemocratic Schooling: Equity and Quality in Mass Secondary Education in Australia*, Melbourne University Press, Melbourne.

Thompson, A. & Gitlin, A. 1995, 'Creating spaces for reconstructing knowledge in feminist pedagogy', *Educational Theory*, vol. 45, no. 2, p. 125.

Thomson, P. 2000, '"Like schools", educational "disadvantage" and "thisness"', *Australian Educational Researcher*, vol. 27, no. 3, pp. 157–72.

Thomson, P. 2002, *Schooling the Rustbelt Kids: Making the Difference in Changing Times*, Allen & Unwin, Sydney.

Thrupp, M. 1999, *Schools Making a Difference: Let's Be Realistic! School Mix, School Effectiveness and the Limits of Social Reform*, Open University Press, Buckingham, UK.

Thrupp, M. 2002, 'Making the difference: 20 years on', *Discourse: Studies in the Cultural Politics of Education*, vol. 23, no. 3, pp. 339–45.

Torrance, H. (ed.) 1995, *Evaluating Authentic Assessment: Problems and Possibilities in New Approaches to Assessment*, Open University Press, Buckingham, UK.

Torrance, H. 1997, 'Assessment, accountability, and standards: using assessment to control the reform of schooling', in *Education: Culture, Economy, Society*, A. Halsey, H. Lauder, P. Brown & A.S. Wells (eds), Oxford University Press, Oxford.

Townsend, T. 2001, 'Satan or saviour? An analysis of two decades of school effectiveness research', *School Effectiveness and School Improvement*, vol. 12, no. 1, pp. 115–29.

Townsend, T., Clarke, P. & Ainscow, M. (eds) 1999, *Third Millennium Schools: A World of Difference in Effectiveness and Improvement*, Swets & Zeitlinger, Lisse, Netherlands, vol. 13, no. 2, pp. 3–9.

UNESCO 1990, *The World Declaration on Education for All and Framework for Action to Meet Basic Learning Needs*, UNESCO, Jomtien, Thailand.

Van Galen, J. 2004, 'School reform and class work: teachers as mediators of social class', *Journal of Educational Change*, vol. 5, pp. 111–13.

Vygotsky, L.S. 1978, *Mind in Society: the Development of Higher Psychological Processes*, Michael Cole et al. (eds), Harvard University Press, Cambridge.

Vygotsky, L.S. 1994, *The Vygotsky Reader*, R. van der Veer & J. Valsiner (eds), Blackwell, Oxford.

Wenger, E. 1998, *Communities of Practice: Learning, Meaning and Identity*, Cambridge University Press, Cambridge.

Westheimer, J. 1999, 'Communities and consequences: an inquiry into ideology and practice in teachers' professional work', *Educational Administration Quarterly*, vol. 35, no. 1, pp. 71–105.

White, R. & Lippitt, R. 1960, *Autocracy and Democracy: An Experimental Inquiry*, Harper, New York.

Whitty, G. 1997, 'Marketization, the state and the re-formation of the teaching profession', in *Education: Culture, Economy, Society*, A.H. Halsey, H. Lauder, P. Brown & A.S. Wells (eds), Oxford University Press, Oxford.

Whitty, G., Power, S. & Halpin, D. 1998, *Devolution and Choice in Education: The School, the State and the Market*, Open University Press, Buckingham, UK.

Yates, L. 2002, 'Effectiveness, difference and sociological research', *Discourse*, vol. 23, no. 3, pp. 329–38.

Yates, L., McLeod, J. & Arrow, M. 2003, *Self, School and Future: the 12 to 18 Project: Report for Schools and Participants*, Changing Knowledges, Changing Identities Research Group, Faculty of Education, University of Technology, Sydney.

Yeatman, A. 1990, *Bureaucrats, Technocrats, Femocrats: Essays on the Contemporary Australian State*, Allen & Unwin, Sydney.

Yeatman, A. 1993, 'Corporate managerialism and the shift from the welfare to the competition state', in *Discourse: Studies in the Cultural Politics of Education*, vol. 13, no. 2, pp. 3–9.

Yeatman, A. 1994, *Postmodern Revisionings of the Political*, Routledge, New York.

Young, I. 1990, *Justice and the Politics of Difference*, Princeton University Press, Princeton.

Young, I. 1997, 'Unruly categories: a critique of Nancy Fraser's dual systems theory', *New Left Review*, no. 222, pp. 147–60.

Young, M.F.D. (ed.) 1971, *Knowledge and Control: New Directions for the Sociology of Education*, Conference of the British Sociological Association, Durham, Collier-Macmillan, London.

Young, M.F.D. 1998, *The Curriculum of the Future: From the 'New Sociology of Education' to a Critical Theory of Learning*, Falmer Press, London.

Zaleznik, A. 1989, 'Real work', *Harvard Business Review*, Jan–Feb, pp. 57–64.

Appendix

The use of coding instruments in the Productive Pedagogies Research, alongside semi-structured interviews, served a number of purposes. First, the instruments were configured to respond directly to the Queensland context, in which both academic and social student outcomes are explicitly valued in schooling. Second, the multidimensional nature of the study opened up the possibility of analysing empirically unanswered questions in the history of school reform—namely, what forms of classroom practice contribute to more equitable student outcomes, and what forms of classroom practice contribute to improved student outcomes for all students. While a substantial body of research has been devoted to analysing these two questions, the Productive Pedagogies Research was one of the first attempts to examine these questions in the context of systemic school reform. Third, the *productive pedagogies* framework formed the basis of *productive assessment*. Analysis of student work samples enabled an examination of the extent to which pedagogies and assessment were aligned to produce high-quality outcomes.

It is important to recall that our intention in creating the observation instrument was for the purpose of coding classrooms, in order to examine in a systematic way the link between teachers' classroom practices and students' academic and social outcomes. Semi-structured interviews were designed to accompany the coding schedule. Coding instruments, of necessity, limit what is observed and said about classrooms: their checklist structure does not register events beyond its descriptive boundaries, and

Teachers and Schooling Making a Difference

interprets those that fall within these in tightly scripted ways. That said, they enable a specified set of items to be considered in a comparable way and, as with other quantitative approaches, offer a scale of study not possible in unstructured observation approaches. The research team was aware that, whatever its original intentions, the coding instrument, once created, could be taken up and used in various ways. We would emphasise the following caveats related to how the classroom coding instrument should be used and understood:

- Coding instruments are not intended to encapsulate all that can be said about classroom practice, and this instrument is no exception.
- This instrument was designed to gather information for research purposes, rather than to judge the quality of teaching practice.
- The presence of 20 elements on the instrument does not imply that all or most elements should be present in every lesson.
- In line with the design of this specific instrument, we would expect elements relating to academic and social outcomes to be present in classrooms in configurations that reflect the specific purposes of the lesson.

Before using the coding instrument in the case study schools, the team further developed and modified the elements through a process of piloting the instrument through collective observations and trials. Table 1.1 in Chapter 1 lists the final 20 elements that made up the *productive pedagogies* model and those that made up *productive assessment* and *productive performances*.

Index